*The Performer-Audience Connection*

# The Performer-Audience Connection

EMOTION TO METAPHOR IN DANCE AND SOCIETY

By Judith Lynne Hanna

 University of Texas Press, Austin

Copyright ©1983 by the University of Texas Press
All rights reserved
Printed in the United States of America
First Edition, 1983

LIBRARY OF CONGRESS CATALOGING IN PUBLICATION DATA
Hanna, Judith Lynne.
  The performer-audience connection.
  Bibliography: p.
  Includes index.
    1. Dancing—Social aspects. 2. Dancing—Psychological
aspects. 3. Emotions. 4. Theatre audiences. 5. Social interaction.
6. Social psychology. 7. Folk dancing—History. I. Title.
GV1588.6.H36  1983    793.3'01    83-6720
ISBN 0-292-76478-2
ISBN 0-292-76480-4 (pbk.)

*To those who want to share and to my family—
all of whom are performers and audiences to each other*

# Contents

# Acknowledgments

This empirically informed essay would not have been possible without permission, cooperation, and support from the Smithsonian Division of Performing Arts, especially Shirley Cherkasky and Sali Ann Kriegsman. I am most thankful for their confidence and involvement in this unique project on the perspectives of participants in performance. To the dancers and managers who took the time to answer questions and the audience members who shared their perceptions, I express my deep gratitude and hope that they and other supporters will not be disappointed with how it all came out. Several participants in the audience survey wrote on the form, "Call me if I can help." In this regard, I appreciate Tamar Lieberman's insightful comments on an earlier draft of the book.

The grant award from the Wenner-Gren Foundation for Anthropological Research and support from the University of Maryland's Center for Family, Housing, and the Community enabled me to carry out the audience survey data processing and analysis under Douglas Coulson's guidance and to complete this study. McKeldin Library and Kennedy Center Library for the Performing Arts provided invaluable assistance. Many colleagues and other scholars shared their thoughts and research findings referred to in this book and thus contributed to the ideas that developed. They are all gratefully acknowledged.

I am indebted to Anni Coplan, Glenna Batson, Lena and Glen Orlin, Anna Maria Veria, and Girma Wubishet for their help in administering audience surveys at some of the concerts. Appreciation is extended to Teresa Ankney for assisting in developing the survey research instrument and code book, helping to administer the questionnaire, coding and partially processing one of the surveys, and commenting, as Anni Coplan so generously did, on preliminary drafts of some of the chapters. I thank Gary Skaggs, for conducting the computer data processing and assisting in the analysis of the audience surveys.

My sincere appreciation is extended to the anonymous reviewers chosen by the University of Texas Press and to Dane Harwood for offering valuable suggestions on earlier drafts of this book. I especially want to thank my parents, David and the late Lili Selmont, who introduced me to performance; my colleague William John Hanna, a constant and helpful critic to whom I owe much; John Blacking, anonymous reviewer of other manuscripts and public speaker who called for attention to feeling (1977); and Scott Lubeck, social science editor; Kathleen Lewis, copy editor; and Shawn and Aaron Hanna, my sons, who encouraged my work on this project.

# BACKSTAGE

CHAPTER 1

# *Introduction*

This book is an odyssey into some puzzling areas of human communication. It is about the communication of emotion in dance: the history of attitudes that create expectations, what performers intend to convey and what spectators perceive, and some traces of past performances that linger in society through metaphors of dance. Because dance is considered so much apart from the American postindustrial society, this work tries to show how a society's culture and history envelop dance and the performer-audience connection, which in turn may influence society. The book introduces dance forms and extends our knowledge of them through historical and symbolic analysis, observation, interviews, and surveys.

SIGNIFICANCE OF DANCE
Dance is a nearly universal behavior with a history probably as old as humanity itself. Since antiquity, paintings, friezes, sculpture, myths, oral expression, and then literature attest to the existence of dance. Dance is embedded in our being. Even when not physically manifest, the concept and vision of dance emerge in our thinking. The dynamics of dance, culture, and society are inseparable.[1]

Drawing upon everyday life and special occasions, choreographers and dancers transform and frame values, beliefs, and expressions of them through dancing. In this way they also introduce new ways of thinking and feeling. In turn, the dances we do, see, and read or hear about often haunt us. Audiences and other members of society draw upon dance as metaphor. Written language about politics, economics, technology, and other social relations evokes the feelings and images of dance in order to clarify nondance spheres of human life. Indeed, dance in its various manifestations yields insight into itself and the broader society.

Dance is an age-old, well-known vehicle to express emotion. The moving human body usually captivates an observer's consciousness. Through perceptions of the multisensory stimulation of sight, sound, movement, touch, and smell, the dancing body excites emotions. Dancing arouses feelings via its associations with basic life functions, pleasures, pain, and guilt. Birth, life, and death are bodily, and the human body is the vessel and vehicle of dance. The potency of dance to persuade and to move people to social action has been recognized in many eras and places, from the antiquity of Aristotle and Plato to contemporary authorities in Africa. For example, in order to avoid ethnic rivalries in a country with about sixty ethnic groups, the Ivory Coast government banned all public gatherings involving traditional music and dance during an election campaign.[2] The government recognized that the arts provoke and intensify heated sentiments.

Why spotlight dance? Dance is an aesthetic form that allows us to encounter a far greater range of emotion than we usually do in the course of daily living. We often repress, suppress, and disavow emotions that surface in crises when passions burst forth. Dance allows a celebration and vicarious participation in the manifold possibilities of humanity. We can gauge the popularity of dance by the level of participation it has reached, the reverence and condemnation it has received, and the number of writers, musicians, and artists it has enamored. Dance concerts; television programs, Broadway shows, and films about dancers; and news publications, articles, and books are a bazaar that has captured the American imagination. Complementing this bounty are dance agents, professional associations, connoisseurs, critics, researchers, memorabilia collectors, therapists, studios, university programs, libraries, and curators. And the dance explosion in the United States reverberates elsewhere in the world.

Since the mid-1960s dance may have been the fastest growing performing art in America. Whereas the national ballet dance audience was estimated at one million in 1964, by the end of that decade it skyrocketed to nine to fifteen million.[3] The momentum and growth continue. In the July 1981 National Council on the Arts "Advancing the Arts in America: Report to the Presidential Task Force on Arts and Humanities," we learn that there were about sixteen million dance ticket buyers, 90 percent outside of New York City, the dance capital. According to the United States Labor Department's statistics, the percentage increase in demand for dancers through the end of the 1980s is greater than for any other artist, worker, engineer, scientist (life, physical, or social), computer specialist, administrator, clerk, food processor, or cleaning service employee. There are yet other indicators of the florescence of dance activities.

Not surprisingly, business has begun investing in dance. Eight major dance companies have joined the National Corporate Fund for Dance in a cooperative fund-raising venture in the business community. Since the founding of the National Endowment for the Arts in 1965, taxpayer support for dance increased until 1981 and the Reagan administration and recession cutbacks. Pollster Louis Harris reported that 51 percent of Americans were willing to pay an additional $25 a year in federal taxes to support arts programs, including dance. Respondents in Harris's recent survey generally said that they would attend more performing arts activities if more and better-quality performances were available. Personal involvement in the arts has also increased dramatically. The proportion of those involved in ballet or modern may have risen from about 9 percent in 1975 to 20 percent in 1980.

The appetite for dance has been whetted. Why? The era of the 1960s rediscovered and accepted the human body. The *Village Voice* senior art critic Peter Schjeldahl suggests that people seek the emotions of the human connection: "As corporate capitalism becomes more enveloping, rationalized and sterile, art is increasingly vested with the function of representing the repressed, factored-out, amputated life of the emotions, the thwarted—and dangerous when thwarted—sum of the sexual and survival instincts. . . . Mere evidence of the human hand, a mere brushstroke, glows today with talismanic intensity."[4]

EMOTION

What is meant by emotion? Emotion, a powerful source of human motivation, is a medium and a message. A subjectively experienced state of feeling, emotion constrains us and inspires us as we create cultural forms and meaning, and as we relate to each other. Often it is what is felt rather than what is reasoned that is most critical in social relations. With physical excitement and conscious awareness, emotion binds us to friends, motivates us to achievement, and energizes us to self-protection and cooperation. This book is concerned with the cognitive aspects of emotion. Experiencing or attributing physical perturbations and arousal, an individual becomes thoughtfully aware and usually tries to understand what is happening. Emotion is essential to survival. No animal will last long if it cannot get worked up when necessary. We shall explore later the question of whether and how dance arouses participants.

Emotion is inexorably linked to movement: we embrace friends, applaud success, and unite in common effort.[5] The Latin verb *emovere* means "to move out." The word *emotion* includes the gloss "motion." Through movement, emotions announce themselves inside our bodies; hearts pound, backs stiffen, stomachs churn, hands tremble, and faces blush. Because emotions and their movements convey meanings that influence special and everyday activities, we traffic in clues to distinguish different emotions.

Important events in our lives such as birth, love, marriage, and death evoke particular emotions. Shifting, kaleidoscopic feelings reflecting our ups and downs infuse our daily movements. All humans express, disguise, or suppress emotions as they confront the problems of living.[6] In everyday communication there are momentary exchanges that color our impressions of people and actions. We act upon this information.

Emotion is essential not only to the survival of a species but to the existence of politicians and the political structure, and to the success of performers. Presidential and other advertising campaigns recognize that conveying emotion on the household-captivating television is more significant than any other form of publicity. Emotion even makes its mark in the rulings of the august Supreme Court. In his autobiography Justice William O. Douglas recalls Chief Justice Charles Evans Hughes's view that 90 percent of any constitutional decision is emotion.[7] Because of the potential effects of emotion on individual and collective judgments and actions, all societies have guidelines for managing emotions and rules about to whom, when, and how to display them. Societies attempt to command and control the expression of some feelings, especially the passions of love and hate, through customs and rites. It is that special feeling sometimes called *soul* or *charisma* that distinguishes the average performer from the star.

Specialists on emotion, who come from several disciplines with different theories and methodologies, do not agree on the definition of an emotion. They recognize that emotions have unique antecedents, consequences, and variations in intensity and duration. They are aware that emotions are affected by an individual's moods, traits, and defense mechanisms and not simply by the situation or environment. There is no agreement about the relationship between emotion and cognition, although there is agreement that they interact and that ideas trigger emotions. Carroll Izard put it this way: "Emotion and cognition are intimately interrelated. Cognitive processes can trigger emotions and play a part in their regulation. Emotion, in turn, can influence perception and cognition."[8]

An anthropological-sociological-semiotic theory of emotions is most applicable to the study of the performer-audience connection in a *live* exchange.[9] Herein, the individual is enmeshed in cultural norms that guide intentions and perceptions about emotion in social relations. The semiotic focus is on semantics, or the meaning of movement in terms of emotions of a "text" or segment of a performance, and pragmatics, the context for creating and identifying emotion. Elaine Batcher put it this way: "Emotion is meaning and understanding at close range to oneself. . . . It is communicated by the context of its expression, the assumption of similarity of others to ourselves, by recall of past experience, and by the loop of comprehension, which of itself has the power to create emotional experience."[10]

In this book emotions are what the participants in the performer-audience interaction say they are. Although most words have multiple meanings, they also have common associations.

## NONVERBAL COMMUNICATION

We know that words and their arrangements convey feelings. However, we know less about how people communicate emotion to each other through nonverbal means, including dance. Is the nonverbal worthy of our attention? Students of communication recognize that words cannot say everything. Sometimes the scope, depth, and nuances of ideas, feelings, and things are better conveyed nonverbally. The renowned dancer Isadora Duncan stated emphatically, "If I could *tell* you what I mean, there would be no point in dancing." Gesture, locomotion, or posture may be faster than the use of sequences of words to get across the equivalent meaning. Body language may carry a more immediate wallop because of its strong potential to evoke sensuous associations. Of all possible media of communication the body is the least removed from our associations of personal experience. When both verbal and nonverbal communication occur, body language often contradicts verbal language. Furthermore, the nonverbal often has an ambiguity that prevents the discomfort that arises from explicit statements about interpersonal relations.

When an individual or group intentionally sends a message to someone who infers a shared meaning and responds, we call this activity *communication*. It is most effective—that is, there is a good connection—when people share knowledge about when, where, how, and why messages are sent, as we shall see in the discussion of the live concerts. Of course, messages should be sufficiently lucid to be perceived despite distractions and from a distance, as in a theatre. People may send or, more accurately, convey unintended messages. Observers make inferences from or assign meaning to what they see.

## FOCUS

We realize that emotion is important in private, public, and theatrical life; we also know that nonverbal communication is a significant vehicle for conveying emotion. Yet we have much to learn about what people sending messages of feeling and those receiving them actually share. What are the intended and missed messages? How can we find out? Since the arts and society reflect and influence each other, dance performances provide a nonexperimental laboratory to explore what is apparently shared in the broader society.

More than merely reflecting society, the arts also challenge it. Dancers draw upon our concepts of time, space, and effort, our history and ecology, and our attitudes and acts of love, hate, war, and joy. They transform these notions of offstage life for the dance performance. But the theatrical changes are not so great that they distort the meanings that the performers and some observers hold in common. Because of the interrelation of dance and society, we can view dance performances, at the very least, as a window on the nondance world and a way to gain insight into the human condition.

A noted anthropologist, Clifford Geertz, emphasizes the significance of exploring public performing arts: "In order to make up our minds we must know how to feel about things; and to know how we feel about things we need the public images of sentiment that only ritual, myth, and arts can provide." [11] These public images have a special power.

By exploring what transpires in the dancer-audience exchange, we can acquire a what-and-how repertoire of the powerful ways that moving images communicate emotion. The common denominator of the dancer-audience relation (and others, such as teacher-student, therapist-client, and politician-constituent) is power. The power to influence attitudes, opinions, and feelings is critical to the stage performer aspiring to success. The first means of power an individual possesses is the body: a baby sucks, makes sounds, and later grabs. The body's real and symbolic power persists through a person's lifetime. This power is critical in understanding the potential of dance, for the body is the instrument of dance. A lively, skilled dancer epitomizes power and the strength and discipline most ordinary people might feel they lack.

Since we have used the word *performance*, it is useful to elaborate upon its meaning. When humans act in accord with some systems of rules, we often speak of performance. Viewing social life from a dramaturgical perspective, theatre is merely a node in a performance web that also includes everyday encounters and special events.[12] Individuals present versions of the reality of situations by choosing the setting, posture, gesture, and so on, to manage an impression. Creators of production material, performers, and observers are the performance participants. For a performance to occur, there is a catalyst to which a creator and performer (who may be the same) react. When a performance occurs, participants have momentary or more lasting responses which affect the ongoing performance as well as future acts. The assumptions that participants acquire through their theoretical and practical experience also affect the performance, with its intertwining messages of feeling and intellect.

Thus, in this book, it is appropriate to begin by identifying the historical perspectives on communicating emotion in performance. These views set the stage for presenting the various perspectives dancers and audience members have at a particular live performance—the subject of the second part of the book. Then the last section traces some of the implications of the staged for the offstage; artists and their publics stimulate each other in mutual exchange. Although the great majority of the world's dancing is performed by people for themselves, many of the popular and folk forms become theatricalized and otherwise transformed.

## EVOLUTION OF THE ODYSSEY AND THEORETICAL ISSUES
How did this book begin? Years ago I became addicted to dance. It started when a pediatrician diagnosed my case as *pes planus*. Dancing would make my feet strong. It did not help my feet much, but it led to other things. I thought about dance.

In *To Dance Is Human: A Theory of Nonverbal Communication*, I suggested how people communicate ideas and feelings through dance.[13] I put forth a case for the intellectual dimension of dance in an attempt to redress the overemphasis on the expression of feelings in dance found in the theoretical and descriptive literature. The emphasis on feeling in dance has ancient roots. According to Lucian of Samosata, writing in the second century A.D., "It is the dancer's profession to show forth human character and passion in all their variety; to depict love and anger, frenzy and grief each in its due measure . . . there is meaning in his movements; every gesture has its significance; and therein lies his chief excellence."[14] The next chapter sketches other relevant thought along these lines. More recently, in 1921 Wilhelm Wundt was the first to advance the theory that gesture is a primitive form of language arising out of emotional states.[15]

When a dance department chairperson asked me, as an anthropologist who studies communication in dance and everyday life, to speak to the faculty, she proposed the reciprocity of emotion and movement as the topic. Then she added, "But we don't want you to talk about culture." By *culture* I mean the values, beliefs, norms, and rules shared by a group and learned through communication.[16] Implicit in the chairperson's remark was the common assumption of a universal way that dancers express emotions through movement and, conversely, how their emotions motivate (make happen) movement. Writing in 1760, Jean George Noverre, a dramatic choreographer and zealous proselytizer, spoke of a universally understood language of dance. Under the influence of Charles Darwin's theory of evolution and concept of universal human behavior, François Delsarte (a movement theorist) carried on this theme in the nineteenth century, and Rudolf Laban (noted for his system of movement notation) and Lincoln Kirstein (scholar and co-founder of the New York City Ballet) perpetuated this notion in the early twentieth century. However, there is cultural variation in nonverbal communication, as some scholars have documented. I found it in my study of a multicultural, multisocioeconomic class school in an American city. Consequently, some performers in dance and other activities who assume a universally understood language of movement may not be communicating effectively.

In a study of elementary school children's social life, I asked boys and girls in grades two, four, and six how they can tell if a child feels different emotions.[17] Several clues identified the same emotion. For example, in answer to "How can you tell if a child is angry?" several children focused on arm-hand action and physical contact: "Sometimes they slug you," said a sixth-grade boy. A second-grade youngster put it this way, "They balls his fist—they push." The appearance of the entire body was a clue for other children: a sixth-grade girl remarked, "Sometime they puff up." The stomping of feet also indicated anger. Children said the face attracted attention: "They roll the eyes at you, get all hunched up"; "When a boy gets mad, his lip start sticking out." Occasionally an expression intended to be friendly was interpreted otherwise, and this triggered a fight.

Given the historical background on universalism, it was not surprising that the dance teachers dismissed culture. Furthermore, the debate raging in the field of nonverbal communication is whether humans universally express and comprehend behavior or culturally express and understand feelings on the bases of, for example, ethnicity, age, or sex. There appears to be support for both arguments in research and criticism. At stake is the issue of whether humans have choice as actors-directors who monitor their own behavior or merely react innately and mechanistically to a stimulus within their developmental experience as other animals do.

Since World War II, after a gap of nearly fifty years, there have been an increasing number of studies of nonverbal communication in the social and behavioral sciences. Charles Darwin, the first major synthesizer of ideas about the nature and expression of emotion, heralded this investigation in the nineteenth century (1872). He postulated that there are innate universal emotional inner states and physical processes that manifest themselves in expressions of the face and body. These movements are vestiges of reactions of early humans that were effective in survival. Darwin's theory of evolution and concept of universal species-specific behavior gave impetus to the work of psychologists such as Paul Ekman, Carroll Izard, and Robert Rosenthal and ethologist Irenäus Eibl-Eibesfeldt.[18]

Psychiatrist Albert Scheflen and anthropologists Weston La Barre, Ray Birdwhistell, David Efron, Edward Hall and Frederick Erickson, are among those who counter Darwin's position. They suggest that culture guides humans in knowing what emotions to express and how.[19]

We may expect some universally understood movements in dance because they are innate to or result from common human experience. After all, movement is available to everyone; it is part of all human commerce. The musculature of an emotional expression may be the same in all people. The smile of happiness has wrinkles, tensions, and certain positions of facial features. However, groups graft cultural meanings onto the physical medium of the body. Culture creates the meanings of a smile. It could mean embarrassment, anxiety, or warning that unless a provocation ceases an attack will follow. Compared to Americans, the Japanese control facial expressions of disgust, pain, distress and fear, and they mask these actions with smiling, a social duty.[20] Orientals use the face less, while Italians employ the hands more than Americans do in everyday encounters. Bodily energy and appearance convey information about the individual's sex, age, social group membership, and so on. We shall see to what extent dance is universally or culturally understood in actual performances.

Culture may be ethnically, generationally, educationally, aesthetically, or gender-based. Social researchers have found, for example, that women are better than men at both displaying and interpreting nonverbal signs. Differences may exist because women are nurturers and in this role share emotions with others. Because women have lower social status and participate less in key events in society, they may draw upon extra resources such as sensitivity to nonverbal cues to survive.[21]

Sociologists trace their recent interest in emotion, not specifically nonverbal communication, to Emile Durkheim, who acknowledged that social interaction promotes emotion and individuals' feelings assure social processes. "It is only by expressing their feelings, by translating them into signs, by symbolizing them externally, that the individual consciousnesses, which are, by nature, closed to each other can feel that they are communicating and are in unison."[22] Susan Shott, Arlie Hochschild, and Theodore D. Kemper are among those who explore the management of emotion and emphasize the social structure as a key determinant of feeling rules.[23] Elaine Batcher found in her study of a classroom that, whereas emotion is central to a child's experience, it is considered difficult to control and contain and therefore inappropriate to school life as it is now.[24] These sociologists take a symbolic interactionism perspective that human social relations require conscious symbolic behavior that is a product of body language. Actions occur on the bases of people constructing meanings in their engagement with each other.

None of the above scholars of nonverbal communication or emotion has examined communication in the arts. Only recently have semiotic studies turned to the performing arts.[25] (The subject matter of semiotics is the exchange of messages and of the systems of signs that underlie them.) Therefore, the second part of this book is an attempt to use the medium of dance to explore these issues in the universal/culturally specific debate.

The fact that dance as emotional expression has received so much attention for so long and dance as a universal language has gained such preeminence seems to beg for discovering what actually occurred in dancer-audience encounters. Consequently, this book is unique in taking dance as a laboratory to investigate the communication of emotion in performance and its links to the larger society. For the first time, within a historical perspective, performers' and audience members' perceptions about conveying emotion in a live performance are presented. Although there have been audience studies, these have generally been surveys that assess attendance characteristics for arts management. They ask how often people attend concerts, what their educational backgrounds are and so on.[26] Other indicators of audience views are the critics' reports. However, very few write about a particular performance, and they are not typical of most concertgoers, as I point out later. There are also (mostly unrecorded) like-dislike reactions through applause (its pace, place, and intensity), standing ovations, box office sales, departures before the end of a performance, sounds of body restlessness, or disapproving vocalizations. Experimental studies of observer intellectual, affective, and behavioral reactions to arts have concentrated on stationary visual works. There are books that explain how artists interpret meaning. However, in these different projects, both sides of the communication equation—sending and receiving—are not addressed. Studies of how accurately, according to a researcher's standard, individuals perceive messages of emotion have not included on their agendas the sending/receiving power in a naturalistic situation. Furthermore, most research in nonverbal communication has focused on a single cue or channel, such as the face, gestures, touching, and gaze. Dance is a multiple cue phenomenon.

*I.*    Chapter 2 provides the backdrop for dancers' current ways of communicating feeling and spectators' expectations. History's legacy of attitudes, beliefs, and experiences with the human body affect contemporary performances and audience reactions to them. Personal and social meanings are grafted onto the physical medium of the human body in dance. R. Dale Guthrie's *Body Hot Spots* and Olivia Vlahos's *Body: The Ultimate Symbol* suggest many of these meanings.[27] Historical attitudes resonate in the present.

Nature or culture? Reflective humans like to set themselves apart from other animals and therefore attempt to mask their animality—the instinctual expression of feeling. People repress or rechannel emotional expression into "acceptable" forms. Some societies attempt to deny passions; others label them sinful and evil. Illustrative are the Greeks' fears of the passionate masses. The Christian church's negative attitudes toward the body and religious dancing which crossed too daringly from the sacred to the sensual led to proscriptions against dance. Church fathers, recognizing that dance intermeshed with many pagan religions, thought that by banning dancing they could destroy the non-Christian religions. Impossible to uproot, however, dance traditions underwent transformations and acquired new meanings. After the French Revolution, the bourgeoisie urged people to harness the body to the production of material goods. Thus economic factors added to charges of immorality brought dance to its demise. Yet even when suppressed, dance rises phoenix-like to evoke its power.

The Greeks, Romans, Hebrews, and Christians in the Western tradition and the Indians in the East seriously reflected upon both emotion and its expression in dance. More recently, as I note later, Constantin Stanislavski pondered how best to convey emotion in theatre; François Delsarte, in opera; and Curt Sachs, Rudolf Laban, and—most significantly—Susanne Langer, in dance.[28]

Whereas Laban and his predecessors believed that dancers express real emotion, Langer, a philosopher, put forth the notion that dancers, in the poet Wordsworth's sense, recollect emotion in relative tranquillity and then dance in such a way that they symbolically convey the intended emotion effectively "with authenticity." However, Langer and her precursors did not ground their notions in evidence of what actually transpires in live social encounters. The theorists provoke many questions. What do dancers think is the relationship between emotion and movement for their performance? What is the effect of movement itself on dancers interacting among themselves onstage? What is the audience's role? When dancers communicate emotion, do the expressions control interpersonal relations, display the dancer's emotional state, or evaluate something?

Choreographers, critics, and poets write about dance performances in dance manuals, notations, newspapers, and books. Yesterday's writers become today's historical resource. Thus we have traces of a series of transformations of the Western ballet tradition. Emotions of dignity and hauteur prevailed in the courts where ballet arose. The nobility borrowed folk forms expressing joy and gender differences and elaborated the dances within the decorous restraint and protocol of the courts and their political machinations. Ballet, then, as later in Russia and China, was in the service of the state. Dance performance conveyed feelings of power and social hierarchy. At first court members performed the court ballets. Professional dancing came later. Formalized technique and virtuosity were increasingly key concerns. Ballet entered a phase of fairy-tale stories and romanticism, sometimes punctuated with sensual figures, usually peasants.

What is called *modern dance* breaks with tradition, and feeling, once again, reappears in the spotlight with pioneers Isadora Duncan, Ruth St. Denis, Mary Wigman, Anna Sokolow, and others. Form supplants feeling as a reaction against realism in the work of such masters as George Balanchine and Alwin Nikolais, and later in what was called *post-modern dance*. In a society that values innovation, the demand for novelty became especially strong in the arts. The stylistic swing of the "point and counterpoint" pendulum then begins to herald a return from an emphasis on form and virtuosity to the human sentient condition.

The history and attitudes toward the body and emotion and the expectations for different dance styles linger among contemporary performance participants. We shall soon explore what audiences and performers share in common.

*II.* "Onstage," the second section of the book, is about a pilot study of performer intentions and audience reactions at live concerts in Washington, D.C., that were part of the varied Smithsonian Institution Division of Performing Arts Dance Series. One is called the American Dance Experience and the other, World Explorer. The series present diverse dance genres and cultures; they have comparatively small (seating at the several theatres ranges from 280 to 550), multicultural audiences of males and females ranging from youngsters to senior citizens. The audience typifies the broad dance concert audience in the United States in being, for the most part, middle class, white, female, and having higher education.[29]

The World Explorer Series performances from living cultures provided opportunities for audiences to learn about cultural areas that have rich forms to express fundamental thoughts and feelings. The series included "Kuchipudi" performed by Indrani of India, "Kabuki Dance," by Sachiyo Ito of Japan, "The Philippine Dance Company" directed by Reynaldo Alejandro, and "Kathakali" presented by a company that is based in India. (The other performers now reside in the United States.) These dances exemplified the vitality and creativity which are a universal part of the human experience and added meaning and context to the stationary collections of the museum (e.g., the exhibition of Indian instruments at the Museum of Natural History and the carvings at the Freer Gallery).

The American Dance Experience Series sought to enhance appreciation of dance in America. Concerned with forms and artists nurtured in the United States who explore their inner worlds and outside environments, this series is conceived as a living, moving Smithsonian exhibit. Audiences are "encouraged to view and participate in many ways— through performances and encounters with leading artists, in relation to their own bodies and lives, and within a matrix of American culture and history." The series presented two endangered traditions—the black jazz "American Tap Masters" and the creations of trail-blazing choreographer-performers, "Modern Dance: The Early Years." The series also brought to the Smithsonian two of the numerous avant-garde forms that move beyond traditional genres, "Post-modern Dance: Douglas Dunn" and "Dance and the Camera: Sage Cowles and Molly Davies."

In the second section of the book, I present each concert separately, following the sequence in which I saw the performances. A sketch of the history and characteristics of the specific dance genre and the performer's professional life prefaces the exploration of performer and audience views. Background material, or performance ecology, on the dance form and dancer is presented because it mediates the relationship between the performance and reaction to it. The historical and cultural baggage that shapes expectations goes by many names: cognitive map, scheme, frame of reference. The background material situates the performance, acquaints us with the performer, and provides the basis for audience evaluation. Emotional expressions, perceptions, and responses derive from a complicated set of interactions of the physically and culturally conditioned self.

Out of each performance emerged an issue which concerned participants. The concerts brought to the fore the conflict between tradition and change, as well as what individuals expect when they go to a performance that has a particular billing. Several performances raised the problem of the validity of dance as a "living museum" and historical testimony. Other concerns included dance as cultural identity, social solidarity, gender role definition, and receptivity to alternate ways of seeing.

The discussions of the concerts are not uniform because of the variable themes, salience of emotion, and uneven literature on dance genre and specific dances. Some forms of dance have ancient codified and recorded traditions to draw upon; others are unrecorded folk traditions about which little is known. There are new styles with an evolving mythology. Although there were series subscribers at the concerts, each dance genre also attracted a following with unique orientations. For example, postmodern dance appeared to have a more analytically oriented audience than did the modern dance performance group. This was manifest in the greater and more detailed survey participation of the former audience. In addition, the discussions of the concerts vary because of the similarity of the choreographic and research processes. Both of these creative approaches sometimes come to fruition as intended; yet at other times they do not fully materialize due to unanticipated developments. Dancers have their own views and ways of working that may be incompatible with the choreographer's or researcher's procedures.

Included in the report of each audience survey with its fixed questions and open-ended comments are the emotions that were perceived and their frequencies, patterns of how people thought the emotions were conveyed, the relationship of spectator responses to their background characteristics, and the coincidence of dancer (sender) intentions and audience (receiver) intentions.

A summary chapter follows the presentation of the individual concerts, with commentary on the similarities and differences within and among performances: performer views on emotion, how spectators identified emotions onstage and whether viewer background characteristics made a difference in perception, mutuality of intention and perception, audience feeling in response to emotions perceived, common themes, and application of research findings.

## APPROACH

How did I explore the live performer-audience connection? I drew upon both humanities and social science approaches in an attempt to identify a slice of life in a virgin area of investigation. Each research method simultaneously provides a way of seeing and a set of blinders, both anticipated and unexpected situations, and a host of problems. These issues are discussed further in the appendix, which provides more detail on methodology than in the following discussion.

Psychological laboratory research, with its measures for validity and reliability, is usually atomistic in manipulating one or two variables or channels of communication (for example, face or face and hands) in artificial settings with posed or specifically created stimuli and chosen respondents. Actual life exchanges, however, are multichanneled and determined by the situation.

This exploratory study, grounded in anthropology/semiotics and symbolic interaction, seeks a more open-ended "native's" interpretation of what transpires in a natural setting (not controlled by a researcher). The approach is in some ways similar to that of clinical psychology. Emphasis is more on how participants in an event construe meaning rather than on eliciting responses in more rigid, predetermined categories. The data are what respondents conceive of as emotions. Of course, in presenting responses, I am influenced by the literature on dance movement analysis, especially the work of Laban as interpreted by his many followers. While moving out of the laboratory into naturalistic settings affords ecological validity, self-report data have their response biases. Research that focuses on the process of social exchange and takes into account context and situation loses the rigor required for statistical tests and limits the kinds of conclusions that can be drawn.

A live encounter in theatrical performance or everyday life has the excitement of the possibility of the unexpected that filmed performance lacks. Film also creates some distortion in what is presented and how (e.g., detail, expanse, and angle). In addition, film's two dimensions twist out of proportion the three-dimensionality of performances.

Following Charles Morris, the semiotic approach has three foci: semantics, syntactics, and pragmatics.[30] In this empirical study, the semantic question is, what is the emotional meaning of sent and received messages of a particular portion of a concert? The syntactic question is, what are the clues to identify an emotion? The pragmatic question is, how do people feel in response, what influences shape people's perceptions, and what are the policy implications of the degree to which performer intentions and audience perceptions dovetail? Historical research on the dance form as well as expectations about feeling, the body, and dance illuminate relations between the performance and its context.

In this work *perception* refers to meaning added to sensation on the basis of the perceiver's anticipation, personal life, and social groupings. Perceiving and imagining involve choice. Ulric Neisser has pointed out that we are largely responsible for what we come to know. A person's perception of emotion may be impeded by the perception of other stimuli onstage; for example, moving images that counter one's aesthetic—that is, notions of appropriateness and competency, as in an avant-garde performance. Context, in this case, is obviously relevant. The historical context, the contemporary social structure, and the process of unique events are taken into account, for they shape expectations that create meaning.

The anthropological ethnographic field work approach incorporates eliciting the perspectives of the "natives" or participants in the performance event, dancers and audience members (critics and nonspecialists alike). The analyst's view appears in the kind of information elicited and the way the material is presented. In this study an attempt was made to foreground one of several aspects of performance, that is, of aesthetic signs on stage, and to draw out reflexivity from performance participants about emotion.

Anthropological semiotics does not merely focus on the "text" (in this case, the dance before the first intermission of a concert) to be analyzed by the researcher, but also the "writer" (choreographer), "speaker" (dancer), and multiple "readers" (audience members), and the performance event context, which includes its history and economics, which bear some degree of referentiality. The dance is a complex, not straightforward text with various components, most of which are spelled out in appendix table 3. The dance is "read" in light of knowledge of the historical development of the dance genre and other expectations and experiences that color a participant's perception and interpretation. The same stimuli onstage evoke different readings, especially when—instead of seeing a ballet that follows a dramatic story spelled out in program notes—dance viewing demands creative participation on the viewer's part. Consequently, there is no one code to crack in discovering meaning, although I attempt to identify patterns that emerge from individual interpretations. The meaning of a performance is the interplay of sender-receiver intention-perception within its context.

I describe social discourse gained through my participant-observation role as an audience member and usher at a series of events that occurred over a year in an urban society characterized by a varied population. As a dance participant and consumer in this urban society, I was not in a strange setting—that is, there was shared culture and experience. Participants in two, not mutually exclusive, "communities" of ticket subscribers and independent ticket purchasers shared their views primarily through a survey. The form identified the researcher and sponsor, and it promised anonymity to participants. I also interviewed the choreographers/performers. The process of discovery to arrive at a focus, a key aspect of ethnography, included earlier work on performance and an examination of the relevant literature.[31]

My concern is with the process by which the emotional content of a dance is formulated. The process includes the choreographer's intentions, dancer's actions, and audience perceptions and clues to them. Signs of emotion become such through the perception that arises in the performance interaction.

Thus this book encompasses the symbolic interactionism perspective. It centers upon immediate, irreproducible experience in which a person defines, interprets, and imposes meaning. Premises crucial to this approach, developed by George Herbert Mead, Erving Goffman, and others, are that humans act toward each other on the bases of the meanings they have for each other and that these meanings emerge through social interaction. Performance participant perceptions may broaden our knowledge of meanings that affect social relations.

Prior to performances, before, during, and after rehearsal, as time, convenience, and performer preference permitted, I spoke with choreographers and performers (often the same). With the individual's permission, I tape-recorded open-ended questions and answers for later transcription, analysis, and comparison with audience responses. I asked, "As a dancer, what emotion(s) do you want to communicate to the audience in the dance before the first intermission? How do you think you get the emotion(s) across to the audience?"

I also asked performers how they motivate a movement, that is, how they consciously infuse it with a reason for happening. "What feeling(s) do you have to have to dance? Does the feeling motivate the movement or does the movement motivate the feeling?"

Since it was obviously difficult to talk in person with all members in a theatre audience who were willing to share their reactions to a performance, I used a written form to elicit their views on the dance before the first intermission. This part of the concert was chosen so that people could have recall and writing time during intermission. As audience members entered the concert theatre, my assistants and I, who acted as ushers, gave them survey forms that explained the study and asked them to identify the emotion(s) they perceived on stage, clues they used to identify the emotions, and how they felt in response to the emotion conveyed. In addition, the form had spaces to indicate the respondent's background characteristics, such as sex, age, ethnic group, religion, occupation, education, income, and dance knowledge, so that associations between perceptions and aspects of a person's background might be identified. There was a relatively large space for audience members to make comments of their own choosing. Many people provided unique insights.

The voluntary responses of one-third to one-half of the audiences at entertainment/arts events comprise a selective sample. Yet it goes beyond the one or two critics who usually provide the sole commentary on a performance and who may not address the questions of what emotions are conveyed and how. Furthermore, the critics' commentaries are often truncated or otherwise edited in newspapers or magazines due to limited space.

A discussion of audience perceptions must, of course, include the critics' reviews. The critics are our most consistently articulate audience members. Their work involves fact plus value. To find value, they need understanding, feeling, and educated, discriminating taste. Critics give their personal reaction, sometimes, as noted critic Clive Barnes points out, relying on questioned values and advocating their own prejudices.[32] In their search for characteristics of artistic significance and merit, they act as a bridge between the artist and the broader audience. Critics guide and explain. For audience members who have seen a dance, these writers often articulate responses they themselves had. For those who did not have these reactions, the critics may arouse their curiosity or disagreement. Critics may create a "surrogate performance" through which readers become a surrogate audience. In this situation, readers who have not seen a performance construct what their own experiences would have been had they been at the dance itself.

The public expressions of the cognoscenti may have an impact on the performer-audience connection before and after the performance. A review of a dance performance is promotion (or anti-motion) and advertisement. Thus critics, arbiters of public taste, often determine the existence and nature of future performer-audience exchanges. Some leading critics are opinion leaders for other critics. The press packet for a concert often includes quotes of praise and endorsement of writers at major publications who have already reviewed the performance. Their imprimatur often influences other newspapers and magazines. The critics are important to performers. As the well-known dancer, teacher, and writer La Meri put it at the Dance Critics' Conference in 1981, "That's the way you pay the rent. The dancers need the public, so you care." About some forms of dance, however, Spanish dancer Marriano Parra pointed out, "Critics' reviews don't get people jobs anymore."

In this book I consider several aspects of emotion: emotion to perform, emotion on stage as experienced feeling, emotion as a symbol for real feeling, and emotion that an audience member feels in response to the emotions performers convey onstage. In addition, my concern is how messages of emotion are conveyed and perceived.

For each concert I explore the following questions: Do performer intentions and audience perceptions of the emotions conveyed on stage and clues to them coincide? What are the differences?

Do the means of conveying and perceiving emotions generally vary according to the dance genre? Darwin's research directed attention to the face as the mirror of emotion. We speak of the eyes as the windows of the soul. In its outward manifestation, according to Mohan Khokar, an Indian authority on expression, the "face becomes the register" of emotion.[33] We consider the head as the command center of the body. Yet, in a form of expression that uses the body as its instrument, is the face focal in conveying emotion?

How do audience members feel in response to the emotions they see on stage? Empathy refers to the capacity to participate in another person's feelings and ideas. Is there a pattern that suggests a dancer's power to evoke feeling?

I also explore the issue of whether the perception of emotion in movement and the use of different clues vary with the background characteristics of a performer or audience member. People often assume that they see, feel, or think much the way that others do. Yet some emotion and action concepts must be learned. Such variables as age, gender, and ethnicity often affect what we learn. We do not know whether groups selectively pay attention to one or another channel of communication. Of course, an individual's perceptual learning and intellectual interests may lead to unique experiences when viewing the same visual patterns from the same spatial position. Some people have acquired sophisticated acumen and subtlety in being able to recognize and describe fine nuances of feeling. Others lack such discrimination and articulation.

On the basis of cultural variations that research has identified, my hypothesis is that people who differ by age, gender, ethnicity, education, income, occupation, and knowledge about dance will differ in perception. People in these demographic categories tend to share culture—some common values, beliefs, and attitudes that are transmitted historically. I also expect that there will be shared perceptions irrespective of background characteristics.

SURPRISES

As I found to be the case in most of my research, this study of feeling shattered some assumptions I held and led to byways unforeseen when I embarked upon the project. For example, at the first performance of the Smithsonian series, "American Tap Masters," I assumed the performers would want to get across the same feelings to the audience. After all, these men attended the same "dancing school"—the street, where youngsters freely picked up, elaborated, and polished their art, continually creating new sounds; the dancers came from the same ethnic background and were age mates. But Bunny Briggs's intention was to convey the feeling of relaxation; Sandman Sims wanted to get across the feeling of a "kid with a new toy"; and Chuck Green's goal was to communicate the feeling of authenticity by which sounds would stimulate the listener/looker's visual imagery and own creative story.

There were other kinds of surprises. I unwittingly found myself the subject of a dance performance. Douglas Dunn was told about my study before I had the opportunity to explain it to him. In his lecture-demonstration prior to the concert, he was illustrating how he collaborated with his musical composer/performer. Each independently created his own work and then they performed simultaneously. During this demonstration Dunn moved about the stage and told stories. He started one about an anthropologist who wanted to talk with him before his premiere and to give questionnaires to the audience which he felt would shape their expectations. He displayed unhappiness onstage but did not finish the story. (When we talked the next day at a mutually convenient time, he explained to me that he reacted negatively to my request because he keeps the day of a concert to himself to make the performance really special.) After the demonstration, Dunn invited the audience to ask any questions they wished. Someone asked what was the ending to the story about the anthropologist. Dunn replied, "We haven't talked yet." Making dances and making studies bear similarities, especially the way Dunn works. As Alan M. Kriegsman put it: "His laboratory is the dance studio; and his test tubes and reagents are fellow dancers and movement impulses. His experiments take the form of testing movement hypotheses— if a dancer moves thus-and-so, he asks himself, how will this relate to his or her neighbors, to the ambient space, to the movements that came before and those that follow? But the questioning is acted out first, and articulated, if at all, only afterward."[34] Researchers, too, follow certain protocols and then modify procedures to accommodate the reality of live people, spaces, and sequences, especially the unanticipated, in naturally occurring behavior.

IMPLICATIONS OF THE STUDY

The suggestive answers to the questions raised at the Smithsonian dance concerts can expand our knowledge of emotion, movement, and communication. Reporting on the sender-receiver equation and receiver variation will shed light on human diversity. What is learned could enable those who perform in a variety of fields—dance, drama, education, and public service—to reach their audiences more effectively. The long-term implications of understanding the nonverbal communication of emotion for the quality of human life are important. Performers may fail because of faulty communication. Therapists may erroneously assume universal and easily read internal states. Community development workers and political figures may unwittingly offend constituents who differ from themselves in some ways. Because the body is still generally a repressed aspect of our culture, we tend to believe the sincerity of the politician who calmly looks us in the eye over television. Awareness of the body's power and resourcefulness protects us against its exploitation and manipulation. The way a person expresses emotion may invite assault through what a policeman called an "aura of muggability."[35] Prisoners at Rahway State Penitentiary in New Jersey noted five movement characteristics common to all potential easy victims: walking by picking up the whole foot and putting it down, using exaggerated strides, moving the same arm as leg, moving the top of the body at cross purposes, and moving so that limbs appeared to be propelled from outside the body instead of from within.

In United States urban life and in international relations, cultural exchanges such as the performing arts are claimed to promote understanding. Thus we have ethnic festivals in cities and visits of the Peking Opera from China. However, receptivity to performing arts events often depends upon understanding what occurs. And a negative reaction to the group's performance is unlikely to promote positive feelings toward an unknown or disliked group. Whereas Elizabeth Taylor Warner refers to art transcending language and being universally understood,[36] Kriegsman writes about a Korean dance performance: "The cause of the boredom was simple enough, the inscrutability of a strange and symbolically intricate narrative when rendered in a language unknown to the spectator."[37] Of course, there are universally communicative scenes, such as the pathos of the death of a child.

Cross-cultural communication misunderstandings often work to the detriment of the so-called disadvantaged. Without the ability to see the world as another person does, teaching, advice, directions, reinforcements, rewards, and punishments become ineffective. In multicultural communication, a person who is unable to evoke shared meaning might merely dismiss the other person in negative terms. Misunderstandings may reinforce the existing prejudices and xenophobia which well-intentioned people are attempting to eliminate. Furthermore, misunderstandings may create new ethnocentric attitudes and behavior, or lead to confrontations.

Being misunderstood and misunderstanding others can create emotional stress for an individual. Although this stress may motivate the individual to create understanding, it more often leads to failure and frustration, which in turn affect mental health and overall life adaptation. For example, individuals who are less accurate in labeling facial expressions of emotion appear likely to engage in antisocial behavior which may cause difficulty for themselves and others.[38]

*III.* The final section of the book, "The Punch of Performance," shows how the emotional impact of dance in informal and theatrical settings ramifies through other aspects of human life. Dance performance can have a strong and lasting impact upon a viewer. Reactions to dance may be immediate, delayed, and/or prolonged. We know that powerful emotional experience may alter an individual's life course.

A dramatic illustration of the performer-audience connection occurs among the Kaluli in Papua, New Guinea, at the Heyalo dance. In this nonliterate society, guests dance for an audience of their hosts. At the Heyalo dance as many as twenty dancers enter a loghouse which is illuminated by torchlight. They accompany their dance with simple, nostalgic songs about different landmarks in their hosts' land. The hosts may burst into tears because of the strong sentiment that is aroused. "Then, in reaction to the sorrow they have been made to feel, they jump up angrily and burn the dancers on the shoulders with the torches used to light the ceremony. The dancers continue their performance without showing any sign of pain."[39] After the night-long dancing and singing accompanied by weeping and burning, the dancers, frequently feeling second- or third-degree burns on their arms and shoulders, pay compensation to these individuals they sorrowed. In the Kaluli performance, the communication of feeling occurs through the sung place names which remind people of the past, particularly of beloved friends and relatives now absent or dead. Another example of a powerful performer-audience relationship occurs in the Sinhalese healing rites.[40] The exorcist attempts to sever the relationship between a patient and malign demons and ghosts. The exorcist's performance of various dance sequences progressively builds up emotional tension and generates power. The power created in the energy of the dance leads to entrancement of the healer and/or patient. Their bodies become the demonic spirit's vehicle, constitute evidence of its control, and convince spectators of the need for a change in social relations that will transform the patient from a state of illness to health.

Such behavior does not follow performances at the Smithsonian Institution, where there is more emotional distance and restraint. However, theatrical and everyday life share analogous qualities.

All the world's a stage
And all the men and women merely players:
They have their exits and their entrances;
And one man in his time plays many parts . . .

Theatrical and other stages have conventions and rebellions against them. All stages involve some predictability, depend upon certain prescribed roles, and have repercussions. Theatrical and other forms of life often merge, most notably in the political arena. Of course, nontheatrical life may be more open-ended, with a greater number of junctures at which "actors" negotiate rights and obligations.

Although assessing the specific impact of the Smithsonian dance concerts is beyond the scope of this project, it is possible to suggest how the emotional impact continues to influence people through the language they use. Language mirrors human mind and emotion.

The metaphor of dance links humanity to its history and vitality. To dance is an innate human propensity built into the psychic, bodily, and cultural potential of an individual. Through historical time and across geographic space, one discovers that concepts about dance are an ingenious way to communicate ideas and feelings in the attempt to cope with human existence. People's metaphorical use of dance in language reveals the punch of performance even though they may not participate in doing, viewing, or otherwise appreciating dance. Metaphor is a means of commenting on one kind of experience in terms of another. We find it hard to define what something is unless we do so by analogy, that is, by showing what it is like. Our most basic concepts—love, work, status, happiness, and health—are understood metaphorically. Havelock Ellis wrote *The Dance of Life*.[41]

Metaphors organize vast amounts of information into a familiar package and go beyond themselves in a creative, insightful way. While the process of conceptualizing meaning through metaphor is universal, the specific meanings of analogies are culturally relative. Sophisticated, industrialized societies depend heavily upon words. Their preeminent status is seen in childhood education, with its scant attention to developing the skills of nonverbal communication. Yet we see the significance of dance in the way the concept with its denotations and connotations of feeling and form has permeated the vernacular and literary language.

There are contrasting perspectives on dance. One is that dance offers a model of human potential. Although the process of assembly line production or computer direction in industrialized countries has deemphasized the creativity and adaptivity of dance, dancers have not abandoned the meshing of mind and body, ideas and feelings transformed into the visual kinetic patterns we call dance. The choreography of a solo or groups of dancers is a matter of managing bodies—reflecting possibilities for the individual in space, duos in interpersonal intimacy, individuals and groups in families, businesses, work teams, and so on.

Literary analysts devote treatises to the use of the dance concept in Shakespeare, nineteenth-century novels, and contemporary poets. Through newspapers and media, the metaphors of dance with its genres, tempi, and interpersonal contact reach the homes of everyone. For example, Robert G. Kaiser describes the presidential candidates' debate between John Anderson and Ronald Reagan as a "mannerly forensic minuet."[42] The debate had the style and pace of the minuet's slow, graceful forward balancing and bowing, courtly toe pointing, and planned and controlled performance devoid of spontaneous emotion. About the 1980 Democratic convention, a *Washington Post* editorial remarked that for some observers,

> Every little movement of the podium polka on the last night of the Democratic convention must have had a meaning all its own. For some students of such performances, obviously the firm handshake accompanied by the glassy I-don't-really-hate-you expression of both men was not adequate. Some traditionalists, including apparently more than a few in the president's trailer, were candidly admitting disappointment that the evening's program did not include the Joint Vertical Arm-Raise, known indelicately by some in the photographic community as the "armpit" shot.[43]

The polka is an informal people's recreational dance. On the oil crisis, a critical issue in public life, Jack Anderson cautioned us: "before visions of bargain fuel begin dancing in your heads. . . ."[44] Here the metaphor of dance refers to the fanciful feelings of joy.

In this book I not only present a historical backdrop and then spotlight dance performance and the converging or diverging of participants' perceptions of flesh-and-blood dancing but also trace the way people have used the dance concept. In everyday life and in the world of letters, the people who dance, the dance process of production, and the performance itself appear as metaphors for character, social stability, change, conflict, and the feelings that people have toward them.

Feeling is the glue and lubricant in the human connection we all seek for our survival. The subject of emotion evokes a swirl of questions that humans have sought to identify and grasp. This book on feeling in dance and society is an attempt to answer some questions; it also raises many more that we cannot answer. We can experience and enjoy a performance without understanding it intellectually or reacting analytically. Contemplation, of course, has its special advantages. Hopefully this book will offer insights to stimulate further research and to be a positive influence on the human connection. Knowledge of how emotion is communicated should enable performers in clinical, everyday, and theatrical life to reach their clients, constituents, and audiences more effectively.

## CHAPTER 2

# First Steps: Feeling through the Ages

Attitudes toward the body and emotion emerge in making and perceiving dance. These perspectives, as we shall see in the discussion of the eight live concerts, affect who participates in a concert and how they react. About five decades ago elder statesman of dance criticism John Martin called our attention to the associations of the body:

> Any theory of dance that attempts to make use of the body as an instrument of pure design is doomed to failure, for the body is of all possible instruments the least removable from the associations of experience. There is no movement of any of its members that can conceivably be separated from implications of usefulness, whether they are positive or negative implications. The body has developed through the ages, slowly and carefully, with that stark economy which is nature's own, solely in terms of its serviceability; even its aspects of decorativeness and beauty are not merely superficial appurtenances but actually associational concomitants of use. It is totally out of the bounds of possibility for a man to raise his hand or kick his foot or bend his torso without implying something in the movement. If he tries to do so, he merely says in effect to the spectator: "I am now actually thrusting, or pulling, or fleeing, or reaching, or rejecting; but excuse it, please, for what I want you to see is only the line and balance of forms as elements in design." [1]

Dancers and audiences respond to the body usage of their times. Deborah Jowitt observed, "The vanguard of dance, it seems to me, very quickly reflects how we as people feel about our bodies. The choreographers of the '60s complained about the puffed-out ribcages and rigid spines of trained dancers, even as the flower children fled from what they saw as inflated and rigid military and social conventions." [2]

The body is the vessel of feeling and dancing. Vestiges of past attitudes linger through time. Consequently, a historical sketch of attitudes toward the body and emotion sets the stage for exploring participants' views of emotion in live performances and then the impact of such performances as revealed in language using dance as a metaphor.

## SACRED AND SENSUAL: THE DANGERS OF DANCING

Through urges and feelings of pleasure and pain, the body signals its constant presence. Humans cannot escape a history as a species—primate, mammal, sexed, a form of life in a universe older than that very life. All animals experience and show basic emotions and drives: fear, hunger, well-being, anxiety, sexual arousal, aggression, reassurance, and submission. Humans, however, while sharing this behavior, attempt to distinguish themselves from other animals. The anthropologist Claude Lévi-Strauss has noted that whereas animals eat raw food, humans eat cooked food. So, too, humans attempt to modify, channel, or withhold the instinctual expressions of feeling observed among other animals. Recognizing the brute potential of passion, humans fear the uncontrolled. Furthermore, they are self-reflexive. Through aesthetic forms they also communicate emotion removed from an immediate stimulus, distanced in time and space, and with deliberately chosen rhythm, style, structure, and purpose.

Humans discovered that certain activities affect feelings. Dancing, for example, can lead to an altered state of consciousness. Brain wave frequencies, adrenalin, and blood sugar in the body change. Intense, vigorous dancing provides a fatigue which abates rage or alleviates depression. Rapid motion may induce catharsis. Turning leads to a state of vertigo. Masses of people in movement change into a charged electric body. Anthropologists and sociologists recognized that aesthetic phenomena express shared values which excite sentiments that bind people together.[3]

Significant influences on body/emotion attitudes that resonate today come from a variety of sources: the Hebrew Bible, Greek and Roman literature, Christianity, the industrial revolution, and the revolt against a mechanized society.

In the Jewish literature we learn that Jews danced to praise their god and express joy for his beneficence. Dancing was an act of using one's total resources. The Old Testament referred to dances arising out of a need to rejoice with the whole being or dances that were commonly performed for traditional festivals. These references are illustrative:

> Then Miriam, the prophetess, . . . took a timbrel in her hand; and all the women went out after her with timbrels and dancing. [Exod. 15:20]
> Is not this David, of whom they sing to one another in dances . . . ? [1 Sam. 29:5]
> And David danced before the Lord with all his might . . . [2 Sam. 6:14]
> Let them praise his name with dancing, making melody to him with timbrel and lyre! [Psalm 149:3]
> Thou hast turned for me my mourning into dancing; thou has loosed

my sackcloth and girded me with gladness . . . [Psalm 30:11]
   A time to mourn, and a time to dance . . . [Ecclesiastes 3:4][4]

The Talmud, ancient Rabbinic writings that constitute religious authority for traditional Judaism, describes dancing as the principal function of the angels.

Socrates, speaking for Greek elite sentiment, esteemed dance for health and physical development as well as for its ability to give pleasure. However, the Dionysian dance, popular with women and lower classes who were excluded from participation in the sports of the various city-states, found disfavor among the elite. The upper class feared that dance could not be controlled and would incite people to disrupt society.

Plato approved of slaves and aliens performing what he called comic dances, including those for bacchanals, because their performances could be state-regulated. Considering dance to be identical with education as a whole, Plato deemed the uneducated man *achoreutos* or danceless; the educated one, *kechoreukos*, endowed with dance. But there were two kinds of dance, the noble and the ignoble. Plato thought that heavy penalties should be imposed upon citizens engaged in orgiastic dance rituals, for humans must not move as other animals do—with abandon.[5] Believing in the division of mind and body, Plato assumed that emotion was unbidden and uncontrollable. He condemned the arts for arousing the passions and consequently undermining the state. However, Plato did recognize that the violent bodily movements freed troubled individuals from inner conflict.

Aristotle, Plato's pupil, developed the proposition that the arts may produce catharsis by purging the audience through pity and terror. Experience in these arts permitted individuals to relive and therefore resolve earlier painful experiences which were unfinished. The reawakening occurs in a context which is sufficiently safe so that the distress experienced is not overwhelming.

Aristotle's *Poetics*, written in the fourth century B.C., is a well-known treatise on dramatic arts that remains a respected theory of criticism for dances with dramatic structure or origin. It continues to influence contemporary viewers' expectations. Aristotle would regulate dancing to serve as moral training. The idealistic rather than the realistic or grotesque could help purge a youth's soul of unseemly emotions (*Politics* 8. 5−7).

The concept of causality and effect stems from Aristotelian canons. Another perspective was that music should be selected to serve the dance. Contemporary viewers immersed in Aristotelian aesthetics thus find dances that are composed of randomly selected and ordered movements performed apart from an integral relationship with music difficult to understand or like.

Both the Greeks and Romans had professional dancers. Lucian, quoted in chapter 1, argued that professionals should portray all the human emotions.[6]

Christianity built upon the Hebrew tradition. In Matthew 11:17, Jesus remarks, "We piped to you, and you did not dance." In the "Hymn of Jesus," apocryphal Acts of John written about A.D. 120, Jesus says, "Grace danceth. I would pipe; dance ye all. . . . The whole on high hath part in our dancing. Amen. Who so danceth not, knoweth not what cometh to pass. . . . Thus having danced with us the Lord went forth."[7] Ambrose (bishop in 374–397) advocated that dancing be the companion not of delight but of grace. Chrysostom (ca. 386) warned against "unseemly motions," and Augustin (ca. 394) against "frivolous" dancing.[8]

Although the Bible discusses two kinds of dance—prayerful dance that propitiates god and immoral dance—it seems that the latter drew more attention and concern. The Israelites demonstrated through pious dance that no part of them was unaffected by the love of god. However, Salome's dance, for which she received John the Baptist's head in reward (he angered her by not reciprocating her interest in him), and other kinds of unrestrained sensual dances, led to the periodic proscription of dance.[9] Plato's attitude, through his rediscovered writing, also affected some Christian writers' negative opinions of dancing.

The Christian religion has had a love-hate relationship with the body. Christ was flesh, God's creation. Christians call the church the "body of Christ." In the Revised Standard Version of the Bible we read, "Do you know that your body is a temple of the Holy Spirit within you, which you have from God? . . . Glorify God in your Body."[10]

The Bible recognizes body communication. For example, "A worthless person, a wicked man, goes about with crooked speech, winks with his eyes, scrapes with his feet, points with his finger" (Proverbs, 6:12, 13).

Yet flesh was scorned as inferior, animal-like, and decaying. It was the root of all evil, forbidden but desired and attractive. The ubiquitous body was to be transcended. In St. Paul's view, it was to be mortified.

During the early Middle Ages (500–1100), dancing accompanied church festivals and processionals in which relics of saints or martyrs were carried. The church denounced "degenerate" secular productions. The later medieval period (1100–1400) witnessed the church's efforts to create its own dramatic portrayals. Dance was an accepted liturgical art form in mystery and miracle plays. From the fourteenth to the seventeenth century people danced for relief from disease or to ward it off. The Dance of Death was a response to the epidemic of the Black Death (1347–1373) in Italy, Spain, France, Germany, and England.

In the fourteenth century the Chorizantes' ecstatic dancing sect engaged in fantastic visions, such as wading in a stream of blood and then extricating themselves through dance. Christianized pagan fire dances were performed at Pentecost.

The Renaissance (1400–1700) developed elaborate and dramatic presentations. Religious dances flourished until the crippling effect of printed tracts, pamphlets, and books and the ascendance of the mind. Royal and rich middle-class people expressed themselves in the metaphor of dance. They spoke to each other of romantic love, chivalry, social propriety, and status through their steps and gestures, turns and bows. The court ballet involved people acting as performers and watchers, the dancing master being the only professional outsider. Later, with the trend toward the virtuoso technique, professional dancing developed.

There had been periodic attempts to curtail the frenzied, grotesque, and sensual dances: the councils of Auxenne (573), Toledo (589), Chalon-sur-Saône (639), Rome (826), Avignon (1209), and Paris (1212). During the sixteenth century the church launched a virulent campaign against the condemned abuses of dance. The church, determined to return to traditions of the Middle Ages, removed many dramatic interpolations; and the 1566 synod meeting at Lyons threatened dance leaders in churches or cemeteries with excommunication. Synodal diocesan decrees of 1585 and 1601 also threatened penalties against dancers. Still dance continued. The church allowed religious dances that were created for special occasions, such as the canonization of cardinals, or the commemoration of their birthdays. In the post-Renaissance period, the Roman Catholic and Protestant churches eliminated the sacred dance in the oratorio, interpretation of hymns and psalms in services, and allegorical ballets. The Reformation generally succeeded in suppressing church dance.[11] Margaret F. Taylor describes some of the exceptions.[12]

The Puritans went further and viewed dance as the sport of the devil, branding it sinful.[13] By the eighteenth century, religious dances were scarce and scattered.

One unusual exception that has inspired American choreography was the Shaker sect that developed at the end of the eighteenth century.[14] Believing that the day of judgment was at hand, the Shakers considered salvation possible only by confessing and forsaking fleshly practices. Notwithstanding the negative attitude toward the body, they used it to dance with the ecstasy of a chosen and exalted people. Impulsive movements evolved into ordered patterns. Shaking the hand palms downward symbolized that they were shaking out "all that is carnal." Turning the palms upward petitioned life eternal.

Thus history reveals that the Hebrews danced in praise of god and his beneficence. The ancient Greeks valued balanced mental, emotional, and physical development. Over the centuries this balance tipped. Theological and philosophical traditions of Christendom devalued the body, some emotions, and dancing. Protestantism and the industrial revolution placed overwhelming importance upon mind and reason. The body, already implicated in sin and deemed the enemy of spiritual life, now also became the foe of economic productivity.

FROM SIN TO ECONOMIC SUBVERSION

Because members of the emergent French bourgeoisie attributed the collapse of the French monarchy in part to moral laxity, they were anxious to protect their power. They therefore transformed the "immoral" body from an instrument of pleasure into one of production. To use the body otherwise was to subvert the economic and political order. In addition, the body became a victim of social snobbery—a brute linking the bourgeoisie to the lower classes. The bourgeoisie considered physical labor to be for the lower classes, who were "close to animal life." The body, a bestial adversary of mind and spirit, had to be denied or overcome. It became a well-ordered shell for hidden and denied aspects of life. "The will to power has been marshalled over many years to discipline the haphazard and instinctive movements of the body and to create the control necessary to make artful . . . moving forms," wrote social historian Stephen Kern.[15]

Even though technology violated the natural order, it opened new possibilities for the human body in action. Ballet was at once anti-technology in its nonmachine creativity and pro-technology in its emulation of the machine. Ballet experienced an increasing development of technique; fouettés (rapid turns on one leg as the foot rises *en pointe*, while the other makes circles at hip level) flashier and more numerous, elevation higher, speed greater, bodies sleeker and as angular as the skyscraper, and movements sharper. Recoiling from the machine to avoid enslavement, some people turned toward ballet in their view of the body as less an encumbrance than an instrument and idealization of human potential and self-disciplined rule over the flesh.

In spite of some interest in ballet, the dominant secular forces that gradually replaced the influence of the church considered dance of little practical value; it was merely light entertainment. When Protestant asceticism, republican theory, bourgeois acquisitiveness, and modern capitalism fused in the United States, work, frugality, sobriety, and rational mastery of self-passion and sensual appetite predominated in the hierarchy of values. Self-control meant control of the body and, further, control of people who were primarily of the body. The deprecation and relegation of dance to the nonessential or vulgar and primitive created an obstacle to the growth of dance in the United States.

The critique of industrialism in the nineteenth and twentieth centuries took a variety of forms. Affirmation of the human body was one. A few clairvoyant individuals celebrated the human body: for example, Rimbaud, Walt Whitman, Nietzsche, William Morris, Thomas Hardy, Havelock Ellis, D. H. Lawrence, and especially Freud.[16]

Dancers were at the vanguard of body resurgence. They became exemplars of the integration of mind, feeling, and body. Part of the feminist movement, Isadora Duncan and Ruth St. Denis rebelled against male-dominated norms and customs, especially those that constricted women's potential achievement. Having been excluded from the world of men, women were not constrained by all of its norms, especially about dancing and feeling. Herb Fredricksen, male leader of a Washington, D.C. area folk dance company, said men often are conditioned from childhood to keep their emotions "bottled up." Dancing is emotional. As a result, women take more readily to dancing because they are freer with their emotions.[17]

The 1960s gave yet another impetus to body resurgence. The cornucopia of literature and activity on diet, physical fitness, sexual freedom, and narcissism proliferated.

## THEORISTS AND CHOREOGRAPHERS ON FEELING AND DANCE

Theorists on the body, emotion, and movement who wrote during the latter part of the nineteenth century and the first half of the twentieth have influenced the attitudes of contemporary dance participants. Among such theorists are François Delsarte, Wassily Kandinsky, Constantin Stanislavski, Rudolf Laban, Curt Sachs, and Susanne Langer.

The French philosopher François Delsarte, with pseudo-scientific theories about the body as a mirror of the soul, articulated principles whereby humans give form to feeling through the body. He developed a system of spiritual labeling of the body. Delsarte classified each bodily gesture in terms of an emotional significance. He described how emotions changed as body position changed. From 1839 until his death in 1871, he developed and taught the "laws of expression." His "science of applied aesthetics" provided rules for controlling body movements in order to express a character in a natural manner. Believing that all arts and science have a trinitarian basis, Delsarte conceived of the human being as comprised of intellectual, emotional, and physical divisions that were conditioned by the natural laws of time, motion, and space. For Delsarte, nothing was more deplorable than a gesture without a motive. He designed the system for opera singers, having suddenly lost his own operatic voice through incorrect training.

Although Delsarte's ideas did not have much influence on ballet, they did have an impact upon Rudolf Laban and what came to be called

American modern dance. "Papa" Ted Shawn spent about forty-five years studying and teaching Delsarte to his disciples at the Denishawn School. Shawn wrote *Every Little Movement: A Book about François Delsarte.*[18] One of his key principles was that "emotion produced bodily movement, and if the movement was correct and true, the end result of the movement left the body in a position which was also expressive of the emotion."[19]

The expressionist movement in visual arts influenced dance, especially the German modern dancer Mary Wigman. Kandinsky's aesthetic theories pointed to the need for inner feelings to moderate performance and for this artistic experience to evoke empathy in the spectator. He believed:

> A work of art consists of two elements, the inner and the outer.
> The inner is the emotion in the soul of the artist; this emotion has the capacity to evoke a similar emotion in the observer . . .
> The two emotions will be like and equivalent to the extent that the work of art is successful . . .
> The inner element, i.e., emotion, must exist; otherwise the work of art is a sham. The inner element determines the form of the work of art.[20]

Kandinsky argued that the ability to experience the works of other artists stimulated the soul through sensitivity, vibration, and enrichment. About dance he wrote:

> In dancing as in painting we are on the threshold of the art of the future. The same rules must be applied in both cases. Conventional beauty must go by the board and the literal element of "story-telling" or "anecdote" must be abandoned as useless. Both arts must learn from music that every harmony and every discord which springs from the inner spirit is beautiful, but it is essential that they should spring from the inner spirit and that alone.[21]

Stanislavski's principles of acting have been applied to the dancer's interpretation of character in dramatic choreography and to the dancer's projection of nuances of human emotion, or its absence, in other forms of dance. His method included acting with the whole body—not merely from the neck up. The training technique of affective memory evoked the past of the character, actor, and audience. Entering into the skin of a role by way of the emotions helps a performer handle the body to illuminate a character and situation. Sense memory is a basic pillar in the method. It is important for an actor to recall incidents of his or her past and to re-experience the physical emotions surrounding them. Drawing upon their own lives, performers renew works of art in the present. The raw material of sensory perception gives movement on stage its credibility. Spontaneous, free movements must be repeated as veraciously as in inner life and organic humanity. Stanislavski devised physical exercises that would stimulate desired feeling reflexively. In addition to costume and makeup, inner preparation was needed to reach the subconscious.

If a performer displayed sincere personal emotion on stage, he or she should, according to Stanislavski, awaken similar feelings within the audience: "It is necessary that the spectators *feel* his inner relationship to what he is saying."[22] However, actors should not play to audiences or acknowledge their existence.

Rudolf Laban, well known for inventing a system of movement notation that is widely used in the dance world, also had ideas about emotion and movement that have influenced dance and dance therapy. Laban described himself as a dance-poet.[23] Influenced by the mysticism of the dervish rituals and the dogma of Balkan monastic institutions, Laban believed that motion, emotion, form, content, mind, and body were inseparably united. Accepting the now questionable naturalistic doctrine that dance is a free discharge of surplus energy or of emotional excitement, he also assumed universality in the bodily expression of emotion.

A charismatic personality, Laban attracted many followers, primarily women, who developed his ideas about many aspects of dance. The Laban "cult" has grown and propagated the guru's theory as articulated in his followers' publications. Within the cult, for the most part, new knowledge that has evolved since Laban's creative work has not been incorporated to modify relevant aspects of his theory. Some people argue that Laban's work was misused, misinterpreted, and badly represented. John Foster, who assessed the influences of Laban, wrote that the Laban Art of Movement Guild "appears to invoke a fanatical following of Laban's theories more than their imaginative development."[24] The writing is characterized as "over-generalized, contains sweeping statements, is often sickly and cloying in its terminology, and smacks of veneration of the master and his works."[25]

Musicologist Curt Sachs's *World History of the Dance* is a classic. Sachs set up typologies and attempted to formulate universal patterns. He described dance as beginning as "pleasurable motoric reaction." Unfortunately, he confused the ritualistic movements of nonhumans with the dance of humans. In his expressive theory of dance, "every dance is and gives ecstasy."[26]

The most prominent philosopher of dance in the mid-twentieth-century is Susanne Langer. She recognizes that dance consists of expressive gestures of emotion that are not symptomatic, immediately felt emotions, in response to a stimulus. Rather the gestures are recollected and imagined by the dancer and transformed into forms symbolic of the idea or structure of feeling. "Everything illusory, and every imagined act (such as a feeling we imagine ourselves to have) which supports the illusion, belongs to the symbolic form: the feeling of the whole work is the 'meaning' of the symbol, the reality which the artist has found in the world and of which he wants to give his fellow men a clear conception."[27]

Langer has assessed the dance literature of the time and describes the writings of the most thoughtful dancers as difficult to read. "To a careful reader with ordinary common sense they sound nonsensical; to a person philosophically trained they seem, by turns, affected or mystical, until he discovers that they are mythical. Rudolf von Laban offers a perfect instance: he has very clear ideas of what is created in dance, but the relation of the created 'tensions' to the physics of the actual world involves him in a mystic metaphysics that is at best fanciful, and at worst rapturously sentimental."[28] She objects that Laban constantly insisted that gesture springs from actual feeling although she notes that he nonetheless understood that dance begins in a conception of feeling, an apprehension of joy or sorrow and its expressive forms. Could there be both actual feeling and symbolic feeling in dance? Sometimes, as we shall see later, the movement itself or the interaction of the dancers as they perform generates emotion, and the performers express the emotion they feel while they are dancing. And yet, not all movement expresses emotion from either the dancer's or spectator's perspective. Psychologists argue that in bodily communication the contrast between emotion and cognition is not clear.[29]

Aptly for a philosopher, Langer sees contradictions: "Only in the literature of the dance, the claim to direct self-expression is very nearly unanimous. Not only the sentimental Isadora, but such eminent theorists as Merle Armitage and Rudolf von Laban, and scholars like Curt Sachs, besides countless dancers judging introspectively, accept the naturalistic doctrine that dance is a free discharge either of surplus energy or of emotional excitement."[30] Then Langer directs us to "one curious circumstance. . . : namely, that the really great experts—choreographers, dancers, aestheticians, and historians—although explicitly they assert the emotive-symptom thesis, implicitly contradict it when they talk about any particular dance or any specified process. No one, to my knowledge, has ever maintained that Pavlova's rendering of slowly ebbing life in 'The Dying Swan' was most successful when she actually felt faint and sick, or proposed to put Mary Wigman into the proper mood for her tragic 'Evening Dances' by giving her a piece of terrible news a few minutes before she entered on the stage." Langer concludes: "It is *imagined feeling* that governs the dance, not real emotional conditions." She explains: "It is *actual movement*, but *virtual self-expression*."

Langer finds the antinomy most striking in the work of Curt Sachs. He groups the antics of apes in the category of genuine dance and fails to realize the momentousness of the step from this behavior to genuine art forms. I have discussed this at length in *To Dance Is Human*, extending

Langer's arguments on the basis of findings in the social and behavioral sciences since she wrote her books. What other animals communicate in motor patterns are programmed action sequences (these appear with maturation and interaction with their own species in a natural setting). These animal dance-like displays are stereotyped, usually repetitive, and involve immediate emotion and drive (for example, fear, hunger, well-being, aggression, sexual arousal) and autonomic rhythms. In human evolution, the programmed action sequences characteristic of other animals tended to be replaced by actions in which social learning and individual choice played a more important role.

According to Langer, expression is not the artist's own actual feelings but what the performer knows about human feeling: "It is a developed metaphor . . . that articulates what is verbally ineffable. . . ."[31] Langer distinguishes between verbal and nonverbal communication. Her distinction between discursive and presentational forms differentiates the kind of communication conveyed by a language from that conveyed by visual structures. Language has fixed vocabulary, syntax, and units that have independent meaning irrespective of context. A presentational form provides information at once rather than in bits strung out over time.

Langer developed these distinctions prior to developments in linguistics, sociolinguistics, and nonverbal communication that blur the dichotomy. Her criteria which characterize nondiscursive symbols are inadequate in terms of Joel Davitz's studies of nonverbal messages in nondance life and others' studies of dance.[32] There is in fact a vocabulary of symbols that people use in communicating with any given mode. There may be discursive aspects of dance in a sequence of unfolding movements and movement configurations. In addition, some dance forms have language-like syntaxes. It is important to point out that dance is more like poetry than prose.

Choreographers (often also dancers) who have written on dance or whose disciples disseminated their views have contributed to attitudes and expectations about specific dance traditions and dance performance more broadly. The noteworthy choreographers include Jean George Noverre, Loie Fuller, Isadora Duncan, Michel Fokine, Ruth St. Denis, Mary Wigman, Martha Graham, Alwin Nikolais, George Balanchine, and Merce Cunningham.

Jean George Noverre (1727–1810), trained at the Paris Opera, attracted disciples who carried on his concepts of ballet. In 1760 he wrote the following: "A well-composed ballet is a living picture of the passions, manners, customs and ceremonies . . . of all nations of the globe, consequently, it must be expressive in all its details and speak to the soul through the eyes; if it be devoid of expression, of striking pictures, of strong situations, it becomes a cold and dreary spectacle."[33] He also argued a questionable point: ". . . painting and dancing have this advantage over the other arts, that they are of every country, of all nations; that their language is universally understood, and that they achieve the same impression everywhere."[34] We shall explore just how universally understood dancing is.

A minority strain in American dance derived from the flamboyant, much admired Loie Fuller, who danced in Paris in the 1890s. She eschewed projection of the emotion or personality of the performer, a perspective to be developed in the 1960s. Fuller thought that human emotion is best expressed if it is bereft of the technical knowledge of how it should or could be done. "The moment you attempt to give dancing a trained element, naturalness disappears. Nature is truth, and art is artificial."[35]

Another American dancer who triumphed in Europe and laid the groundwork for the lineage of expressive dance was Isadora Duncan. Dances expressed her deep personal emotions. The serious music of composers like Beethoven, Schubert, and Chopin aroused profound emotion and inspired her. She began her dance through her own body, trusting it to tell her what she needed to know. The solar plexus was the central spring of all movement. Envisioning her body as the center of the universe or the stage, she believed, would generate the clarity and intent of its performance. Her beliefs thus dictated the use of the entire body in dance, contrary to the balletic, peripheral deployment of the arms and legs. For Duncan, as noted earlier, if the message was the sort that could be communicated in words, there would be no point in dancing it.[36]

Duncan influenced American dance and also inspired the Russians with her 1905 performance. Michel Fokine, trained at the St. Petersburg School of the Imperial Russian Ballet, was struck by the beauty and grace of the natural human body he observed in museum displays and in Duncan's dancing. "The New Ballet," a 1916 article he prepared for the Russian periodical *Argus*, presents his views about laws and traditions. "The traditional ballet . . . essayed to express a psychological feeling by a fixed movement, or series of movements, which could neither describe nor symbolise anything. . . . a dance is the development and ideal of the sign. The ballet renounced expression and . . . became empty." Fokine sought to remedy the mechanical state of dancing. "First, one must study oneself, conquer one's own body, and try to learn to feel and develop an ability to perform various movements. . . . The whole body to the smallest muscle should be expressive."[37]

He believed that dancing and mimetic gesture have meaning only insofar as they express emotionally the ballet's dramatic action. Mere divertissement or entertainment apart from the scheme of the entire ballet was out of the question. Fokine's new thrust advances the principle of expressiveness from the individual body to the expressiveness of a group of bodies. This contrasts with older ballets, where groups of dancers served an ornamental purpose. Fokine also required an alliance of dancing with other arts only in a nonsubservient role; for example, dance should not be overshadowed by music. His principles suggested an emotional expressiveness in dance unknown during his predecessor Marius Petipa's reign in the Russian ballet.

In the early twentieth century Vaslav Nijinsky also revitalized ballet through his attempt to make the audience "feel" his work. He wanted to create a maximum kinesthetic response. Kinesthetic sympathy occurs when we see a human body movement that we experience vicariously in our nerves and muscles; the movement evokes associations we would have had if the original movement had been ours. Nijinsky's ballets "L'après-midi d'un faune," "Jeux," "Le sacre du printemps," and "Til Eulenspiegel" communicated ideas through feeling and blurred the mime-dance dichotomy.[38] He said, "I think little and therefore understand everything I feel. I am feeling through the flesh and not the intellect. . . . I must show the meaning of life and death. . . ."[39]

Ruth St. Denis, in the early 1900s, parented the most flourishing lineage of American modern dance. She viewed the body as a manifestation of the spiritual condition. Elizabeth Kendall said that St. Denis was the first in commercial theatre to have a dancer's body realize its own natural pace and begin to occupy all the space and time on stage that it craved.[40] She used dance to "give expression to Divine Intelligence."

The German dancer Mary Wigman, influenced by Kandinsky, referred to earlier, thought that dance could come into being and exist without music, because her feelings motivated dance. In 1926 she said, "When I dance I must above all be hungry. This is the easiest way for me and my troupe to be overcome by ecstasy."[41] She explored trance motions and mysterious rituals. Foremost in her dances was the "assumption that the human body could mirror spiritual states of being."[42] She wrote:

Without ecstasy, no dance.
Without form, no dance.
The creative moment . . . creates in us out of longing need, an urge to communicate the psychic state of which the idea is born.[43]

Wigman thought creative dancers should evoke an unreserved emotional reaction in the spectator to forge a strong performer-audience connection. In 1933 she wrote,

The primary concern of the creative dancer should be that his audience not think of the dance objectively or look at it from an aloof and intellectual point of view,—in other words, separate itself from the very life of the dancer's experiences;—the audience should allow the rhythm, the music, the very movement of the dancer's body to stimulate the same feeling and emotional mood within itself, as this mood and emotional condition has stimulated the dancer. It is only then that the audience will feel a strong emotional kinship with the dancer: and will live through the vital experiences behind the dance-creation.[44]

Wigman also thought that dance was a language *all* human beings could understand.

Martha Graham, a student of Ruth St. Denis and Ted Shawn, sought the "inner hidden realities behind the accepted symbols."[45] She looked inward to her own feelings and experiences. During one phase of her career she said, "Life today is nervous, sharp, and zigzag. This is what I aim for in my dances."[46] By 1926 she was generating tension through opposed muscles inside her body. Taking themes from the twenties, Graham developed the allusions to power expressed in women's torsos, arms, backs, and necks as well as strong thighs for jumping. Her stylized movements expressed passionate emotional states and violent crises of spirit.[47] Graham recognized the need to communicate with the public and to realize that "we are trying to reach each other across a gulf."

Alwin Nikolais, in the modern dance tradition, took another path. He sought to wipe out vestiges of personal emotion. On the ballet scene, George Balanchine, choreographer of the New York City Ballet, attracted the labels "abstract" and "formal." Coming from Russia, he felt that American dancers had a "kind of angelic unconcern toward emotion."[48] He said,

A lot of people go to the theater to see their own life, their own experience. We don't give them that in the ballet. We give them something less. When you see flowers, do you have any emotion? You're moved by the color and the beauty—but what does it mean to be moved? Some people think that you have to cry to have emotions. Suppose you don't—then people believe you're cold and have no heart. Some people are hot, some cold.[49]

More recently Balanchine said he thinks as a dancer, "in steps." The dancers do not have "to 'act' a part—it's all in the music."[50] Balanchine thus deemphasizes the importance other ballet dancers/choreographers attribute to emotion to motivate movement and to performers to express emotion and evoke emotion in the audience.

Choreographers of the 1960s and 1970s, in what came to be called *post-modern* dance, emphasized "naturalness," by which they meant movement drained of emotional overlay, the forsaking of dramatic emotional story of the expressionist genre. Their choreography was often consciously polemical against earlier traditions. The post-modern choreographers sought the integrative physical experience and the doing of dance. Minimalism in dance meant that dance as form was all-important, and dance as a social force was relegated to the discard file. Progenitor of the post-modern, choreographer-dancer Merce Cunningham liberated dancing from specific references beyond dance movement itself and for its own sake. Going beyond its progenitor, the Judson Dance Theatre and the post-modernists freed dancing from the technique and overt virtuoso display of Cunningham's performances as well as the dramatic-psychological concerns he eschewed. The trained body strapped with a particular style hid the real beauty of naturalness and spontaneity of movement that was the general post-modern manifesto. Thus ordinary people who had interest, a "presence," and feel for movement performed pedestrian movements onstage in what was called dance.[51]

During the 1970s choreographers in the modern dance tradition such as Paul Taylor, Erick Hawkins, and Alvin Ailey drew upon folk and ritual traditions as models to instill vitality into the theatre. They sought to bring back the feeling in human life extruded by mechanization and technology. In an article titled "Choreographic Novelties," *New York Times* critic Anna Kisselgoff calls the visible trend within the young avant-garde "seeking an emotional response from the audience that the earlier formalists specifically avoided."[52] Illustrative of this development is the Movement Research, Inc., organization of dancer-choreographers formed "to address the unique needs of the post-modern dance community." Judy Padow is part of this new direction. She is re-creating emotional experiences through formalistic concerns and developing narratives of mood qualities. In Padow's "Cameo," critic Janice Paul writes, "The feel of intimacy and privacy reminiscent of the self-preoccupation and fantasies of a young adolescent girl" prevail.[53] Padow says, "Now my pieces are more about the organization of total perception, about composing and organizing perceptions and feelings."[54] From structuring phrases by rules, she has moved to creating phrases by thought and mood. This change leads to a deepening of feeling. "The movement dynamics are like emotional dynamics; and the richness of the dancing is found in the equal intensity of the pure physicality and the emotional tone of the movement."[55]

Johanna Boyce, another dancer/choreographer in the new trend toward concern with emotion, writes: "The dance for me is a physicalization of urges, or impulses. I feel more able to release or express myself through kinesthetic responses, through movement, than I do through talking."[56] Growing up in a home where there were reminders of universal love and with her father serving as president of the Experiment for International Living, she was propelled toward expressing questions about mutual accommodation and the importance of cultural differences and their contexts.

Deborah Jowitt, *Village Voice* critic, points out that the continuing thread of expressing social consciousness is arousing passions toward social action:

The association of modern dance with liberalism and dissent dates from the '30s, and has traditionally produced several different forms of action. Prominent choreographers of the period performed benefits for the International Labor Defense or the American League Against Fascism, just as the important figures in the Judson Dance Theatre of the '60s offered their works on programs and rallies that protested American involvement in Vietnam. Choreographers have also made dances that could be seen as a response to the political and social climate of the times, however oblique or abstract those dances might be. Martha Graham's "Chronicle" and Doris Humphrey's "With My Red Fires," both made in 1936, were extremely individual, high-level responses to the Spanish Civil War and the rise of fascism in Europe.

Some choreographers have also made unabashedly propagandistic dances—dances designed to arouse or rally "the people," rather than simply to stir the dance audience. Beginning in the '60s, quite a few black choreographers made political dances that were as unshaded and as upfront in their sentiments as posters. [57]

There are a few overtly political dances in the late 1970s and early 1980s. Sharon Hom dealt with the cultural dilemma of Chinese-Americans. Susan Griss treated the labor-management hassles that led up to the ghastly fire in the Triangle Shirtwaist Factory early in this century. "The influence of the women's movement on dance has been subtle, but powerful. Although Graham's company of the '30s like Twyla Tharp's company of the '60s was all female, in the '50s it seemed that if you saw a large group of women onstage in a modern dance concert, you could assume they were waiting for the men to come home from the sea. Women could be featured as antagonists, but you rarely saw them touching and supporting each other to the extent that you do now." [58]

Jowitt describes the Wallflower Order Dance Collective from Eugene, Oregon, as a group of five women who are "rampant about nearly every worthwhile liberal cause you can think of." She continues:

Since the Wallflower has performed in prisons and for various kinds of activist groups, one of their paramount concerns is getting audiences to identify with them and/or get what they're driving at. . . . Sometimes they communicate simply by the intensity of their emotion. . . . The only issue the women soft-pedal at all is lesbianism, which comes up obliquely in a moving but slightly self-righteous poem by Judy Grahn . . . the accusatory "Have you ever held a woman's hand?" is answered by words like "Yes, I have held the hand of a woman who was dying. . . ." [59]

We have moved from the early writing of the Hebrews to the present. In this sketch of the history of dynamics concerning the body, emotion, and dance, we see conflicting attitudes and expectations. These remain alive in the contemporary dance scene to attract (or repel) audiences to dance generally or to specific kinds of dance. The pendulum periodically swings and captures predominant sentiment in favor of one attitude or another. Sometimes there are dysfunctions between artistic creation and the general public. It may become indifferent or hostile. The avant-garde or foreign dance public tends to be limited. Do the appropriate audiences and performers mesh at the Smithsonian concerts? The next section of this book explores this issue.

ONSTAGE

## CHAPTER 3

# Hoofing to Freedom with Soul and Sole: Briggs, Sims, and Green

"Tap," explained Chuck Green, venerable elder of the black genre, "really is jazz itself. It's all about freedom." Sandman (Howard) Sims, another esteemed performer in the Smithsonian American Dance Series concert, calls the tap dancer "a free man" who shows soul when he dances. Tap dance is autonomy to express and dominate oneself and to test one's strength, wits, and creativity against anyone who is willing to try to meet the challenge. It is the opportunity to transcend the everyday, to climb out of poverty into fame and economic well-being, and to liberate for a moment the downtrodden, materially deprived, or depressed through distraction and shared rejoicing.

To be a man in America is to be free, strong, macho, and competitive. Brought unwillingly to United States soil, blacks lost many freedoms and much of their African culture, including their dances and drum accompaniments. Because the 1739 Stono, Virginia, slave insurrection used drum messages whose beats reached from one plantation to the next, the 1740 Slave Act prohibited the use of drums. Some whites recognized that potentially arousing African dances intertwined with pagan religion. Consequently these whites proscribed the dances and demonstrated their preference for docile, god-fearing Christian workers. Yet, as is historically the case, significant aesthetic forms in the lives of humans reemerge in new transformations. Dance, the primordial art in many of the more than 1,000 groups in Africa, each with its own special dances, underwent changes in manifold transplantings to assert black freedom.

## CONTINENTAL CONTINUITY
The meaning of tap dancing—performer intention, preparation, concert, and audience perception, lies, in part, in its history. After several hundred years of gestation, tap has roots running deep and long to two continents: Africa and Europe. Wrenched from their African homelands, brought to the United States, and separated from kin and cultural patterns, slaves clung to certain traditions. When prohibited from traditional drumming,

some of it melodic as well as rhythmic, slaves often let their feet take up the rhythms, and their voices, the tones. When prohibited from dancing their religion as they had done in their natal villages, blacks frequently "felt the spirit" in church with fancy footwork, clapping, and bodily action, all reminiscent of traditional African dances.

Some European dances that the black slaves saw whites performing in the United States were, with modifications, compatible with many movements in the African heritage. Numerous African groups have complicated, sprightly steps in their dance traditions.[1] Many blacks in America appreciated the energetic, complicated footwork with toes and heels in the springy Irish jig, a dance in triple rhythm performed with the upper torso held rigid, arms close to the side. Reports from about 1894, perhaps a bit exaggerated, suggest that skillful dancers could execute as many as fifteen taps per second. The clog sonority, rhythmic potential, and improvisation of the English Lancashire clog dance performed with thick, wooden soled shoes beating out rhythms on the floor also attracted black observers. Hard shoes became fashionable to cope with inclement weather or appalling factory conditions. Step dancing by the mid-1700s had taken on competitive characteristics. Men competed in the local Yorkshire pubs, and the man who danced best or longest won a pint of beer. As competition got greater and tempos faster, clogs became dangerous. By the early 1800s dancers' wooden soles gave way to more flexible leather shoes, and English copper pennies were fastened on heels in order to emphasize the sound.

Although the style and intent of tap was a blend of different continental contributions, this black genre most deeply reflects an African heritage. Black Americans carried on the African tradition of accepting the natural sensuousness of the human body. In contrast, the Anglo-Saxon tradition viewed the body as shameful and sinful. Thus Afro-Americans added torso fluidity, bending, and crouching atop the intricate, energetic footwork of the European jig and clog. The spine could curve or ripple; the shoulder, shake. Movement impulses emanated from deep inside the chest and pelvis and flowed out to the limbs.

Natural acceptance of the body and receptivity to its messages appear in rhythm. Sims says, "The greatest essence is time. Everything runs by time. You hear beats in time. It just comes to you." In Africa, in Dallas classrooms and playgrounds, and on Harlem streets, I have seen Afro-American children uninhibited by Anglo-Saxon middle-class mannerisms spontaneously dancing.

In Africa the use of multiple meters, overlapping rhythms, and syncopation is common. Often dancers contribute yet another rhythm to the distinct rhythm of each instrument in the musical ensemble accompany-

Lionel Hampton, Chuck Green, Sandman Sims, and Bunny Briggs in George T. Nierenberg's film "No Maps on My Taps." *Courtesy of George T. Nierenberg.*

ing the dancers. This African rhythmic heritage is prominent in black tap dancing, as is "shading the count" or emphasizing the off-beat.

The Afro-American method of learning tap is the same as in many African village "dancing schools": imitation. Dapper statesman of tap Honi Coles said that dancing was not a learning process—it was fun. Aspiring young tap dancers attached themselves to great dancers performing in streets, bars, and theatres. They learned to dance by observing. Sims explained that dancing schools are for rich kids in the United States. Hoofers got ideas—not steps—from other dancers. During the twenties, thirties, and forties, the Hoofers Club met in a downstairs back room at the

Comedy Club gambling establishment on 131st Street and 7th Avenue in Harlem to hold challenges and stimulate one another.

The free improvisation in many secular African dances continues in America and characterizes black jazz tap. In this genre, dances are not "set" and passed on from one person to the next or even performed the same way at each concert. When the sixty-year-old Green telephoned his eighty-year-old "teacher" John Bubbles in California, Bubbles, one of black vaudeville's all-around entertainers and innovators, encouraged Green to follow his nose, to keep on creating steps. Bubbles invented a style called rhythm tap and introduced syncopation. With deceptive nonchalance, he incorporated extra tap sounds and unique accents by dropping his heels and clicking them together as well as adding a rhythmic turn. Green tells his own protégés to do what they can do best: "Don't do someone else." Coles said conformity was "sound-wise not body-wise."

The graceful, poised demeanor of the black tapper hails from an African heritage as well as from imitation of the white plantation owners who carried on the European courtly style of the quadrille, reel, cotillion, and waltz. Stereotypically African dance is wild, hip-swinging, orgiastic movement. Yet, as I observed in work that took me to thirteen countries in Africa, and as I read in the reports of others, there is a wide variety of dance genres among the approximately 1,000 different groups on the African continent, as well as among the various social ranks. Especially notable is the centuries-old, stately, decorous dance style of many African groups' leaders.

Tap retains some stylistic patterns common to African agricultural groups whose survival depends heavily on the beneficence of the earth: dancing with an upper torso earthward-oriented, the knees gently bending and slightly straightening with each step. Sims said, "We're not strictly tappers. We're hoofers. We dance with the whole foot, not just the heel and toe." The use of the flat foot, gliding, dragging, and shuffling steps are widespread in Africa.

Thus African torso mobility, rhythmic complexity, and improvisation added to the European lively improvisatory footwork echoing through tapping shoes. There were running trills of restfulness, terrific rolls of mounting sounds, staccato ripples, and tantalizing off-beats. Various steps had different names depending upon the tapper or place.[2] There were toe slaps and slides, heel drops, digs, struts, scoot backs, lunges, jig hops, chugs, cross turns, brushes, shuffles, step ball changes, and tap patter. The buck and wing generally had swinging rhythm, clogs, jigs, song and dance (soft-shoe), acrobatics, and syncopation. The five tap wing, perfected by the Irish, was danced on one foot, the other raised backward below knee height. The dancer hopped into the air and on the way down made five clear sounds on the floor with his foot. Tappers made feet go like trip-hammers and sound like all manner of drums. In addition to style, the purposes and functions of tap dance owe much to Africa. Let us consider the freedom dance offers in Africa and Afro-American tap. Specialized dance is actual power for a performer. Through practice an individual marshals power to discipline the instinctive movements of the body. As a result, the dancer gains control over the body in order to win freedom to use it in a particular way. Dance achievement testifies to self-control, dominance, and ascendance, similar to the human conflict with nature found in Spanish bullfighting. Tappers, like many African dancers, control the rhythms of life and make the difficult look simple in testament to human competency and potential.

The freedom to express oneself in dance and distinguish oneself from others is pervasive in Africa and Afro-America. African women and potential in-laws discriminate among men in terms of their dance performance. In *Song of Lawino*, Okot p'Bitek writes about Acholi dance: "A man's manliness is seen in the arena, / You cannot hide anything, / All parts of the body / Are clearly seen in the arena, / Health and Liveliness / Are shown in the arena!"[3] Young men of the Nuba Tira tribe recite their exploits in raiding and mime their skillful actions, pugnacity, and endurance in the *habodha* dance. They try to attract the attention of girls standing in the center of the ring formed by the dancers, who will select a favorite and throw themselves against him. In the slave era, dancing skill often relieved a person from hard field labor and supplied the performer with conveniences as a reward for entertaining whites. Tap, too, is an avenue to self-distinction. On the street, in back alleys, onstage, or in film black dancers participated in the "compete," "tap off," "dance off," challenge dance which Sims described as "like fighting." The challenge "brings out the best of our own steps that took a lifetime to perfect." Peers evaluated each other, and many of the outstanding performers followed a professional career when tap was popular.

The Nigerian Ubakala Igbo women and youth, among whom I lived, were excluded from their traditional society's political and ritual bodies. However, they used dance as a vehicle to express their interests in a manner similar to that of lobbyists in the United States. Dancing served to mediate conflict and moderate political control. The Igbo, like many African groups, permit greater freedom of expression in dance than in ordinary conversation and movement. Dance allows a special kind of license which protects the individual and group from what would be libelous in other forms. Indeed, the colonialists paid heed to dance performances, instruments of satire, sometimes at the expense of dominant whites. Slaves, too, parodied the manners of masters and mistresses and diverted themselves with mock parades and messages of innuendo, allusion, and double entendre.

Coles put it this way: "Tap has the potential to describe a whole variety of feelings." Although it is usually happy and "up," he said that it can be stately. He gave the example of tappers dancing at dancer Baby Laurence's funeral at Reverend John Gensel's jazzman's church in midtown Manhattan: "With no music, we did a toom-chicka-toom-chicka-toom right in front of the coffin, and with the echoes of the church and all, it was truly solemn."[4]

Tap permits the dancer to become free from the everyday and to transcend it. As in Africa, dance is a means to reach altered states of consciousness or spiritual euphoria. Sometimes trance and possession dance are vehicles to reach such states. Since dance intertwined with religion throughout Africa, it was not surprising that some professional dancers got their inspiration in Afro-American Christian churches.[5] In the eighteenth and nineteenth centuries, the shout was allowed in the churches even when dancing was proscribed. "Hit ain't really dancin' 'less de feets is crossed," explained a participant. Because the slave reverie of the future negated the present, shout dancing permitted visions and feelings of transcendence. With body and soul, blacks reached out beyond the world that confined them, to imminent rebirth. Dancing persists in what a black middle-class colleague denigratingly called "those emotional churches!" Sims danced in his parents' Holiness Church. He said, "I believe it's the Holy Spirit that comes into me when I dance." Partaking of the Holy Spirit is a momentary freedom from the natural and a transcendence into the supernatural realm.

As in Africa, dance observers often empathize with performers in their transcendence. The pleasure of a tap performance absents them temporarily from necessity, coercion, and constraint. They forget their troubles after voluntarily paying their ticket money: the tapper delivers them from the trials and tribulations of the daily routine to a joyful state. For Green, tap is an escape to freedom: "Maps are full of roads and signs and detours and destinations. Maps are full of limitations. But when I tap, I can get lost in dancing. I don't have no maps on my taps." Blacks in America have had limited opportunities to break the bonds of political, economic, and social domination. Dance performance and sports achievement have led to some aspects of freedom.

DECLINE AND REEMERGENCE

After thriving in the early part of the twentieth century, tap performance in theatres and movies bottomed out in the 1950s. The renaissance of interest in tap dancing that began in the 1960s is a rewriting of popular history. Notwithstanding the roots of tap running across the Atlantic to the European and African continents and the flowering of tap among blacks in American ghettoes, the nation at large assumed that the greatest tap performers were white. They had more opportunity for visibility since whites dominated society. As a result of segregation in America, tap evolved into two different genres. Sometimes styles merged when blacks parodied white slave masters and white minstrels copied the mannerisms of blacks. In the 1840s New York City offered an arena for equal competition between newly freed slaves and recently arrived Irish immigrants. Here the Lancashire tradition of the dance challenge and African competitiveness reigned supreme. Legendary confrontations between Irishman John Diamond and a black man, William Henry Lane, also known as Juba, King of Dancers, led to Juba becoming the only black dancer to be accepted by white minstrel companies. Reacting to the black exclusion from white theatre stages, Sherman Dudley promoted a Theatre Owners Booking Association, TOBA, or "Tough on Black Artists," in the 1920s in order to promote opportunities for blacks. The first major appearance of TOBA performers on Broadway was in *Shuffle Along* (1921).

The wide dissemination of motion pictures with Fred Astaire, Gene Kelly, Eleanor Powell, Ginger Rogers, and Donald O'Connor created the myth of the great white tappers. With the exception of Bill "Bojangles" Robinson, brilliant, innovative black artists never received widespread recognition. Since the 1930s Robinson had been dancing and bringing laughter to many people. He gained renown through his appearance with child star Shirley Temple in the 1935 film *The Little Colonel*. Robinson performed his immortal "Stair Dance," in which he ad-libbed a dance up and down a flight of stairs.

Before its decline, tap had thrived in streets and back alleys, in black clubs (such as the Apollo and Small's Paradise Club in Harlem) that drew black and white audiences, and in splashy Broadway houses. Sims blames the popular attraction of rock for the ruin of tap and big-band jazz. "You couldn't hear the taps or see them anymore, because of the loud music and flashing lights. When we danced with the big bands, and I've danced with all of them, we were really out there as part of the act." Coles attributes the decline of tap to Agnes de Mille's success with *Oklahoma*. Broadway decided that dancing should carry a story forward, and the old set piece that was tap was dropped.

The renaissance of tap is part of the nostalgia boom that has witnessed the revival of old musicals and fads for clothes, hairstyles, and furnishings of earlier times as well as interest in the preservation of American heritage. Whites have been at the forefront in preserving forms that blacks have rejected in pursuit of the most recent fads promoted by peers and the media. This is also true for blues singers and players. Mama Thornton illustrates the case of a singer abandoned by young blacks who performs for mostly white audiences, is managed by white promoters, and is interviewed and written about by white writers and scholars. Middle-class black intellectuals may discover black behavior as art forms through contact with white college students. Jazz historian Marshall Stearns brought some of the great old black tappers to the Newport Jazz Festival in 1962/63 as a living repository of black dance history. The emergence of the black power and Black Is Beautiful movement in the 1960s did not, however, acknowledge tap dance as a glorious black achievement. The reason probably lies in the association of black hoofers with servile, demeaning roles in movies, a white enterprise.

In recent years, theatres have been resounding to the percussive rhythm blacks play out through dance. New, adoring spectators come from modern dance and ballet audiences and tap studios.[6] College dance departments, too, are grabbing tap as living history. Sims's reaction was that "tap dancing never got lost—the people just lost the dancing." In spite of the new public and belated recognition of a national treasure, black jazz tap may still be an endangered species.

### THE HUMAN CONNECTION

George T. Nierenberg saw Sandman Sims dance and then decided to make a film portrait of dancers who love their art and struggle to keep it alive. The sixty-minute 16mm color film took five years to complete. During this time George organized a series of live tap shows. The Smithsonian "American Tap Master" program featured the award-winning film "No Maps on My Taps." It shows vintage photographs and film clips of the heyday of tap. This provides the backdrop for intimate portraits of three authentic, prestigious hoofers. A live performance by the film's stars, the legendary Sandman Sims, Chuck Green, and Bunny Briggs, followed. In concert, Lloyd Mayers was on piano; Keter Betts, bass; and Mike Shephard, drums. Nierenberg introduced the concert, explaining that he does not dance, but his mother was a tap dancer. At the height of her career she gave a performance in Sing Sing. One of the inmates fell in love with her. "He's not my father," said the filmmaker.

The film conveyed pride and grief, occasional despair, awe, pathos, enormous vitality, and good humor. The audience generally recognized the nostalgia for lost forms and the sadness of people inadequately rewarded. They appreciated the men's love of dance and life's sadness. One person summarized the general sentiment: "the filmmaker captures the essence of dancers' lives and motivations." Another said it was "more cerebral than gut," reflecting the diversity of audience response.

*Performer Intention.*   In order to talk with the tappers about their intentions for the live, largely improvised performance, I met them at the Baird Auditorium for the rehearsal to run through the evening's program. The musicians—piano, bass, and drums—had not played together as a group. None had played for the dancers. And this was my first "formal" discussion with dancers about what feelings they wanted to get across to the audience. The "interview" was in keeping with the tradition of improvisation and freedom in the black jazz idiom.

I had a preconceived notion that I would get the same kinds of answers from the three tap dancers. They came from the same ethnic background, learned to dance in a similar manner, danced as featured artists in comparable places, and were roughly of the same generation. Briggs was 58; Sims, 53; and Green, in his mid-6os. My assumptions proved wrong.

Sali Ann Kriegsman, American Dance Experience Series organizer, introduced me to Briggs, who was only too willing to talk—"I'm the chatterbox." An elixir of energy, he appeared unfazed by the effort of traveling into town from New York City and offering a workshop for the D.C. high school of the performing arts earlier in the day. Born and raised in Harlem, Briggs started dancing as a toddler. He danced at basketball half-times performing the "Bugle Call Rag." As his skill developed, he danced the fast tapping buck and wing. Whenever and wherever possible he earned rent money for the family during unbelievably difficult economic times, well remembered. Famous in the 1920s as a child star, he had leapt from Harlem sidewalks to the Four Hundred haunts of high society. At eight years of age he sang and danced with pianist Charles "Lucky" Roberts and his Society Orchestra. During the Depression, he danced at Harlem's Ubangi Club and developed his "Paddle and Roll" style at Kelly's Stables, where he worked with jazz stars Earl Hines, Dizzy Gillespie, and Charlie Parker. Briggs's credits include tours with Count Basie, Lionel Hampton, and Duke Ellington. At the 1963 Newport Jazz Festival, Ellington dubbed Briggs the "superleviathonic tapsthematician-ologist." His tap career went from black entertainment spots, Broadway theatres, and movies to Catskill and Pocono resorts. Now he performs at sea on the cruise ships *Doric*, *Oceanic*, and *Queen Elizabeth*.

Briggs has been described as doe-eyed, cute, cuddly, and a bashful sentimentalist performing soft and sassy routines with camel walks and struts. Critics have noted his lightning speed and attack, heels and toes vibrating faster than the eye can see, and a cool, winning, and sometimes melancholy edge to his dancing.

Before the Smithsonian performance, I asked Briggs, "What kind of feelings do you try to get across in dancing?" He replied:

Well, the first thing is relaxation; that's how I feel. When the person puts their money up in the box office, that's a compliment right there. Because, like, he can say, "I'll go home and get me a six pack and watch Johnny Carson." That's the first thing. Now, when they sit down there, I want to make them forget about their telephone bill and electric light bill, how high the prices are for beef and that kind of thing. So when I dance, the first thing I say is, "I want to entertain." And I dance that way to make them relax, not to sit on the edge of their seats. I want them to relax. If they're with their wife or their girlfriend, I want them to put their arm around them and say "hey," and make them forget. So that's how I feel when I do my performance.

When I asked how Bunny got the feeling of relaxation across to his audience, he explained, "Well, I dance relaxed, I dance relaxed, I dance, thank god, relaxed. I'm trying to convey that to the audience. I want them to relax. As soon as I dance, you're going to relax. Now, you might say it ain't no good, but you will be relaxed, because I don't do dancing that makes anybody feel uneasy. I will not dance that way. When I dance, you're going to sit back and, to me, that's the biggest compliment that I could get—when I see somebody relaxed while I'm dancing." Briggs thought that performing difficult dances makes a person "get on edge." He continued, "I don't like to do that. In other words, I hate violence. And I try to convey that through my dancing and, thank God, so far it has worked."

I was curious to find out if there were any other feelings that Briggs tried to get across to his audience. He said, "Yes, a lot of them. I like people to love, because to me it's the greatest thing in the world. And I'm not just talking about going out huggin' and kissin'—love everybody! Just plainly love, because, to me, that's the ultimate in life."

After talking with Briggs, I approached Sandman Sims. To me, he looked like a tough guy on a Harlem street corner. In sharp counterpoint to his colleague with whom I had just spoken, he did not initially exude warmth and relaxation.

Sims was born in Los Angeles. When he got through crawling, Sims said he stood up and danced, even though he was the clumsy one of his family. At four or five years of age, egged on by brothers and sisters, he began street dancing. He was the awkward little kid who followed his brother and tried to match his level of expertise. When he met the challenge and then some, his brother quit, and Sims kept on dancing—on his own. He aspired to boxing, but a broken hand put him out of the ring. Anyway, he explained, "People enjoyed me more dancing in the resin box than they did me boxing."

In 1944, Lionel Hampton saw Sims dance and invited him to join his show at San Francisco's Golden Gate Theater. Two years later Sims began a seventeen-year stint at the Apollo, first as a comedian and then as a dancer. A "flash dancer," Sims, as one critic remarked, "aims at the eyes." He developed a unique speciality to add to his light, fast, athletic style. He dazzles audiences with shuffles, chugging, "nerve roll" leg shakes that force the feet into spasms of tapping in a "sand dance" that creates gritty, abrasive sounds soft and loud, punctuated with crystalline accents. "First I tried gluing sandpaper on my shoes and then I wore the mat out. Then I glued sandpaper on the mat and wore my shoes out. Finally, I just put sand on the board and became the world's greatest sand dancer," said Sims. He uses a three-by-five board covered with a sprinkling of fine sand from California.

When Sims could no longer find work as a hoofer during the decline of tap, he took up carpentry and auto mechanics. Now he works with tough youths in Harlem and "turns on" to tap when he gets gigs.

I asked Sims what kind of feelings he wanted to convey to the audience in his dancing. He snapped briskly, "I don't want them to feel!" I must have looked amazed. He continued less pugilistically: "I want them to hear. When they hear, they'll feel what I feel." "What do you feel?" I queried. "Like a kid with a new toy," Sims replied. He wanted to convey the feelings of happiness, playfulness, and surprise. When rehearsal began Sims marked the movements, yet he did not really dance them with his heart. He went through the paces and steps. Then he began to loosen up. He smiled. The ice thawed. During the performance the audience was ecstatic—his solos got standing ovations. And Sims joyously played with the steps and rhythms, "hoofing," as he put it. Not just a toe-heel and counts. But all the foot and transformations of counts. When we talked at the reception after the performance, Sims radiated warmth and elation. He obviously enjoys himself onstage and on the night of the Smithsonian performance he certainly carried the audience with him. He did not talk about the power of persuading people through his dance to feel his feelings of joy and delight at the improvised steps and the way they all fit together. However, that was the challenge, and it was well met.

Chuck Green, regarded by many as the reigning genius of black tap, began as a boy in Georgia by using bottle caps on the soles of his feet to create sounds. At about seven years old, he and James Walker met as dance contestants and became a comedy and tap team—Chuck and Chuckles, heirs to the illustrious Buck and Bubbles team—and toured the United States, Europe, and Australia. At nine years of age, Green went to New York City and became a protégé of hoofer John Bubbles. Later Green took Briggs and Sims "under his wing." Sims said Green would not teach steps. He just said, "Do your own thing." Green was the acknowledged master in his heyday, "an inspiration for all the dancers in the Harlem belt," according to Sims. Green's effortless rhythm tap dancing, continuous melody of taps, and beautiful balance gained him such epithets as the "Bach of tap." Critic Arlene Croce called him "the King Lear of tap. . . . Age completes him."[7]

A poetic, visionary, and profound man, yet described as silent, mysterious, introverted, and resigned, Green was given to depression and was institutionalized for fifteen years. He never lost the poetry of his feet. At the Smithsonian on film and onstage, critics recognized his fluid movement with elegant simplicity, his head bent forward in concentration, his arms loose and butterfly-like. Moving in a small space, with the floor as instrument, he played out complex cross steps, turns, slides, stiletto taps, and air turns with heel clicks, interspersing quick slides and pulling the legs together, balancing on one foot while clicking out complex rhythms. His large frame was covered with a boxy tuxedo, vented coattails, ankle-length pants, and finished off with long bump-toed shoes.

In our conversation, this big, gentle, soft-spoken man said he wanted his audience to feel "credibility" when he danced. Green spoke of being "on the edge of happiness." The sounds, he explained, should evoke images. These images should lead the imagination like a moving pencil to etch and fill in visual concepts and events, and stories. Stories? "Yes, stories." Green said he had danced on radio. In those days, all people had to go by was the sound. When Green spoke, poetic imagery and metaphors came fast and dense. Unfortunately, the poetry was lost before I could absorb it—and alas, my tape recorder had broken unbeknownst to us. For the first time in hundreds of taped interviews, the tape spilled out of the cassette. When I went to the Sony repair shop the following day, the man who helped me was a black jazz guitarist. He said, "When they heavy in the head and heavy in the heart, that's when they get the respect." As mentioned earlier, Green had earned respect among the star tappers. Briggs remarked, "When he dances, he gives everybody lessons. Pick your feet up!"

Green seems to experience transformations of sensory forms—from mind to body action to sound to mind once again. He spoke of "penetrations." Dancing a ballad should evoke the prelude to a kiss. "Caravan," he said, is "the story of family getting together, oasis." A poet concerned with communication, Green referred to someone he admired: the man spoke with beautiful diction, like a nobleman from a foreign country. It was Green who inspired the title of the film "No Maps on My Taps" with his metaphor for the improvisational nature and freedom of tap dancing. Green dances evocations to images provoked by music performed by a group or merely his own rhythmic sound creations presented primarily through footwork. His friend, English dancer Dee (Dorothy) Bradley, said, "When Chuck dances, I can't keep my eyes off his feet." The rhythm also, of course, emanates through his body and into the long, loose arms and hands.

Briggs, Sims, and Green had different intentions regarding the feelings they wanted to get across to the audience. If the performers' intentions in tapping were diverse, were the audience perceptions also varied?

*Audience Perception.* Who were the 110 respondents in the audience survey?[8] Most, 67 percent, were female. Of those who gave information, nearly half (48 percent) were in the 41–65 age group, followed by 30 percent between 21 and 30. Eight percent were under 20, 5 percent between 31 and 40, and 3 percent over 65. Seventy-eight percent were white and 7 percent, black. Educationally, 36 percent were postgraduates, 31 percent college graduates, 20 percent had some college, and 8 percent high school. Family income information revealed that more than a third (36 percent) earned over $40,000; 23 percent, $21,000–$30,000; 15 percent, under $20,000; and 12 percent, $31,000–$40,000. Forty-six percent of the respondents were professional; 13 percent managerial-administrative; 10 percent students; 8 percent sales and clerical; 5 percent other skilled labor; 3 percent housewives; and 7 percent retired and other. Sixty-four percent of those who filled out the form indicated that they were somewhat knowledgeable about dance; 25 percent not at all; and 8 percent very. This skewed population distribution is similar to performing arts audiences everywhere, as noted in chapter 1.

What emotions did spectators perceive onstage as the dancers performed solos and together? As indicated in appendix table 1, 67 percent of the respondents observed happiness, 36 percent playfulness, 23 percent vitality, 21 percent caring, 18 percent sadness, and 11 percent surprise.

Audience perception and performer intention overlapped most closely for Briggs and Sims. Briggs wanted to make people feel relaxed, happy, and loving while they were at the concert. Most of the spectators who filled out the survey form thought that the tappers conveyed feelings of happiness, carefree delight, warmth, and affection.

Sims wanted the audience to get the sense of surprise. Respondents acknowledged surprise generated by the dancers' spontaneity, free movement, unexpected leg gesture or other movement, and sense of playfulness. As one spectator put it, "Even the performers haven't seen this dance before!"

The feelings of surprise and playfulness are part of the freedom ethos in tap. Through the sense of "perfectionism," "sheer ecstasy," "exhilaration," and "devotion," the dancers conveyed to the audience their freedom to dance into an altered state of consciousness. For several observers, the dancers got across a contagious "high," especially "whenever inner music and outer tapping came together and merged." Dancing transported several audience members to an altered state of consciousness—pure joy. So much so, they said, that talking or filling out forms would detract from this state.

The audience perceived the tap form as a vehicle of self-expression and competition. People saw the dancers' "extreme pride in what they do pre-

sented with every inch of themselves." They noticed the fierce concentration of the tappers and how they challenged each other with banter,
teasing, and general "hamming it up." Not only was the "egging on performers" spotted, but also the friendliness and respect the competitors
had for each other. They moved out of each others' way and followed
each others' movements. An observer remarked, "What was fascinating
was how differently each man expressed himself through his dancing."

Audience member reactions certainly varied. There were a couple of
respondents who did not believe tap dancing was supposed to be very
emotional. The drummer expressed this sentiment: "Emotion is not the
thing. It's entertainment, cutting up, having fun [joy, happiness], that's
what it is about. I was so engrossed with what they were doing with
rhythm I didn't think about what emotion they were trying to convey to
the audience."

Individuals who perceived sadness were responding to the context of
the dance—the plight of performers dedicated to an art that was no
longer able to sustain livelihoods as it had in the past—rather than to the
dance itself. There was regret that a native American form might be going
the way of the dodo.

Let us now turn to how respondents thought the emotions were conveyed.[9] As indicated in table 1, happiness was mostly seen through action, primarily gesture and locomotion (40 percent of the total number
of clues to this emotion) and body parts (45 percent). Eyes were also
identified as clues.[10] Playfulness, caring, and vitality were similarly identified through action and body parts, the categories of "face" and "all
parts" figuring prominently.

Respondents identified the feelings they perceived through the performers' playfulness "with beat and feet," as someone put it, the smiles,
happy feet, and total commitment. Interactions with the audience and
humor and banter among the performers also contributed to the tone of
joyousness. The dancers' camaraderie and reluctance to leave the stage
suggested their fun and enjoyment in performance. "When the men dance,
sparks fly; each dances in rapport."

Is there a relationship between the tap concert respondents' perception
of emotion and clues to them and a perceiver's background characteristics? No differences were found based on gender, ethnicity, occupation,
education, income, age, or knowledge about dance. The common audience perceptions may be the result of the long and broad exposure tap
has had, first in popular film and later on television shows.

Audience members generally shared in the freedom of tap. They admired the willful pursuit of what one believes in despite adversity. Tappers and audience shared moments of joy, distraction from burdens or

## TABLE 1. TAP CONCERT: HOW AUDIENCE PERCEIVED EMOTIONS

|  |  | *Perceptions through* | | | | | |
|---|---|---|---|---|---|---|---|
| *Clues per person: 4.45* <br> N = 61 <br> *Emotion* | *Action* | | *Body Parts* | | *Quality of Movement* | | *Nondance Factors* |
| *Happiness* | Gesture | 25 | Face | 20 | Energy | 3 | 9 |
|  | Locomotion | 20 | All | 19 | Time | 5 | |
|  | Other | 10 | Eyes | 8 | Space | 1 | |
|  |  |  | Feet | 6 | | | |
|  |  |  | Other | 8 | Other | 3 | |
| Perceived clues | | 55 | | 61 | | 12 | 9 |
| % of total |  |  |  |  |  |  |  |
| (136) clues | | 40% | | 45% | | 9% | 7% |
| *Playfulness* | Gesture | 10 | Face | 10 | Energy | 4 | 2 |
|  | Locomotion | 7 | All | 4 | Time | 5 | |
|  | Other | 6 | Other | 10 | Other | 2 | |
| Perceived clues | | 23 | | 24 | | 11 | 2 |
| % of total |  |  |  |  |  |  |  |
| (60) clues | | 38% | | 40% | | 18% | 4% |
| *Caring* | Gesture | 9 | Face | 7 | Energy | 2 | 1 |
|  | Locomotion | 6 | All | 5 | Other | 2 | |
|  | Other | 5 | Other | 7 | | | |
| Perceived clues | | 20 | | 19 | | 4 | 1 |
| % of total |  |  |  |  |  |  |  |
| (44) clues | | 45% | | 43% | | 9% | 3% |
| *Vitality* | Gesture | 5 | All | 6 | Energy | 2 | 2 |
|  | Other | 8 | Other | 8 | Time | 1 | |
| Perceived clues | | 13 | | 14 | | 3 | 2 |
| % of total |  |  |  |  |  |  |  |
| (32 clues) | | 41% | | 44% | | 9% | 6% |

*Note: Percentages have been rounded off.*

distresses of life, relaxation, surprise, and the marvel of human creation. I do not know to what extent Green's dancing evoked the kind of "authenticity" he talked about. Although spectators often commented on things about the performance that were not asked on the survey form, there were no remarks about the dancing eliciting "stories." But then, poets are few!

# Touched by the Timeless Female Creator and Destroyer: Indrani Dances Kuchipudi

## RELIGIOUS ROOTS

The meaning of the Kuchipudi concert and the ultimate performer-audience connection lie within a rich heritage. Indians trace their dance history to the Vedas, the earliest known literature of India, perhaps written prior to 5000 B.C. There is also archaeological evidence of dance from the civilizations of Mohenjodaro and Harappa in 2500 B.C. As in the Judeo-Christian heritage, the Hindu worship included dancing. There is even a Hindu god of dance, Shiva, destroyer and renewer, who determines the rhythm of the world (considered further in chapter 10). Ancient Hindu texts state that no place is fit for human habitation without earth, water, and a deity. Consequently temples housing the gods became pivotal in all aspects of life.

Kings usually built the temples and supported their various rituals and services, which included dancing. Female dancers called *devadasis* were "dedicated" to god in ceremonies called Bottu Kattal, in which they became his brides and servants and were given to particular temples. The women helped with temple duties such as cleaning devotional vessels and decorating shrines. More significantly, they propitiated and entertained the deities and danced before their images. Within Hindu philosophy, dancers expressed the divinity within themselves. By imitating the gods they partook of the cosmic control of the world. The women received lands and emoluments from the king as well as royal protection. *Devadasis* had their own social customs. If they wished, they could choose a mate. Any children they had were considered legitimate. Children assumed the mother's father's name and could inherit his property as well as the mother's. Daughters usually took their mother's profession, while sons often became musicians.

The temple dance, known as *nac* or *sadir nac*, was a votive offering. For this reason rigid rules governed the dancers' training and method of performance. Their teachers were male professionals who came from he-

Indrani illustrating Durga's gestures. *Courtesy of the Performing Arts Department of the Asia Society.*

reditary families of teachers and musicians who were also attached to the temples.

*Devadasis* not only performed before temple shrines and when the image of the deity was taken in ceremonial procession, but also danced at private parties and at the royal courts, especially for marriages. Some of the dancing girls and immoral women (*dais*) who exploited the dance became associated with prostitution or were kept as concubines by well-to-do patrons. Unfamiliar with the Hindu tradition, the British rulers (in league with Indian reformers) waged an "anti-*nac*" campaign at the turn of the century to prohibit temple dancing and the "dedication" of girls to the temples. The campaign was successful. In 1947, Madras State forbade temple dancing.

Yet, as human history testifies, when dance is suppressed, it rises phoenix-like to live again. The ethereal beauty of Anna Pavlova's 1929 ballet performance in India may have rekindled enthusiasm for Hindu dance. She astonished India not only because of her artistic distinction, but because she performed dances based on Indian themes accompanied by an Indian partner, Uday Shankar, and semi-Indian music composed by Cemelata Bannerjee-Dutt and posed the simple question to the Indians: "Where is *your* dance?"[1] When dancing was revived, the renaissance brought major innovations. Daughters of respectable families, including Brahmans, took up the traditional classical dancing. The high school and, in diluted form, the cinema, stage, and private gatherings also embraced this kind of performance.

For all of the arts, Hindu spiritual and philosophical thought requires that the goal of the artist is to suggest, reveal, or re-create the infinite, divine self. Artistic creation was conceived as the supreme means of realizing the Universal Being. Art was a sacrifice, a dedicated offering of the best that one has to the best that one seeks.

In the Indian context, however, dancing combined the religious and the secular. Not only were art and religion inseparable but so, too, were spiritual and sexual ecstasy.[2] These orientations and the tribal, folk, and art or classical dance forms have continually interacted and merged. Over many centuries the technique of dance offerings has evolved with the characteristics of the different regions of the country to create unique styles.[3] There are generally five classical styles; Bharata Natyam, Kathakali, Orissi, Manipuri, Kathak, and the dance-dramas of Kuchipudi, Yakshagana, and Kutiyattam. The Indian dancer Indrani brought to the Smithsonian World Explorer Series a concert of styles from several parts of the country. However, the focus of discussion about performer intention and audience reception was on the Kuchipudi dance from the Andhra Pradesh region of southeast India.

Three types of dance in Andhra affected the evolution of Kuchipudi dance: the devotional dances of the *devadasis*, the religious Yakshagana dance-dramas of the Brahmans, and the secular dances of the Raja Nartakis. Kuchipudi is one of India's classical dance styles with traditional roots reaching back to 1500 B.C. The emergence of the cult of Bhati that worshipped god through the "path of devotion" between the sixth and tenth centuries A.D. gave impetus to the art of Kuchipudi. These religious mystics believed that devotion to god could be most effective and rewarding through the rapture of participation in sacred performing arts. According to some accounts, more than 1,000 years ago the religious atmosphere of the temple and the standard of the temple dance had declined, in part due to economic stresses. Consequently, in Kuchipudi, as elsewhere in India, male scholars and pundits well-versed in the arts of music and dance organized in groups called Brahmana Melas to preserve the purity and quality of these performing arts. The Brahmana Melas were exclusive to the religiously pure men, in contrast to the traditional Nattuva Melas, gurus and experts who about 100 years ago began teaching dance to women performers who formed the Bhoga Mela or Natya Melas. These dancers performed solos which varied according to the different families in Andhra.

The origin of the Kuchipudi dance that was performed at the Smithsonian is as follows: in the village of Kuchipudi, situated in the estuary of the River Krishna, lived the ascetic Siddhendra Yogi. He was a disciple of a saintly poet and musician called Tirtha Narayana Yati. Siddhendra was inspired by this man's fervent songs about Lord Krishna's early life. Later, in a revelation, Lord Krishna told Siddhendra to write out and stage a dance-drama. Siddhendra persuaded the Kuchipudi Bhagavatas, the dance-drama performers, to present his new work. The Brahman boys performed before the ruler and noblemen of the Vijayangara Empire (1336–1565 A.D.), great patrons of the arts. They were so pleased with the performance that a Muslim nobleman, the Nawab of Golconda (1672–1687), gave the village of Kuchipudi as a gift to the performing party on the stipulation that the village would continue to train people in the newly created form. Herein, the dancers speak as well as dance and sing. Furthermore, dance and mime are not separate and *sabdas*, or solo dances, may be performed. Long significant in religious ceremonies, festivals, and royal court entertainment, Kuchipudi is performed in the Telugu language. Kuchipudi combines a balance between *nritta* or abstract sequences of dance movement, *nritya* or dance-drama, and *natya*, or acting with dance. Accompanying the dance is the *sadam*, a poetic composition in praise of some deity or patron. Although Kuchipudi dance-theatre began exclusively with Brahman male dancers and actors, at some time they taught the art to the guilds of teachers who instructed women. Today women are responsible for its survival and performance.

## SPOTLIGHT ON A DANCE

Chamundeswari Shadbam is the specific Kuchipudi dance in our exploration of the performer-audience connection. This episodic dance tells the tale of the unconquerable Goddess Durga and the evil buffalo-headed demon Mahishasura. Durga is a universal spirit, a deity with male and female qualities. She represents female energy on earth and the potential to destroy evil and bring justice. Mother of all living things and creator par excellence, Durga also possesses the characteristics of power and victory, protection and grace, love and peace. She is savior of the gods and killer of demons.

The majestic Durga is an important divinity in the sacred Indian tradition. She rules the heavens with Lord Shiva. They are a loving couple devoted to divine children. Hindus believe Durga and Shiva dwell on the high peaks of the Himalayas and in humble temples. Capable of taking any form, they are timeless creators, rulers, and destroyers of the world. Their cosmic dance dissolves and re-creates the world. When these deities are angered, they strike the offender. When they are pleased, they bring joy.

The evil demon Mahishasura received boons from Lord Shiva as reward for his devotion and asceticism. However, he later created havoc on earth and went on to terrify all the gods who were unable to withstand him. The demon declared himself god and destroyed good holy people. Shiva rose in anger, and Durga appeared to save the gods.

The *sabda* solo dances dramatically render mythological episodes and portray the characters. Pieces in the *sabda* repertoire are composed in the Paathya musical style that combines intoned recitation of descriptive or narrative verses (*slokas*), rhythm syllables (*sabdas* and *darus*), and song.

Indrani danced the impersonations of Goddess Durga, Lord Shiva, and Mahishasura. She set the mood with *abhinaya*, an expressional abstract dance, and a Sanskrit hymn of praise to Goddess Durga. Then the dancer in the role of narrator depicted the demon's conquest of the universe and the defiance of the gods. Indrani impersonated his boastful proclamation of supremacy and danced his challenge. She presented the anger and dismay of the gods, who appealed to Lord Shiva for assistance. Then she danced Shiva's reply. From the divine, radiant splendor of all the gods, the dancer portrayed the creation of Goddess Durga. Indrani became Goddess Durga and displayed her divine weapons bestowed by all the gods. Indrani then swiftly assumed the role of the monstrous demon. In the battle dance she alternated the roles of the two combatants, dancing to accented drumming. The dramatic sequences climaxed Durga's supreme victory.

What are the sources and characteristics of the dance? For the most part, the Sanskritic scholar Bharata Muni codified the basic principles of Indian classical dance, gesture, and mime in the ancient treatise on dance, the *Natya Shastra*, in the second century A.D. The canonical work called the Fifth Veda provides textual sanction for the Kuchipudi theory and practice as well as the other local classical styles. Classical dance includes the *nritta*, an abstract, pure decorative series of movements without theme, story, or symbolism. Herein, hand gestures create abstract rhythmic patterns to the accompanying music, which does not have words. There is also the *nritya*, mimetic expository dramatic dance that depicts a story or poem sung by a singer through symbolic hand gestures, facial expressions, and dance movements. Dance themes come from the mythological epics, the *Ramayana* and *Mahabharata*, and the Puranas or legends about lives and loves of the gods, who are conceived in human images with all the human moods and passions. The kinetic visualization of this material provides a source of religious education, especially for the common people. *Natya* refers to drama. There are masculine, vigorous (*tandava*) and feminine, delicate (*lasya*) movements. The mimetic art (*abhinaya*) includes enacting through words and mime (*vachika*), physical movement (*angika*), costume and decor (*aharya*), and subtle physical manifestations of emotion (*sattavika*).

Although Kuchipudi is similar to the Bharata Natyam classical style in technique, with its geometrical dance postures, sharp movements, subtle mime component, and sophisticated rhythms, Kuchipudi has a more abandoned manner. It also has more obvious storytelling mime. When Indrani dances Durga and the demon, there are prayer-like movements, clawing, rapid eyelash batting, arm slashing, thumb twitches, torso ripples, and foot stomps. It is as if the dancer intended the symbolic actions to bring about what they expressed.

There are nine basic feelings (*rasa*) in the classical dance: love, anger, laughter, disgust, sorrow, fear or terror, amazement, valor or chivalry, and peace. Within the Indian tradition, these major emotions are believed to be embedded in the human soul. The classical dance forms have stylized poses and movement to convey the meaning of these emotions.

Any object or feeling can be described with separate parts of the body, including the face. *Angas* are the major parts: head, hands, chest, waist, hips, and feet. The *upangas* are the eyebrows, eyelids, eyeballs, nose, lip, chin, and mouth. *Pratyangas*, the minor parts, are the arms, shoulders, belly, thighs, and calves. Some Indian dancers also include the neck, knees, wrist, and elbow. *Mudras*, or gestures, convey a poetic language to initiates. Each *mudra* may combine two or more of the twenty-four basic *hastas*, or hand poses. These are accompanied by choreographed movements of the arms, body, feet, legs, and face.

Poses emphasize balance or perfect stillness. The joints and bone structure of the human body, rather than its musculature, receive attention. In the principal stance, the dancer's body comprises a triangle with one line joining the knees, which are bent and stretched out to the sides, the apex at the heels of turned-out feet. A second triangle consists of the waist as apex with a line joining the knees as the base. A third triangle has the waist as apex and a line joining the shoulders as the base. Movements emerge from the knee, pelvis, shoulder, and neck joints. Especially common in Kuchipudi dance are the distinct postures of *alidha* and *pratyalidha* that express heroic and furious moods. From these postures, the dancer wields such weapons as the bow and arrow, spear, and sword. The space between the feet in dance postures and movements is specified according to the *tala* (rhythmic and spatial) pattern. *Tala* (coming from the "word for palm surface of the hand, the beating of which originally indicated a measure of time"[4]) are measured by the space between the tips of the thumb and middle finger when the hand is fully stretched. The *danda* (staff) is a stiffened arm that conveys anger or defiance.

Steps and dance sequences are clearly defined. Beating the ground with the sole, heel, and toe are not left to chance; the dancer's ankle bells must coincide with the drum rhythms. Steps are *adavus*, combined into *jethis*, which form a *thirmana*. There are conventional rhythmic gaits (*caris*). *Bharmya*, "earthly," *caris* are stepping movements. *Akasika caris* are movements in which the feet are raised in jumping or lifting and bending.

A level pose of the head conveys serenity and usually begins a dance. Raising the head indicates dignity or divinity. Vigorously nodding the head expresses anger, threat, or boasting. Moving the eyeballs in circles conveys valor, passion, and fury. Up and down movements of the eyeballs express wonder; horizontal shifts suggest heroism, fear, direction, and mystery. Diagonal movements denote grief. Eyelid fluttering conveys excitement and terror. Sidelong glances express dalliance, whereas a projected wide-eyed look signifies anger and challenge.

Of the five chest movements that Bharata described, "drawn in," denoting fear and modesty; and "heaved up," for pride, courage, and anger, are common to Kuchipudi. Relevant waist movements are "turned aside," as in wielding weapons; "shaken," the stretching involved in wielding weapons. Folding in the waist expresses female shyness; undulation, seductiveness.

Although there are clearly recognized symbolic gestures (some are part of everyday Indian life), the sage Bharata forbade realism so that godlike and unlimited ideals may be expressed by the artist and imagined by the spectator. The Hindu relationship between dancer and spectator has both sacred and profane dimensions.

## THE MOOD: PERFORMER-AUDIENCE CONNECTIONS

Indrani is the first professional dancer to present the Kuchipudi dance style abroad. Her mother, American-born Ragini Devi, married an Indian physicist, Ramlal Bajpal, and later became India's classical dance pioneer in the 1920s. Devi became a celebrated dancer praised by Indians and Westerners alike and a key researcher. She describes the Kuchipudi style in her essential text *Dance Dialects of India.*[5]

Born in Delhi, India, Indrani began dancing at the age of five. She studied with her mother and various other Indian masters. Indrani has performed on five continents and received one of the Indian government's highest awards, Padma Shri. And in 1982, India's President Neelam Sanjiva Reddy recognized Indrani for her art and contribution to its propagation. She has taught at the Julliard School, State University College of Arts at Purchase, New York, and Harvard University Summer School Dance Center.

Because of the religious origins and purposes of the classical dance in India, the initiated spectator, the *sahradaya*, connects with the skilled performer in a way that goes beyond the noninitiated's entertainment or secular altered state of consciousness. From Bharata to the late medieval writers on Indian aesthetics, the process of creation is considered complete when the ideal viewer responds.

Artistic creation is "the expression of a feeling of passion . . . freed from distinctions in time or space," according to the scholar and advisor in the Indian Government Department of Cultural Activities, Kapila Vatsyayan (Ph.D.). The dancer expresses moods or *bhavas*. Through the inner force of creative intuition, the dancer tries to evoke in the spectator, in whom the different states of being lie dormant, the states of consciousness called *rasa*. The ultimate state of bliss is known as *ananda*. Within the Indian aesthetic, the process of artistic creation is fulfilled when it is communicated to the trained or initiated spectator.

Faubion Bowers correctly points out that the concepts of *rasa* and *bhava* are elusive for Westerners. "Roughly put, *rasa* means feeling or flavor and is the permanent mood with which dance . . . concerns itself. . . . *Bhava*, on the other hand, consists of the situations and acts which evoke specific responses. . . . *Bhava* may be either enduring or transitory, a cause or effect, or even an ensuant or excitant. Taking the *rasa* of love, for example, its *bhavas* can be the casual one between a husband and wife or between two strangers. The *bhava* of effect will be that of undying devotion, if it is permanent, or longing, despondency or doubt, if it is transitory. The ensuants can be sidelong glances or coquettish smiles, and the excitants, moonlight, a beach, or a soft zephyrous breeze. When all these minute *bhavas* are properly portrayed, the *rasa* appears as a kind of telling reaction from within the spectator, and this *rasa* is an overpowering aesthetic delectation which according to the Hindus only true art can arouse. . . ."[6]

Aestheticians regard life as a continuing opportunity to expand and cultivate feelings. Vatsyayan explains, "The culture of emotions, the training of feelings, assumed a significant place very early in the history of Indian modes of living and [were] given a value which belonged not only to the realm of aesthetics but also to the realm of spiritual realization."[7] Participants in the aesthetic experience, dance and spectator, thus seek to expand the unique self toward the universal divine self. Art and religion intertwine. No dancer begins a performance without the Ranga Puja, the invocation in obeisance to the gods, gurus, and audience.

For Indians the thrill of their dance "lies in the unfolding of the known but dormant, and not with the confrontation of the strange, the unique or the highly subjective."[8] The dance themes are highly literary in character and comprise legend, mythology, and poetry; the stances are sculptural and iconographic, reflecting chiseled temple figures with the same themes; the music has finished *ragas* (musical modes) and *talas* (rhythmic cycles with specific numbers of unaccented and accented beats). Indian dance combines techniques of several art forms. It may use a piece of poetry with a specific mood which is set to music with a particular melody and metrical style. These synchronize with the dancer's movements to evoke a certain mood. In a way, the parts of the body become like the notes of the music. Vatsyayan explains that

> Variations, interpretations and synchronizations are all built around the pillars of the metrical cycle and the musical role. The delight of the initiated spectator comes from the prismatic unfolding of the different lights and shades where he can see and recreate the innumerable permutations and combinations of a self-imposed limitation of time, measure and space; in the pantomimic sequences, the understanding of the word and the musical note are essentials as the word provides the foundation for the countless varieties in dance patterns.

She emphasizes that "this stylized layering of movement patterns for a particular sequence of dance upon unchanging musical and literary compositions constitutes the cardinal principle of the classical Indian dance."[9]

PERFORMER INTENTION
The ancient classical tradition of Kuchipudi has maintained the preeminence of feeling in dance. The mood is the essence. I asked Indrani what feeling(s) she wanted to communicate to the audience at the Smithsonian, which was primarily a non-Hindu group. She replied:

This is a very complicated question. . . . When we are trained, we are trained to communicate through the technique the feeling, themes, and so on of the dances, and that in itself already conveys a great deal. Using the old dance technique, the medium of the body, and the story (because our stories are universal), so much is conveyed which is . . . timeless.

Indrani went on to explain that there was something beyond the training that a performer draws upon to convey emotion.

There is so much as you live in life. Whatever your medium is as an artist, you are trying to convey so much. . . . And that's where there is something universal, the universal inside the individual. I'm trying to convey that universal which you feel you have experienced or been touched with or seen into and try to convey that to others who may or may not have that experience—to try and give something of that.

The traditional form carries out the mood. Indrani remarked:

It's very old, and strangely enough, it amazes me how the old things convey so marvelously, at least to me and certainly to those who observe and seem to understand the story. We struggle a lot in modern dance, creative dance, and appreciate the efforts. What a struggle there is to express things! And sometimes it's so very abstract, which is also fine, because abstract is also very beautiful. But it is wonderful how very old things can really convey and gratify. But the old is not always popular.

Indrani described the Chamundeswari Shadbam as "a very interesting dance" because it represents two contrasting feminine qualities. Dance, like phenomenal life itself, is a mixture of the terrific and the auspicious. "One of the feminine qualities is the proud and flirtatious. And one is the warrior goddess. It is a very, very strong piece. And the Goddess Durga, she is *chati*, female energy personified. And it is a very serious piece." Thus Indrani tries to convey a variety of emotions. Durga is the warrior goddess who destroys wickedness and evil. Female energy is not only ferocious, but also benign, giving a benediction. Because Indians venerate and fear Durga, Indrani wants to get across these feelings. "Before the soldier goes into battle," Indrani said, "he cries out Durga's name in order to be victorious. . . . She is ferocious, she battles, and then she twitches with the kill for a while after killing the demon and gradually resumes her gracious, benediction-giving self. And all of that is, of course, through the technique of the dance, the mime, the face, and the mood, also. . . . But then, behind it all is the individual's feeling." All the movements are important, none more important than the others except at the very end, when movement finally "concentrates in the face."

Mohan Khokar, advisor for dance, Sangeet Natak Akademi, New Delhi, India, says, "The face of the dancer becomes the register of the feelings and passions that well up in response to the words of the song and their emotionally charged release; the eyes, eyebrows, mouth, lips, and cheeks all become potent instruments of suggestion and insinuation."[10] In this particular dance, there are the body movements of the battling goddess and demon, and there is a contrast between the two characters through body as well as mime.

The traditional training and the idiosyncrasy of the dancer's life experience merge. There are nine basic emotions that dancers convey in the traditional training. Yet the dancer has special feelings to get across. How does Indrani do it? She said:

> It's so hard to explain. When in a good performance and a good time, one tries to totally immerse oneself deeply in the spirit and mood of what the art is trying to convey. And if you immerse yourself deeply and feel, then all the spirits of feelings and experiences that make up what you're trying to give, which is trying to pour itself to flow toward others, it happens; it just happens.

Indrani explained the difference between a fair performance and a fine one:

> Now the technical things may be mastered by many, but how many of the many who master it inspire? What is the difference? And that is something really intangible. Now the things that inspire me, I know at once. I'm deeply moved by things or absolutely left cold. And when I'm moved, I am very emotional and a thing can affect me even for several days. A whole mood if it can keep with me, and if I'm very deeply moved by something I see, I want to run away and not talk with anybody and let it stay a long time quietly and absorb it and revolve it and not have anything break that mood. This has happened to me observing others who have really inspired me and moved me.

Apropos the Goddess Durga role of creator that she performed, Indrani found that the supreme, most moving experience of life was the birth of a child:

> The moment of giving birth itself is to me a fantastic, amazing thing. And I can only feel sorry for men for not having this kind of an experience in the sense that we are, after all, touched by something universal at this time, something very strange and marvelous. It's a fantastic thing to experience and cannot be understood by those who have not gone through it. I would say first that then the emotions of life, all the colors of life, flow through my art. I'm almost a medium to convey to others.

In summary, Indrani believes that several elements must combine: the story, the movement, the moods, the philosophy behind them, and what the performer personally gives to the performance.

Not surprisingly, Indian and American audiences respond differently to Chamundeswari Shadbam. The religious and literary backgrounds of the two groups are markedly different. Indrani said:

> In India when I perform this piece many people jump up in the audience and shout at the end. . . . Because they worship Goddess Durga and they feel as though it's a manifestation and they cry out, "Long live the Goddess" as they would during the ceremonials. And this has been very thrilling. But it's also considered very dangerous knowing they are almost worshipping you and something might go wrong, and they might destroy something. They are very capricious people. But I love the piece, and I don't let that bother me.

Audiences in India chant "jai jai Bhadrakali" when Goddess Durga stands poised for battle against the monstrous demon. Upon her final victory the spectators chant praise and wave lighted lamps.

For American audiences Indrani gives explanations for the gesture language and general story of the dance. She mentioned that such explanations are also necessary in India. Because the British misunderstood the Hindu temple dance, they contributed to the demise of the classical form. Consequently, much of the general population's former knowledge was lost. Furthermore, as Indrani mentioned, what is old is not always popular.

AUDIENCE RESPONSE

We generally assume that Western dance critics represent a sophisticated American view of performance. Anna Kisselgoff of the *New York Times* wrote, "Indrani has the inner concentration of a great dancer. Yet there is a total vividness about her every movement and expression. Indrani offers a gaiety, even playfulness. At the same time, this playfulness can become poetic. . . . Indrani is also a skilled actress—with every mood passing over the face like a thunderburst or a radiant sunbeam." [11] Other critics have noted the vivacity of Indrani's dancing in the fingers and face and the footwork producing intricate movement and music through the ankle bells. Some reporters remarked that in contrast to ballet, the dance form that is more familiar to Western audiences, Indian classicism has a weighed, balanced, and stylized manner.

At the Smithsonian performance, George Jackson reviewed Indrani's performance for the *Washington Post*. A cognoscente, he reported that Indrani was "a gently seductive performer in contrast to such other practitioners as the passionate Rita Devi or the incisive Balasaraswati." [12]

Indrani offered a lecture demonstration in the afternoon before her performance. This audience received Khokar's five-page, single-spaced article "Bharata Natyam and Kuchipudi." Not all of the concert audience attended the afternoon presentation. Consequently, in order to foster an understanding and appreciation of her art, Indrani explained each dance before performing it for the evening concert, demonstrating and simultaneously translating the gestures and expressions into poetic English.

In the audience survey a Nigerian woman reported that Indrani's telling the stories beforehand helped her understand what was going on. "Otherwise it would have been difficult to tell why the emotions were shown." On the other hand, a housewife-teacher remarked, "It might have been more interesting to see what reaction you would get if we had not been told the story."

In spite of Indrani's explanations for the dances, some audience members seeing classical Indian dance for the first time had difficulty in understanding it. A member of the audience who saw the emotions of anger, pride, and vitality told me at intermission that she was overwhelmed by the performance: "It's too much information to absorb." This respondent said she looked at the hands for the story. "And then when I tuned in to the rhythm, I looked at the feet." A housewife wrote on the survey form, "It is most difficult to give any opinion in seeing the performance for the first time—I see this strictly as entertainment with no thought of judging any emotion, except pleasure—in seeing this for pleasure's sake alone." However, she recognized anger through the face, hands, and body motion; happiness through smiles; pride through body bearing and the face; vitality through the hands and body: "Enjoyed performance as outsider looking in." Thus, whereas Indians immersed in the Hindu tradition find the thrill of Indian dance in the unfolding of the known, Americans often find fascination with the strange and unfamiliar.

What were the characteristics of the 139 spectators who filled out the audience survey form?[13] Twice as many women responded as men, 61 percent to 35 percent. The age-group distribution was 37 percent between 41 and 65; 29 percent between 31 and 40; 17 percent between 21 and 30; and 8 percent under 20. More than half (55 percent) of the respondents had postgraduate education. Twenty-two percent were college graduates, 10 percent had some college, and 5 percent high school education. Sixty-one percent in the survey were white, 15 percent Indian, and 8 percent other. A third (32 percent) earned over $40,000; 19 percent $21,000–$30,000; 18 percent, $31,000–$40,000; and 15 percent under $20,000. Half were professionals; 10 percent sales and clerical personnel; 9 percent managers or administrators; 8 percent students; and 7 percent housewives. Forty-six percent of the spectators were somewhat knowledgeable about dance, 30 percent not at all, and 20 percent very.

What emotions did the audience members perceive in the dance before the first intermission? As indicated in appendix table 1, Indrani succeeded in conveying a range of feelings. The overwhelming majority of the respondents (87 percent) recognized anger. Competition and pride were each perceived by 69 percent. Nearly half (43 percent) observed happiness, 34 percent playfulness, 28 percent ecstasy, 15 percent the closely related emotion of eroticism, and 26 percent vitality.

What clues did the spectators find to identify these emotions Indrani conveyed?[14] As shown in table 2, body parts identified anger, overwhelmingly the face, although the hands were perceived 48 times, eyes 42, shoulders and arms 19, and feet 16. Body parts, especially the hands, also identified competitiveness. The face conveyed pride, with the hands and eyes contributing for some respondents. Also, the face primarily indicated happiness. Playfulness was mostly identified through the face, eyes, and hands. Body parts again identified disgust and ecstasy. Most people perceiving vitality noticed a large number of clues.

Some respondents had no difficulty in identifying emotions, specifying the clues to them, and responding. A male government worker, for example, identified the emotion of anger through arm and eye movements; competitiveness through the narrative; playfulness through short, quick steps accompanied by similar eye and head movements; pride through straight posture and big, sweeping arm movements; and vitality through the pace. In response to the performance he said, "I feel admiration for the skills of the dancer . . . all the fine ways of expressing the emotions that she conveyed."

Two computer programmers, former Christians who are now Bahais, were unhappy that the survey form did not include the emotion of spirituality. The couple pointed out that "there is a more transcendental feeling to the whole first half" of the performance than the list of specific emotions suggested. Although the survey form had a place for "other" after the list, I was not "relating to" what they considered most important. The couple noted that the dancer conveyed to them the categoric emotions of anger, competitiveness, happiness, pride, vitality, and empathy.

Although nearly all respondents felt emotions identical or similar to those they perceived onstage, they also had diverse reactions. Responding to the feeling of pride that Indrani imparted, a woman writer-editor said, testifying to the dancer's dramatic ability, "It made me surprised that she looked unattractive." In theatre, it is not uncommon for a performer to undergo contrasting transformations. A female librarian perceived the feeling of transmutation at the end of the dance and felt awed. In response to the strong emotions that Indrani conveyed, some people became excited and held their breath. Spectators became enthralled in response to competitiveness. A college student put it this way:

> I found the dance to be disturbing, jarring, and discordant. It depicted very well a state of chaos, turbulence, and war that would exist in just such a

**TABLE 2.** Kuchipudi Concert: How Audience Perceived Emotions

| Clues per person: 10.65 N = 137 Emotion | Action | | Body Parts | | Quality of Movement | | Nondance Factors |
|---|---|---|---|---|---|---|---|
| *Anger* | Gesture | 35 | Face | 73 | Energy | 14 | 0 |
| | Locomotion | 16 | Hands | 48 | Time | 9 | |
| | Posture | 9 | Eyes | 42 | Space | 1 | |
| | | | Shld/ | | | | |
| | | | Arms | 19 | | | |
| | | | All | 14 | | | |
| | | | Feet | 16 | | | |
| | | | Other | 10 | | | |
| Perceived clues % of total | | 60 | | 222 | | 24 | 0 |
| (306) clues | | 20% | | 73% | | 8% | |
| *Competitiveness* | Gesture | 25 | Hands | 38 | Energy | 13 | 0 |
| | Locomotion | 16 | Face | 33 | | | |
| | Posture | 7 | Shld/ | | Time | 9 | |
| | Other | 2 | Arms | 31 | | | |
| | | | All | 16 | Space | 1 | |
| | | | Eyes | 14 | | | |
| | | | Legs | 12 | | | |
| | | | Feet | 11 | | | |
| | | | Other | 5 | | | |
| Perceived clues % of total | | 50 | | 160 | | 23 | 0 |
| (233) clues | | 21% | | 69% | | 10% | |
| *Pride* | Gesture | 17 | Face | 49 | Energy | 18 | 0 |
| | Posture | 13 | Hands | 22 | Time | 4 | |
| | Locomotion | 11 | Eyes | 17 | Space | 2 | |
| | Other | 1 | All | 17 | | | |
| | | | Other | 23 | | | |
| Perceived clues % of total | | 42 | | 128 | | 24 | 0 |
| (194) clues | | 21% | | 66% | | 14% | |
| *Happiness* | Gesture | 12 | Face | 38 | Energy | 5 | 0 |
| | Locomotion | 10 | Eyes | 12 | Time | 2 | |
| | Other | 5 | Hands | 11 | Space | 1 | |
| | | | Other | 28 | | | |
| Perceived clues % of total | | 27 | | 89 | | 8 | 0 |
| (124) clues | | 22% | | 72% | | 9% | |

*Table 2, cont.*

| Clues per person: 10.65 N = 137 Emotion | Action | | Perceptions through Body Parts | | Quality of Movement | | Nondance Factors |
|---|---|---|---|---|---|---|---|
| Playfulness | Gesture | 17 | Face | 20 | Energy | 3 | 1 |
| | Locomotion | 11 | Eyes | 18 | Time | 3 | |
| | Posture | 7 | Hands | 18 | Space | 2 | |
| | Other | 7 | Other | 33 | Other | 1 | |
| Perceived clues | | 42 | | 89 | | 9 | 1 |
| % of total | | | | | | | |
| (141) clues | | 30% | | 63% | | 9% | 1% |
| Disgust | Gesture | 6 | Face | 24 | Energy | 3 | 0 |
| | Locomotion | 2 | Hands | 14 | Time | 2 | |
| | Other | 2 | Eyes | 7 | | | |
| | | | Other | 16 | | | |
| Perceived clues | | 10 | | 61 | | 5 | 0 |
| % of total | | | | | | | |
| (76) clues | | 13% | | 80% | | 7% | |
| Ecstasy | Gesture | 5 | Face | 22 | Energy | 5 | 2 |
| | Locomotion | 3 | Hands | 9 | Time | 3 | |
| | Other | 3 | All | 8 | | | |
| | | | Eyes | 7 | | | |
| | | | Other | 18 | | | |
| Perceived clues | | 11 | | 64 | | 8 | 2 |
| % of total | | | | | | | |
| (85) clues | | 13% | | 75% | | 9% | |
| Vitality | Gesture | 36 | Hands | 30 | Energy | 22 | 4 |
| | Locomotion | 27 | Face | 28 | Time | 12 | |
| | Posture | 8 | All | 28 | Space | 8 | |
| | Other | 9 | Feet | 21 | Other | 5 | |
| | | | Shld/ Arms | 19 | | | |
| | | | Eyes | 18 | | | |
| | | | Legs | 13 | | | |
| | | | Other | 13 | | | |
| Perceived clues | | 80 | | 170 | | 47 | 4 |
| % of total | | | | | | | |
| (301) clues | | 27% | | 57% | | 17% | 1% |

*Note: Percentages have been rounded off.*

situation as between these two characters. I preferred the earlier dances and singing, which are more harmonious and flowing; even the earlier dances allowed me to become intensely involved in the even flowing rhythm of the dance, feeling the rhythm of the dance rather than actually seeing it performed. This particular dance prevented me from becoming involved in the harmony of music and dance, forcing me instead to follow the story of the dance very carefully.

This student saw fierceness throughout captured by the actions of the body and facial expressions. She became excited and angry. Competitiveness took shape in the middle of the dance through the actions of the hands and facial expressions. The student felt enthralled: the continual vitality transmitted through facial expressions and body and hand movements awed her.

Since the face has been considered so important in the nonverbal communication literature, I asked a woman with whom I was speaking at intermission, "Did you look at the face at all?" She replied, "If there was a real extreme emotion, like anger, when it was framed, when the hand was nearby so your attention was drawn to it. The Indian costumes are so colorful and the bells so intriguing and the rhythms so unusual to the Western ear that you are tempted to focus on those things."

At this concert as at others, some of the audience members expressed their approach to dance viewing rather than responding specifically to the survey questions. Not all people pay explicit attention to the emotion that is conveyed onstage.

My assistant Teresa Ankney spoke with a woman in her fifties who said that she mainly looked at the technical aspects of dance, the costumes, and the music. She watched to see if it was the upper or lower parts of the body that were being used. "I don't look for emotions, I look at the dancers and the way the dance is choreographed and then I let the rest fill me in."

We now turn to the question of the association of background characteristics and perceptions of emotions and clues to them. Income was related to anger-face clues. More respondents who earned over $40,000 (64 percent of 44) and $21,000–$30,000 (69 percent of 26), perceived this pattern more than respondents in the groups $31,000 to $40,000 (42 percent of 24) and under $20,000 (38 percent of 21). I can offer no explanation.

The demographic and cultural characteristic of sex was associated with perception of happiness and competition. More males (54 percent of 48) than females (39 percent of 82) perceived happiness, perhaps reflecting greater male interest in aggression and winning a conflict through physical combat such as Indrani depicted. On the other hand, more women

(76 percent) perceived competitiveness than men (54 percent). Perhaps women could empathize more with the conflict between the dual moral aspects of good and evil of the goddess Indrani was portraying.

Indians (45 percent of 20) saw less competition than members of other ethnic groups (73 percent of 117) and more happiness (70 percent to 39 percent), their perceptions being more comparable to male than female perceptions in regard to happiness. Half of the Indian respondents saw happiness expressed in the face, whereas only a quarter (24 percent) of the other respondents did. Recall the Indian scholar who emphasized the importance of the face in conveying emotion.

Because the Kuchipudi dance style is rooted, nourished, and blooming within a Hindu spiritual and aesthetic philosophy and way of life, it is not surprising that there is a different performer-audience connection when Indrani performs in India than when she performs in Washington, D.C. What amazed me was that so many of the audience members expressed a sense of strangeness, even though Indrani gave lucid explanations prior to the presentation of each dance. The story and gesture language are alien to the dance forms Americans are accustomed to seeing. Yet Americans did recognize universal emotions. Indians are able to place these within the story. Indian dancers strike sculpturesque stances and through a succession of these render moods and attributes that are also rendered in iconography. Whereas Indian sculpture captures movement in a static form, the dancer gives movement to the static form and evokes a state of mind or sentiment, *rasa*.

Within the classical Indian aesthetic, the process of artistic creation was only partially fulfilled for Indrani at the Smithsonian. Most of her audience did not comprise what Vatsyayan described as the ideal spectators, with cultivated and trained emotions as well as familiarity with an art that reiterates in some way every other art. The general audience did not reach the ultimate state of bliss in which finite merges with infinite. On the other hand, Indrani is an international performer, and she shares other aesthetic goals. One was to convey the universal and timeless: woman in her various manifestations. Indrani succeeded in this and in enchanting many audience members. Twenty years ago, Vatsyayan summed up the current situation:

> So long as art was confined to the creators and the cultivated, the creator was constantly stimulated and inspired by the spectator of attuned disposition and similar heart and each enriched the other. With the throwing open of artistic performance to large, heterogeneous audiences, this totality of communication in dance is no longer easy, if even possible. The dancer can and does feel isolated behind the proscenium arch, aware that it is usually he [or she] who makes the effort to reach the spectator, and

seldom, if ever, the audience makes an active effort to reach him [or her] . . . the arts of . . . dance have now to pass through the crucial test of being presented *prima facie* for entertainment while retaining the beliefs which embody an entire culture and civilization.[15]

The stage has become the new temple.

## CHAPTER 5

# Resurrecting a Tamiris Spiritual:
# Repertory Dance Theatre of Utah

## TO DO OR NOT TO

The performer-audience connection and spectator response to the audience survey (see appendix) at the Repertory Dance Theatre of Utah (RDT) were ensconced in history. During the 1970s the past became inviting as dancers sought their roots in the aftermath of the 1960s ethnic group movement to search for one's heritage and document the social and cultural life of this legacy. Dancers attempted to reconstruct dances that were no longer being performed. The issue of reconstructing or resurrecting early modern dance is controversial. Many questions arise. For example, should pioneering efforts of the forebears of American modern dance be revived? Can they be? If so, how? Can the past be recaptured validly through dance? Should the current performances be given as close to the original as possible or be made more contemporary?

Accepting a reconstruction effort as feasible, the task is difficult for several reasons. The pioneers of modern dance held individual freedom to be their manifesto. As a result, they changed their choreography and interpretation because of creative impulses or the constraints of a performance, for example, the kind of stage or audience. There was a flux rather than a codification of dance. The pioneers' students also sought new directions rather than maintaining their teachers' styles and dances. Although some recording of the pioneers' dances by film or notation was done, it was not a regular activity. Furthermore, film and notation distort dances. Reconstructors therefore rely upon the film and notation sources as well as still photographs, performers' diaries and movement notations, critics' reviews, and memories of performers who danced with the leaders or observed their performances. Authenticity is consequently not fixed or noncontroversial.

Another reconstruction problem is that each dance and dancer have a special time and history. Creating a facsimile two, three, or more decades after a dance premiere can create disjunctions. In part, this is because dancers look different today. Their training is more sophisticated, and consequently their movement technique surpasses that of most pioneers. How much technique can contemporary dancers reveal before destroying the style of the pioneers? Most people agree that essences and spirits can be presented. Yet they also acknowledge that it is impossible to create the life of the creator and dancer who made the original a dazzling consummate inspiration for its time. The pioneers had unique charismatic qualities not found in most dancers; qualities inherent in heroic modern dancers disappear with the original performers. A key question is, can the dance be separated from the dancer? RDT members believe that the choreography of pioneers can bear witness to their achievement in creating "art as a work of art" as Kay Clark puts it, and provide a sense of the artistic progress of dance ideas and work.

Some audience members at reconstructions remember the original performances. A long-time critic of the dance scene, Walter Terry, has noted that dancers today have more highly developed dance technique. However, he points out that what the old-timers lacked in developed technique they made up in "soul," "pugnaciousness," and a "radiant mesmerizing projection." [1] A current re-creation can bring the richness of its own experience in respect or tribute. Larry Warren, himself a choreographer and director of a dance company, put it this way: "If a work of art has durability it needs to be able to stand the test of a reconsideration in the light of the sensibilities of a new generation; a new audience and new performers. Even the old masters are occasionally cleaned and reframed. Theater works and symphonic music are reinterpreted with each new presentation." [2]

The RDT decided to tackle the issue of reconstruction. Aware of the inherent problems in such a project, the group referred to it as a celebration of a great past. RDT was formed in 1966 with the assistance of the Rockefeller Foundation, the University of Utah, and the Salt Lake City community. The company began operating as a democratic artistic community with each dancer contributing to company policy. It later changed its organization, and two elder members of the company assumed co-director roles. The RDT repertory encompassed the contributions of ten luminaries of American modern dance. The dances appear in a historical perspective that the dancers narrate. Marcia Siegel, author of *Shapes of Change* and dance critic for the *Soho Weekly News* and *Hudson Review*, wrote the script.

The company is devoted to maintaining the repertory of such individual artists as Isadora Duncan, Ruth St. Denis, Doris Humphrey, and Helen Tamiris. RDT intends to present the works in an authentic manner that does not replicate but captures the spirit of the pioneers, who had their own unique time and charisma. They re-create masterworks to let us know how we came to be where we are and to assess our legacy.

Repertory Dance Theatre in "When the Saints Go Marchin' In." *Photograph by Lisa McClanahan, courtesy of RDT.*

For the most part, theatre dance has been strongly rooted in New York City. While little happened elsewhere in the United States to offer decentralized options for dancers, the RDT created opportunities. It combined its own creative efforts and incorporated the dances of pioneer choreographers. John Martin, esteemed *New York Times* dance critic, had remarked in the 1930s that the stability of dance as an independent enterprise depended upon decentralization.[3]

The RDT "Company Statement" is testament to its intent:

> It was with a sense of adventure, curiosity, and a bit of daring that the members of The Repertory Dance Theatre set about to create a dance retrospective which would include works by legendary figures from the early years in American Modern Dance. . . . Siegel was commissioned to write a text and a narrative script to document the performance.
>
> *Then . . . the Early Years of Modern Dance* is history which not only lives, but breathes, sweats and leaps. The details of the choreography, style, and emotion come from many sources: dance notation, teaching by noted dancers, film and writings. We have synthesized much opinion and data . . . no easy task in a field where even dancers in the same company will differ in their recollections. The synthesis and the sifting continues, but it is made relevant only when it is interpreted by living artists.

The terms "revival" and "reconstruction" do not adequately describe our project. We are celebrating a great era of expression, exploration, enthusiasm and personal statement. One cannot come in contact with these works without being amazed and rejuvenated by them. We decided to embark upon a great collection of early pieces in order to discover our roots as contemporary dancers and in order to share them with others. We chose to regard the pieces as timeless works of art. We chose to abstract or suggest the original costuming in some cases, fearing that exact duplication would seem to mimic or date the choreography.

From the beginning of our search we were affected by the tremendous vitality of the material. We wish not to copy or imitate the individuals of the past, but to dance their works as if for the first time, with all of the conviction and passion of the people who made them.

*Then . . . the Early Years of Modern Dance* was premiered March 14, 1980, at the Capitol Theater in Salt Lake City, Utah. It was performed by the following dancers:

| | |
|---|---|
| MICHAEL KELLY BRUCE | MICHELE MASSONEY |
| ROBIN CHMELAR | RACHEL NELSON |
| KAY CLARK | THOM SCALISE |
| FORD EVANS | STEVE SPENCER |
| JOEL KIRBY | LINDA C. SMITH |

—The Repertory Dance Theatre

Dance critics did not assail the RDT intent to celebrate the past and discover and share the roots of contemporary dance. They certainly recognized that the company did not "copy or imitate" the individuals of the past.

Clive Barnes of the *New York Post* described RDT as "one of the liveliest and most imaginative modern-dance troupes in the world." About the program "Then . . . The Early Years of Modern Dance," offered in New York City a year before coming to the Smithsonian, he said, "Historically it is fascinating, and as dance it is a surprising knockout."[4]

When the RDT opened in Salt Lake, Helen Forsberg of the *Salt Lake Tribune* wrote, "When the concert is over, you'll feel as if you've been both entertained and have also gained a wealth of information."[5] In the *Deseret News*, Dorothy Stowe said, "Thank you RDT, for taking names off a page of history and making of them living, breathing dancers."[6] She described the program as "a leisurely stroll through America's immediate dance past, so interestingly presented that one is loath to leave one scene and proceed to the next." She noted that "entertainment first and education as a by-product" is not an easy balance to attain. Alan M. Kriegsman of the *Washington Post* described the event as an "exhilarating crash course in dance history." The program did "powerfully evoke the atmosphere and aspiration of a crucial era and that alone is a singular and treasurable accomplishment."[7] However, when the company danced the pioneers' works with the intention "as if for the first time, with all of the conviction and passion of the people who made them," some critics howled.

The program was subject to the common charge against reconstructions leveled by Anna Kisselgoff in the *New York Times*: "unsophisticated dilutions" of good intentions and the pieces themselves. In the *Soho Weekly Review*, Nancy Goldner said, "While everybody is being terribly courteous toward the past, few know what they want from it. Presumably we all want pleasure. But when it comes to defining authenticity, or even intuiting its presence at a given performance, confusion and misunderstanding prevail."[8]

Walter Terry noted that no one in the RDT was powerful enough to take on the titanic roles the greats created for themselves. Anne Marie Welsh of the *Washington Star* conceded that the reconstructions had some accuracy.[9] Nonetheless, "In most cases spirit and style were so deadened, individual differences so blunted, that even historical interest could not excuse the lifelessness onstage." She found the program "a monumental, overly ambitious effort of retrieval of a rich, revolutionary, and substantial period of modern dance."

Thus, although there was critical appreciation of RDT's goal to celebrate past contributions and present some aspects of the dance heritage, there was also attention to some of the shortcomings.

### HELEN TAMIRIS

At the Smithsonian, the RDT performance of Helen Tamiris's "Negro Spirituals" was the subject of the performance-audience connection. Born Helen Becker (1905–1966), Tamiris, as she became known, had a creative dance career marked by a history of struggle and determination, semi-flops, failures, and triumphs. A beautiful, glamorous woman, she was recognized for her theatricality in style and dress (she designed her own costumes with spontaneity and zest), her vitality in dancing, and her profound ideas and social activism.

The daughter of Russian-Jewish immigrants living on New York City's Lower East Side, Tamiris came from an artistic family. At the age of eight, she was sent to dance classes at the Henry Street Settlement (before the Neighborhood Playhouse was formed). She later entered the Metropolitan Opera Ballet School, learned Italian ballet, and became a member of the corps de ballet in 1919. On leave, she performed as a principal dancer with the Bracale Opera Company on tour in South America. She returned to the Met for one year, resigning in 1923. Attracted to free, strong, and vital movement, Tamiris tried the Russian ballet of Michel Fokine and tasted the natural dancing of Isadora Duncan. Neither satisfied her. Her career changed directions, and while searching for a form of dance that suited her taste, she appeared as a specialty dancer in night-clubs, revues, and movie-house stageshows. In 1924/25 she was a featured dancer in the Music Box Revue. Then, still dissatisfied with dance as it was, she gave up remunerative work and spent a year and a half searching by herself.

Tamiris embarked on her concert career in 1927. Her debut was in the same year that three New York City newspapers established independent departments of dance criticism. Her solo program "Dance Moods" presented at the Little Theater heralded a new direction. She used modern American composers, even danced without music, and treated jazz rhythms seriously.

If her professional name, dance style, and personal appearance were glamorous, most of Tamiris's choreography was earnest. It dealt with important social themes. Dance was part of "people's theatre" with concern for minority and poverty themes. Tamiris believed that dance has to show the power and strength inherent in life in order to be meaningful. "The validity of the modern dance is rooted in its ability to express modern problems and, further, to make modern audiences want to do something about them." [10] Tamiris choreographed social statements about blacks in America and revolution in Mexico. Her work denounced war and explored the encounter between the haves and have-nots.

In 1928 Tamiris first encompassed the spirit of the black spiritual. She continued choreographing spirituals until there were a total of nine dances by 1942. This work led to the epithet "Harlem savage." Tamiris recognized life as conflict and said so. The "Negro Spirituals," indispensable to her programs, were well received by the public and the press. This suite served to plow the field for more ethnic dance. Tamiris sympathized with the black pathos and joy. She found in black rhythms freedom, lack of inhibition, the challenge of the impromptu, and spontaneous venting of emotion. The spiritual had feeling and human significance, qualities that became her keynote: "Dancing for technical brilliance alone loses its cords into life." [11]

Tamiris was not only socially oriented in her choreography and performance but was a tireless activist in attempting to organize dancers for their common benefit, to improve their status. Recognizing the precarious financial plight of dancers, she was driven toward cooperative action that worked to the sacrifice and denial of her own artistic growth and development. During her career, she organized various groups and produced concerts for other choreographers as well as herself.

Tamiris organized the Dance Repertory Theatre in 1929, the first cooperative venture to be undertaken by American dancers. Recognizing the logic of creative collaboration, Martha Graham, Doris Humphrey, Charles Weidman, and Agnes De Mille participated in this group. Its purpose was to build larger audiences for indigenous American dance. The project collapsed after two years. Other major cooperative efforts were the American Dance Association and later a Federal Dance Theater in the Works Progress Administration of the 1930s.

Tamiris then concentrated on her own group. She did not believe in imposing her style on others. The body itself, she thought, knew how to move and therefore did not require someone to tell it how to breathe, contract, or fall. With Daniel Nagrin, her husband, she established a concert dance company and choreographed for it until her death.

Historian Christena Schlundt described Tamiris as caught between two camps, neither of which claimed her as a member. One was the "big four" of Denishawn training and the Bennington College "circle": Martha Graham, Hanya Holm, Doris Humphrey, and Charles Weidman. The other camp was the social revolution group of dancers like Anna Sokolow. From the perspective of the big four, Tamiris was a glorious dancer who could not choreograph. She did not follow the aesthetic standard that Louis Horst had articulated in *Pre-Classic Dance Forms*. "It was all right for Humphrey to follow the symphonic form, Graham could use stream of consciousness with climactic orgasm, Weidman could use pantomime with dramatic flair, but Tamiris could not make artistic statements that used social themes so obviously," reported Schlundt.[12] From the perspective of the revolutionary dancers, Tamiris's dances were "too illusory, or they did not move her audience, or they were too bourgeois, or her themes dwelt too consistently on the decadent."

Yet Tamiris had her admirers. She gained her widest acclaim with commercial Broadway theatre choreography for *Up in Central Park* (1945), *Show Boat* and *Annie Get Your Gun* (1946), and *Inside USA* (1948). About her dancing Schlundt wrote, "Tamiris in motion excited the most casual observer with her rich loveliness, her heroic and maenadic femaleness, her animal logic, her ease of flow, control, rage. In vigorous affirmation of life, she seemed to wring her dances from her blood and muscle."[13]

From what we know about Tamiris, she would probably be supportive of the RDT collaborative efforts. She would most likely respect their individual and collective freedom to pay respect to her creative accomplishments through new achievements.

### THE PERFORMER-AUDIENCE CONNECTION

As recognized by theatre managers who solicit their attendance with "comps" or complimentary tickets for choice seats (and hopefully choice reviews), critics are key audience members. Some people believe that critics have the power to make or break a company or performer who is not well established with an audience following. Earlier we heard from

the critics about the issue, problem, and success of the overall RDT performance of "Then . . . The Early Years of Modern Dance" that has been
presented in various parts of the United States.

In Washington, the RDT performance followed a spread of what
Kriegsman called "deluctable courses." Several of the company members
taught movement classes at various universities in the metropolitan area.
At the National Portrait Gallery, RDT was part of the series "Portraits in
Motion." The company brought to life one of the Gallery's holdings
through their rendition of "Ruth St. Denis: In Performance." After this
program, RDT gave a lecture-demonstration in which they explained
some of the group's goals.

At the Smithsonian concert, the subject of the performer-audience
connection was the dance before the first intermission, as in the other
performances. This dance was "When the Saints Go Marchin' In" (1941),
the climax to Helen Tamiris's suite of "Negro Spirituals." The sequence
began with "Go Down Moses" (1932), followed by "Swing Low" (1929),
"Crucifixion" (1931), "Git on Board" (1932), "Joshua" (1928), and "L'il
David" (1942). Some audience members responded to the entire suite because they considered it one dance rather than a series of dances.

Critics' responses to the suite were positive. Dorothy Stowe noted that
the "Negro Spiritual" choreography of about fifty years ago looked as
vital today as then. Walter Terry thought RDT captured the thrust of
movement for which Tamiris was famous.

*Performer Intention.* I asked the performers in the group dance "When
the Saints Go Marchin' In" what feelings they wanted to convey to the
audience. Several dancers interviewed mentioned that they wanted to
convey the feeling of jubilation.

"Jubilation," Robin Chmelar said, "a religious fervor type of feeling,
even though I'm not a religious person. In a group piece, I feel sort of like
what my energy adds to the group and what the group adds to my energy
kind of melt together so it's not as individualized as in a solo, like in the
Duncan things. Every time I do it, I can decide if I want it to be really
happy and light or something else because I'm the only one out there. But
in a group thing, you stay with the group."

Michele Massoney also wanted to get across the feeling of jubilation,
joy, and elation to the audience. Ford Evans put it this way: "Jubilation,
sort of ecstatic joy, to use a few words; it's sort of a celebration." Sharing
his sentiments, Art Lee, too, spoke of "jubilation, joy, exaltation, because
that's what it is, and a sharing with everybody there; it's a kind of social
gathering too." Joel Kirby explained, "Since it is the end of the whole
series of showing the plight, the highs and the lows basically, it's sort of
the conclusion. For me, it's a moment of total ecstatic joy and freedom."

I asked, "How do you get the feeling of jubilation across to the audience?" Chmelar answered: "Things like a real energy in the chest, when we do a thing like this [she brought her hands into her chest, extending her arms diagonally upward and outward, and vibrated her hands] and when I open, I just really feel an upsurge of energy upward as if I were yelling something to the sky. I feel that kind of energy up from the chest. And eye contact with the other dancers. I always watch Michele and Rachel doing little things across the floor. . . . It's a really genuine smile and happiness, because I like watching them dancing. So mostly that and putting a lot of energy and clarity in the movement. There are a lot of jumps . . . and my feet are real springy and articulate. Jumping like that is more energetic than if you are just articulating well and using your full energy." Massoney's response was, "There's a big feeling of that [jubilation] within me and I guess it shows through a smile and radiance through the entire body and spirit." Evans said, "The movement has a lot to do with it, the energy going out; it is an opening up, skips, leaps; it's movement that one does to project outward." Lee thought he conveyed the feeling of jubilation "just by being with the other dancers."

"It's all coming from out of my heart, I guess," Kirby explained. "It explodes out and sometimes it comes out in the form of a shaking movement or hopefully on my face, that total joy that centers from right in here. My favorite moment in the whole thing is when we do the jumps-run-circle where we are coming in and opening out because that is the moment when it's giving and giving some more. I think that movement is the most typical to show the feeling of the piece to me."

Rachel Nelson wanted to get across to the audience "the kind of exuberance . . . a little bit like the kind of excitement that comes from the Shakers. Only the Shaker's excitement is born of frustration, the religious fervor born of frustration. And the kind of religious excitement that is in the Saints and the whole spiritual seems to come from joy. It's such a painful section to do, there's so much jumping that doing it once or twice in a day, my feet feel like they're going to give out. But to get above that you have to try harder so maybe that's what makes the section work." She thought that the choreography was responsible for getting the feeling across. "All the movements are uplifted and open across the chest and whole torso which seem to communicate a great deal. And working as a group; all the circular patterns force you to look at everybody you're dancing across from, whereas when you're dancing stage front there isn't as much eye contact, at least not noticeably."

I asked the dancers what kind of feeling they had to have to dance the Saints. Chmelar said, "You have to have a lot of energy, because it's hard. You just have to get a natural momentum. You stand backstage and slap the thighs during the introduction." "Is the movement motivating the feeling?" I asked. "It's both, and it's not just the movement. It's the direction of the choreographer. The person who set the dance said you don't just go straight forward, you watch the people. I don't think there's anything that I do that I can think of where the feeling motivates the movement or the movement motivates the feeling separately."

Nelson remarked, "You have to forget that it's movement and however you motivate it could be a lot of different ways. Some days for me it's picking out somebody and sort of having a movement joke with them. It makes you smile to know that somebody else understands perfectly well that your feet are killing you. You make something out of it. By the end of the piece though, you're so breathless. The finale starts with a sort of giving motion, and it seems to me that you keep trying to give, to give, to give, to give until you have done that and the whole thing ends in a tableau. To me that's really a peak in the piece." She continued, "You start with the idea of the joy, but to make it become a reality, for me, I feel I have to establish contact with everybody in the piece and those two things feed off each other. I can start with an individual feeling but then it has to build as a group."

Massoney said she had to have the feeling of jubilation to dance Saints. The movement affected her feeling, "especially the part where Rachel goes across the stage with all this open stuff; if it's really feeling right, at that point I can actually feel goose bumps or shivers or chills. When I do that, I feel so excited and knowing that someone is doing it exactly with me, it's like the whole group is cheering us on. You can feel the energy from the other people." For Evans, "It happens as we are standing onstage and the music starts; it's a real group sort of thing, the feeling is initiated by the group. . . . We don't have any choice about the outcome, we're just swept up."

Lee thought the dancers just had to have their own feelings to dance the Saints. "It's just allowing yourself to let them out." When I asked about the reciprocity of movement and emotion, he said, "You do have the feeling that this is a fun one . . . when you're out there dancing with everybody else, it becomes even more so. When we come out in the first circle and the second circle and you look across and you see all these faces smiling back at you, it's really a warm and nice feeling. The dance itself is choreographed to be joy. And it works, because that's how we all feel about it."

Kirby said, "I think you need understanding, and I think in working with it hard, because when you rehearse it, it's hard to get that type of energy up, and we rehearse a lot, and . . . it just doesn't work a lot of times in rehearsals, because that joy doesn't come through." He continued, "The movement comes out of the feeling for me. And just having done the little solo I do before that ("Git on Board"), I sort of establish that feeling . . . and again, the slapping before the dancing."

When I asked how he felt after the dance, he replied, "I usually feel real good, especially if I don't bump into anybody. It's a tiring piece, not only physically but also emotionally—if you really get into it and do it. I'm usually quite drained at that point and thank god the curtain goes down. I usually feel good, just being about a social theme like that, the blacks. It makes me feel good to think that I'm helping, showing that at the time there was trouble, there was joy that could come out." Kirby signs for the deaf. Indeed, both his parents are hearing impaired, and his background has given him a sensitivity to problems of minorities. Kirby signed during the "Portrait of Motion" lecture-demonstration.

*Audience Survey.* About the RDT program overall an energy consultant who considered herself very knowledgeable about dance said, "I think this work of the RDT is most significant of anything happening in dance today. It must be filmed and shown more widely. More touring and teaching."

Who were the 30 participants?[14] Women outnumbered men 53 percent to 37 percent. Two age groups were equally represented, 21–30 and 41–65, at 33 percent each. The 31–40 group was 17 percent; under 20, 10 percent. According to the information respondents gave, 63 percent were white, 3 percent black, and 10 percent other. At this concert 40 percent were post-graduates, 30 percent college graduates, 17 percent had some college. A third of the respondents' family income was over $40,000; about a fourth (23 percent) under $20,000; a fifth, $31,000–$40,000; and 13 percent, $21,000–$30,000. The occupational distribution was 43 percent professionals, 10 percent manager/administrators, 10 percent sales and clerical, and under 10 percent others. Fifty-seven percent of the respondents considered themselves somewhat knowledgeable about dance, 20 percent very, and 17 percent not at all.

True to Tamiris's intent for "When the Saints Go Marchin' In," 83 percent of the audience who shared their views of emotion saw vitality and happiness; 73 percent ecstasy; and 67 percent playfulness. In addition, 37 percent perceived eroticism, 30 percent caring, and 23 percent pride (see appendix table 1).

What clues did respondents find to identify the emotions they perceived?[15] As shown in table 3, body parts, especially in combination (coded as "all"), suggested vitality, as did the action of gesture and locomotion. The use of energy and time qualities of movement were also suggestive. More than half of the clues to happiness were body parts, more in the entire body and other aspects than the face. Gesture, locomotion, and energy were also notable. Body parts strongly indicated ecstasy, with action, quality of movement, and nondance factors also making a contribution. Playfulness was noticed through gesture, locomotion, and other actions, body parts, quality of movement, and nondance factors.

TABLE 3. RDT Concert: How Audience Perceived Emotions

*Clues per person: 13.1*
N = 30

| Emotion | Action | | Perceptions through Body Parts | | Quality of Movement | | Nondance Factors |
|---|---|---|---|---|---|---|---|
| *Vitality* | Gesture | 12 | All | 8 | Energy | 12 | 1 |
| | Locomotion | 11 | Face | 5 | Time | 9 | |
| | Other | 6 | Other | 17 | Space | 1 | |
| | | | | | Other | 2 | |
| Perceived clues | | 29 | | 30 | | 24 | 1 |
| % of total | | | | | | | |
| (84) clues | | 35% | | 36% | | 29% | 1% |
| *Happiness* | Gesture | 8 | Face | 13 | Energy | 5 | 1 |
| | Locomotion | 8 | All | 5 | Time | 4 | |
| | Other | 4 | Other | 16 | Space | 1 | |
| | | | | | Other | 1 | |
| Perceived clues | | 20 | | 34 | | 11 | 1 |
| % of total | | | | | | | |
| (66) clues | | 30% | | 52% | | 17% | 1% |
| *Ecstasy* | Gesture | 9 | All | 10 | Energy | 4 | 4 |
| | Other | 13 | Face | 9 | Time | 2 | |
| | | | Shld/ | | Space | 2 | |
| | | | Arms | 7 | Other | 2 | |
| | | | Other | 17 | | | |
| Perceived clues | | 22 | | 43 | | 10 | 4 |
| % of total | | | | | | | |
| (79) clues | | 28% | | 54% | | 13% | 5% |
| *Playfulness* | Gesture | 10 | All | 6 | Energy | 8 | 2 |
| | Locomotion | 9 | Face | 5 | Time | 5 | |
| | Other | 11 | Other | 18 | Space | 2 | |
| | | | | | Other | 2 | |
| Perceived clues | | 30 | | 29 | | 17 | 2 |
| % of total | | | | | | | |
| (78) clues | | 38% | | 37% | | 22% | 3% |

*Note: Percentages have been rounded off.*

A composer offered a unique point of view, and perhaps an occupational bias: "The most emotion is conveyed by the music, second most by facial expressions, third most by stylized gestures, for example, stamping foot, clicking heels in air. Very little by dance itself."

An Afro-American dance movement therapist saw feelings of caring, ecstasy, eroticism, happiness, playfulness, pride, sadness, shame, vitality, and struggle. She felt empathy, excitement, and the desire to move. "This level of expression and sharing in these dances is very exciting to me, particularly the expressions on dancers' faces and audible breathing is very important, I think, in exciting response in the audience. The vision all of this excitement inspires in me is what carries the dancer's spirit on in our/my lives. Thank you for sharing so much with me and us."

From their survey reports, people generally felt the same or similar emotion to the one they perceived onstage. In "When the Saints Go Marchin' In," the commonly recognized feelings of happiness and vitality made respondents feel "upbeat" and "enthused." A potter noted the "energetic, strong, quick full movement, complete body involvement, aware faces lifted to lights" that conveyed happiness, playfulness, and vitality. A transportation planner identified these three feelings through bouncy movement, facial expression, leaping, short movements, and repetitive motions. He shared the feelings.

The energy consultant mentioned earlier perceived caring through arm and group movements. She felt caring in turn. At the end of the piece, from her perspective, the dancers got across the feeling of ecstasy through their arms and torso and made her feel strong. The head tilt and rhythm depicted happiness and evoked the same kind of feeling in this observer. At the end of the dance when the performers captured the emotion of pride through the torso stance, head, and arms, she felt good. The continuous vitality expressed through the dancers' full body and rhythm made her feel strong.

Commenting on the RDT as "very accomplished dancers," an engineer felt the ecstasy the dancers' performance created through arms, body, and legs. A saleswoman felt happy about the feeling of ecstasy that she perceived through the "marching and dancing." A young woman from New Jersey thought that the dancers expressed ecstasy through facial expressions and "much outward expression of movement, not inward." The vitality imparted throughout by speed of movement and complicated steps made her feel "invigorated, a shot in the arm." Anticipation and praise displayed at the beginning and end through facial expression and upward sweeps of broad movement made her feel "confirmed, edified, and blessed."

Were there relationships between respondent background characteristics and perceptions of emotions and clues to them? Because of the small sample size ($N = 30$), conclusions are necessarily tentative. However, it is possible that there are sex differences associated with recognizing vitality. Men (64 percent of 11) saw vitality through the clue of energy more than women (31 percent of 16). Perhaps because they are generally more active in sports than women, men perceived the continuous strength and vigorous effort of the leaps, jumps with springy feet, and expanding chests. Other clues to vitality included the gestural and loco-moter actions, body parts, and brisk pace.

The dancers recognized the piece as a group dance in which their collaborative efforts conveyed emotion. Teresa Ankney spoke with a woman in her mid-fifties who had danced professionally with Martha Graham. The interviewee said, "They did not feel like separate people to me. I saw them more as a group."

RDT seems to have achieved success in reaching its goals of entertainment and historical reporting. Furthermore, the dancers' intentions in "When the Saints Go Marchin' In" meshed with audience perceptions. Spectators reported receiving their messages of vitality, ecstasy, and jubilation.

## CHAPTER 6

# Symbiosis and Short-Circuit in the Avant-Garde: Douglas Dunn

By definition the avant-garde is controversial. Both attracting and re-pelling, it raises sticky questions about public policy and the arts. Do performer and audience connect in an avant-garde concert? Are there short-circuits? What expectations does each have for the other? Are accommodations and mediation needed?

## THE REVOLUTIONARY

Billed as a "post-modern" American performer-choreographer, avant-garde dancer Douglas Dunn appeared with Deborah Riley in the Washington, D.C., premiere of a duet in three acts called "Foot Rules," score by John Driscoll, costumes by Mimi Gross. The work had its world premiere in Berlin and was performed in New York City in 1979. "Foot Rules" has no specific story or narrative line. In the program notes written by Sali Ann Kriegsman, the audience could discover that fifteen years ago "Yvonne Rainer defined a revolution against modern dance":

> No to spectacle no to virtuosity no to transformations and magic and make-believe no to glamour and transcendence of the star image no to the heroic no to the anti-heroic no to trash imagery no to involvement of performer or spectator no to style no to camp no to seduction of spectator by the wiles of the performer no to eccentricity no to moving or being moved.

The target of the post-modern revolution was "modern dance," itself a rebellion against the classic ballet theatre. Ballet had evolved over the past four hundred years into what detractors called an abstract, codified, impersonal movement vocabulary and grammar (way of putting the movement together). Ballet had five positions for the body, arms, and legs. Turnout from the body center with the feet pointed out to the sides in an unnatural stance was de rigueur. Above the ground, only pointed toes were acceptable.

Pioneers of modern dance rejected the rigidities of ballet movement technique and assaulted the fanciful fairy tales and romantic themes. The

American Loie Fuller (1862–1928) dancing in Paris in the 1890s began laying the foundation for modern dance with its freedom of movement and the solo form in marked contrast with ballet traditions. She eschewed the projection of emotion or personality, virtuosic dance technique, and even attention to physical beauty in the dancer. These radical changes lay dormant, to be resuscitated in the 1960s in the post-modern revolution that Rainer defined.

Isadora Duncan, a more renowned ancestor of modern dance, built simple dances with basic locomotor steps in repetitive structures. Her heretical concepts about human freedom in movement are a key legacy to later developments on the American scene. Two other forerunners of modern dance, Ruth St. Denis and Ted Shawn, provided succeeding generations of choreographers training in a wide-ranging variety of movement styles. They exposed students in their Denishawn school to an exotic and extravagant aesthetic against which to rebel during the late 1920s. For example, Martha Graham devoted her energies to heroines of a twentieth-century America concerned with recognition, confrontation, and resolution. She used "natural" breath to contract and release the body and to dramatize emotions of pain and ecstasy. Doris Humphrey, another Denishawn student, used breath to motivate the body in resisting and yielding movements and to symbolize the social triumph of humanity over inertia and gravity. Both Graham and Humphrey costumed themselves in somewhat austere yet expressive garb.

In moving into audacious realms that violated past canons, modern dance ideology articulated tolerance for diverse performance styles and even body structures. Thus modern dance expressed individual quests for personal movement styles, thematic concerns, and theories of movement. For American dancers, Dunn remarked, "Dance has always been a way of adding to or escaping from one's 'ordinary social self.' That's what gives our need to dance such urgency."

Merce Cunningham, a soloist in Graham's company, departed radically from the traditions in which he had been trained and sowed the seeds for post-modern dance. For Cunningham, and his successors, any movement could be dance material; any procedure, a valid method of composition. Thus he made use of chance. Dancing for him could be about anything, but it was essentially about the human body and its movements, beginning with walking. A source of inspiration for post-modern dancers, Cunningham's dances do away with the predictability of following a musical structure, story, psychological patterns, or demands and rules of traditional theatre. But unlike the post-modern choreographers, Cunningham remained embedded in a technique that he invented.

Many post-modern dancers lacked the movement technique and the

Deborah Riley and Douglas Dunn in "Foot Rules." *Photograph by Lois Greenfield.*

slender body structure of contemporary ballet and modern dance. Post-modern dance blurred the borders between "art" and everyday life; it broke down distinctions between different kinds of experiences. The work process became more significant than the finished product. Strategies of making dances without many contrasts and using performers without dance training replaced practices of employing traditional composition approaches and trained dancers and evaluating dance in terms of good or bad. In order to break boundaries between art and everyday life, post-modern dancers even used onstage the actual time that it might take to accomplish something outside the theatre, much repetition, and improvisation; they permitted mistakes, fatigue, awkwardness, and difficulty to show in concert performance. Not only was virtuoso technique antithetical to the post-modern concern; technique itself was demystified through drastically simplifying movement to the extent of placing survival movements like eating or grooming in a dance context. Technology and methodology became the antidote to the subjectivity of dramatic dance. In reaction to modern dance's dependence on literary ideas and musical forms, the formal qualities of movement, often drained of any emotion, sufficed as reason for choreography. The purpose of making dances could be merely to fabricate a frame within which people look at movement for its own sake or as an illustration of a theory of dance. For example, Dunn's dance "101" proposed that stillness constituted a dance. Thus post-modern dancers challenge the audience's prior expectations for performance.

To be sure, post-modern dancers are not a homogeneous group, nor do they share a single aesthetic. Individuals evolve in their own unique ways. Dunn did not begin dancing until he was in college. He studied with Merce Cunningham and danced with his company from 1969 through 1973. The Cunningham influence shines in "Foot Rules." Both skilled choreography and performance technique flow through the three acts. Dunn also danced with post-modern dancer Yvonne Rainer (1968–1970) and from 1970 to 1976 performed with the Grand Union. Dunn's own choreographic work began in 1971. It varies and resists conforming to a single style. His repertoire includes a trove of pure movement inventions, juxtapositions of abstract movements against pure wordplay, theatrical imagery, and a work, mentioned above, that is only stillness. Dunn's dances are generally about themselves and the choreographic process. However, he is open to alternatives. In 1980 Dunn received a commission from Michel Guy to choreograph Stravinsky's "Pulcinella" at the Paris Opera, and he made another piece for the Opera the following year in collaboration with jazz musician Steve Lacey. Dunn was not accustomed to having something like music in his head before beginning to make dances. Consequently, he had to work hard to avoid being trapped into "that dutiful, keeping-the-beat look."

As an aside, in speaking with Dunn and reading about the post-modern dancers I was struck by the fact that the words *choreograph* and *create* were noticeably absent. The word *make* reigned. Dunn explained that *make* means to "do something with a little bit of the intention we have to do things. Make aligns one with the product, gets us out of the romantic artistic trip. The word *create* seemed pretentious and inflated." Post-modern dancers are more like artisans. "If there's inspiration, great. But you invest yourself in your materials. *Choreography* is a long word."

THE HUMAN CONNECTION

To find out what transpired in an avant-garde performance, for the Washington premiere of Dunn's "Foot Rules" duet, I spoke with the choreographer about his intentions in this piece and solicited audience perspectives about what the dancers conveyed to them onstage. My assistants and I also noticed both the riveted attention of some spectators and the exodus of about one-third of the audience by the end of the second act,[1] listened to audience member comments during the intermissions, studied audience reactions written on a survey sheet distributed at the concert, and read the diametrically opposed dance critics in Washington's two major newspapers.

*Performer Intention.*   Turning to Dunn's intentions in act 1, I asked, "What do you want to get across to the audience? What kinds of feelings do you want to convey and how?" He replied: "My intention is just to do the dance. So, both as a choreographer and a performer, I have no idea about the audience. First of all, I don't think of them as an audience; I think of them as individuals, as separate people. And I assume their individuality of response. I think I make something that doesn't require that they all see it the same way. When I perform, I want to be clear. . . . That doesn't always mean it's simple, but it means that whatever movement takes place somehow tries to make itself clear, and I try to be the instrument which achieves that clarity."

Dunn spoke of intention in ballet and modern dance in comparison with his own dances. Modern dancers feel something, say it through movement, and the audience is supposed "to get that." In contrast, Merce Cunningham and John Cage, his avant-garde musician collaborator, are "just like a turn in the road. . . . And it's very interesting to me that . . . you can say, wouldn't it be interesting to try to have choice? All the language about chance and choice is an attempt, I think, to open up the possibilities so that you're not locked into what is ultimately a kind of compulsive idea about behavior and its relationship to feeling. . . . That doesn't mean that you don't have feeling."

Dunn explained: "You put your attention on the structure and then the feeling whatever it is emerges immediately in the form of structure. And the feeling, whatever it is, remains, as far as you and the audience, perhaps, are concerned, open. So I can do my dance, and I can feel one thing, and they can see it and feel another, and there's nothing wrong. . . . It gives everybody a lot of room. . . . It means you can experience your own feeling, so to speak, in relationship to what you are seeing, more than you could before."

The visual is important to Dunn, who likes to look at pictures and studied art history at Princeton University. "I'm interested in what you can see. The meaning should be visual. I've always been very oriented toward shape and the rhythms of shape in space." The visual information, he believes, can connect with the audience member's own life. He admits the audience into a creative role. Thus the viewer's imagination and experience respond to the dancing, and both the dancer and viewer together create meaning for the viewer. "I want it equalized," said Dunn. "You shouldn't 'ought' to see something like structure; it's up to the viewer."

For himself, Dunn wants openness—the choice to set up his own rules which he can choose to alter if he does not like the dance the rules determine. He gives instructions to himself for work and tries to generate imagery by paying attention to the dancers he works with. "I start to make steps, then think of the imagistic possibilities."[2] But not all of the audience shared his goal of openness for them.

*Audience Perception Problems.*    Nearly half of the audience filled out the survey form, although not always as requested. The form demanded from some people what was beyond their expectations for (and perhaps grasp of) dance viewing. They were not prepared to identify emotion. The habit of passively watching television may have carried over to passively rather than actively watching a theatre concert and participating in the creative process which Dunn desired. Several individuals reported that the performance overwhelmingly violated their dance aesthetic. Consequently some of the spectators became anxious, tense, nervous, and even irascible, as I discovered when a few descended upon me at intermission to talk about the performance. One respondent, a former member of a modern dance company, wrote that she did not enjoy the Dunn performance because of the stress level involved. "I have enough stress in my daily life—I see dance as more of a release—I dance for release. . . . I'm more of an Isadora Duncan type." A few audience members indicated that they were tired to begin with and did not want to work at a concert—either by figuring out what was happening onstage or by filling out a survey. Others were merely puzzled. One asked, "An idea: if my life is meaningless, will the dance be also?" in reference to an audience member interpreting a dance by drawing upon personal experience.

An individual's evaluation of dance is part of the attempt to "make sense" out of observations in relation to what dance generally means or feels to him or her. Understanding any behavior requires knowing the rules for the genre.

Some observers find their pleasure in performances well laced with familiar elements of older dance traditions of ballet, folk, jazz, or modern dance. They seek entertainment, defined as the reassurance of being immersed in some recognizable aspects of dance. Consequently yesterday's heritage asserted itself against contemporary creation at the concert, and "traditionalist" reactions to the Smithsonian premiere of "Foot Rules" adamantly opposed this new style of dance. Not only was much of the "Foot Rules" movement abstract, but so was the music. It was "alien." Driscoll's score, "Ebers and Mole," uses "interlocking delay patterns of pulsed material" which he transforms in performance through an array of acoustical modulators. In contrast to most classical ballet, the dance and music were independently created and performed and hence merely coincidental. About the music Dunn said, "It's for the audience, something to hear and fill aural space."

Opposite to traditionalists are people who are adventurous and receptive to novelty. There are spectators, imaginative by temperament, who enjoy interpreting visual stimuli. Some individuals are natural problem solvers and take readily to games like chess. Nonliteral dances tend to demand a greater receptivity and sophistication from the viewer, and thus are enjoyed by a relatively limited population of individualistic types, perhaps akin to sociologist David Riesman's "inner-directed" person.[3]

Peter Schjeldahl, *Village Voice* art critic, put the dilemma for some viewers this way: "We are obliged to remake from scratch the foundations of our taste, as of our politics and our very lives. Old ways of judging linger as unexamined habits, comforting defenses against the recognition of our common lostness. Thus defended, one is deprived of the compensatory joy of current liberty and profusion."[4]

Two incensed couples in the audience directly expressed to me their displeasure with avant-garde dance. Series organizer Sali Ann Kriegsman had announced that I was available in the comfortable "living room–like" reception room just outside the theatre to speak with people who wished to know more about the study of communication they were invited to participate in. The irate couples came over to where I was sitting and instead of talking about the study, they asked me how the Smithsonian could program such a concert. I invited them to sit down and chat. Only one woman accepted; the others maintained their angry stance. One man said the couples wanted a refund. They had come for entertainment and were going to discontinue the series—it cost $7.50 a person, plus transportation expenses, and time. Once seated, the more accommodating woman said she thought an audience could only watch one act. She and her friends had hoped that the second act would differ from the first, but since it did not, they were leaving before act 3. "This concert will turn people off to the series," remarked one man. "The dancers are fine, graceful. But the heavy ungainly movement was like what monkeys do at the zoo." The couples disliked the "sounds." A woman explained, "The music got on my nerves. It should have something familiar, for example, melody." As the couples left, one of the men said of the first American dance revolution, "I didn't like modern dance, so I should have known I wouldn't like post-modern."

*Positive Perception.*   Alan M. Kriegsman's *Post* review, however, summarized the favorable sentiments of many observers in the audience and provided a trained viewer's perception: "Douglas Dunn's 'Foot Rules' is a tour de force in more ways than one—as a conception, a choreographic achievement, and a bravura act of performance."[5] That an "abstract" piece of one hour for only two dancers "could be as consistently absorbing and fascinating as 'Foot Rules' proved to be is only one measure of the work's success, but it's also an index to Dunn's creative individuality." Kriegsman continues: "Though it's abstract, in the sense of depicting no narrative development or unambivalent imagery, the piece has a remarkable sense of 'content.' . . . 'Foot Rules' leads the eye and mind along its complex unfolding of movement and gesture with an unrelenting sense of suspense from point to point. We may never be quite sure what, but we know that *something* is going on—something tense, complicated and involving, something that feels true to our experience of human interaction." The *Post* critic attributes much of the impact to the "presence, authority and charisma of the two dancers." He explains to his readers that act 1 is "prevailingly playful and erotic in tone; the second explores variations on the possibilities of partnering, with Riley the dominant one of the pair; and the third, surprisingly, divides into alternating solos, except for a penultimate cadenza. The level of invention never flags. Driscoll's muted soundscape makes an ideally apt aural backdrop, and Mimi Gross' sporty, modular costuming lends visual energy and accent in just ratio."

Audience members sharing all or some of these sentiments were diverse: dancers, lawyers, engineers, technical writers, housewives, students, and others. One respondent said, "Fresh, new choreography was a welcome change. Well worth the trip from Rockville. All in all, a very rewarding performance." Another remarked, "I am wonderfully involved in the whole concert."

*Negative Perception.*    Opposed to such accolades were a diverse group of spectators who shared the unfavorable views of *Washington Star* critic Anne Marie Welsh.[6] This trained observer attributed the "distinct disappointment" in part to "the mystique that dance critics and historians have begun building around the choreographer and what he represents." She described the three acts as essentially not conveying emotion.

> What unfolded . . . were three workmanlike duets composed about equally of everyday movements, poses and steps clearly derived from academic ballet, and some original variation in skitters and floor work. Each "act" was structurally different. The first was full of unison passages performed parallelly or as mirror images, the second relatively more full of lifts and partnering and the third a series of alternating solos, performed with a remarkable degree of technical proficiency. . . . In keeping with an aesthetic of denial, Dunn avoided—almost with a vengeance—any at-

tempt to create meaning out of the duet form. If the work was about a relationship, it was of the sort a desk and chair rather than a man and a woman might have with each other.

Welsh bemoaned the fact that Gross's brightly colored, contemporary costumes and Driscoll's "fascinating sense-around electronic score kept suggesting human and cosmic imagery that the movement fastidiously avoided delivering." Her concluding paragraph stated: "The resulting work was an exercise in dullness, unrelieved by the theatrical wit and strange beauty of Merce Cunningham whose influence could fitfully be seen, or by the more interesting innovations of someone like Maida Withers, a local choreographer who sometimes works in a similar idiom."

It is noteworthy that when audience members commented on the dancers apart from the choreography both sides of the like-dislike controversy, generally, recognized the dancing as disciplined, well rehearsed, and creative. One person described the dancing as "beautifully and elegantly executed."

Although audience members both praised and damned the concert, those who were dissatisfied with the avant-garde were more dramatically expressive. One respondent ignored the questions on the form and wrote over the sheet of paper in large, strident lettering, "It stank!" Another person who spoke with me at intermission also ignored the form requests and boldly printed on one side: "Very, very boring!!! I would like a forum to complain. The Smithsonian pulled a fast one on the paying public." On the other side of the sheet this man, who identified himself as an urban-born engineer with an upper middle class family income, wrote, "a rip off to have paid $7.50. I think having to pay to see a performance like this is absolutely a SHAM! An absurd performance, especially if you are expecting entertainment. I am including my name, etc., for I wish to discuss this further and would like a refund." I turned a copy of the form over to the series organizer. "Even good dancers can't make a bad program good. Fred Astaire and Ginger Rogers, they're not," was one comment. A bored viewer remarked, "I watched the orchestra. Why am I here?" A teacher explained, "Act 1 did not really communicate with me. The dancers' facial expressions turned me off. Both participants seemed to have a case of acute indigestion."

Who were the 125 audience survey respondents?[7] More than half (62 percent) were female. The age distribution was 9 percent under the age of 20; 35 percent between 21 and 30; 22 percent between 31 and 40; 25 percent between 41 and 65; and 3 percent over 65.

In the categories of ethnicity and place of birth, respondents born in the United States were 73 percent white and 1 percent black. There were another 21 percent white who were born outside the United States. Some 3 percent were Japanese; 2 percent responded as "other."

Educational attainment level among the respondents was 42 percent postgraduate, 26 percent with four-year college degrees, 16 percent with some college, and 8 percent with at least high school education.

Family income level data showed that 31 percent earned over $40,000 per year; 44 percent, $21,000–$40,000; and 26 percent, under $20,000. Occupationally, 31 percent of the respondents were professionals; 16 percent students; 16 percent managerial or sales; 12 percent dancers; 8 percent nondance creative artists; 3 percent housewives; and 1 percent skilled labor. Four percent responded as "other."

With regard to understanding dance, 28 percent of the respondents considered themselves very knowledgeable, 43 percent somewhat, and 15 percent not at all.

Appendix table 1 presents the emotions the audience members perceived on stage. Spectators offered opposite views on whether or not the dancers conveyed feeling in the dance before the first intermission and how they felt in response to what happened onstage. Forty-six percent saw no emotion. Other audience members perceived a wide range of emotions, although they differed in their personal feelings in response to the same emotions. Whereas one observer reported that "the performers expressed the whole spectrum of emotions," another felt angered by the lack of feeling perceived in the dancers: "They are more concerned with movement than emotion."

On the "dancers conveyed feeling" side of the controversy about emotional expression, an oceanographer, like many audience members, spotted several emotions, the places in the dance where each was displayed, the clues he found to identify them, and his own feelings in response. He perceived caring through the dancers' hands and limbs, competitiveness through equal movements of each dancer, fatigue through the stillness of the entire body, playfulness in the bouncy quality of the dancing, and vitality through speedy movements. In response to the emotions he observed, he either felt positive or no emotion. In the blank space for comments he wrote: "The question in my mind was what would an extraterrestrial visitor interpret from this piece about humans? My answer would be confusion."

Although there was perceptual diversity, some emotions were perceived by about a third of the respondents: caring (31 percent), competitiveness (29 percent), and vitality (30 percent). As appendix table 1 illustrates, of the many emotions perceived, 55 percent of the 113 audience respondents noted the playful feeling of the performers. Yet, others (46 percent) faulted the dancers for a lack of playfulness. "I'd say they take themselves so seriously, play or communicating seems the last thing they think of doing. They've forgotten how to have fun. A sense of play is one of the most important things, along with truth, beauty, and so forth, in all art, and they need a reminder."

Forty percent of the respondents observed eroticism. A male engineer perceived this feeling in the intertwining and rolling of the couple on the floor, and he said it made him feel "horny." Another person viewed the dancing as "X-rated." A male lawyer saw ecstasy as the dancers were "lying as if spent," and he felt "excited." Remember that half of the respondents reported that they saw no emotion!

Among these respondents, those who offered comments in the space provided on the survey form tended to describe the movement style as mechanical, stilted, robot-like, computerized, and possessing a tense, bound quality. "An intellectual, nonemotional quality was projected," remarked a viewer. Another said the dance has "the feeling of New York art, especially the costumes and made me feel like I was watching androids or mechanical mannequins."

Some observers responded to the first act of "Foot Rules" with emotions similar to the ones the dancers conveyed to them, as noted above. The perception of sharp moves and music dissociated from movements as well as lifts depicted and evoked surprise. A student who saw the dancers express shame through relaxing the chest and hips and then tightening them again felt sad. Stress and tension conveyed to an observer through the dancers' taut body carriage, especially in the shoulders, and lack of flow from one combination of movements to the next evoked stress and tension in the observer. The dancers' running and free-style movements made a musician feel energized. The feeling of boredom communicated through tempo or "no emotion" evoked the same feeling. The dancers' lack of facial expression and connection created a sense of alienation for some respondents, who in turn felt distant.

Audience reactions to emotions perceived onstage were also sometimes different from these. "Self-centered independent movements" conveyed pride to an attorney and stimulated his feelings of sadness and happiness. Disgust seen through "winged shoulder blades" evoked a performing artist's sentiment of pride. Jerky movement elicited anxiety.

The genre of dance may determine a viewer's emotional response to a performance. A dance critic and TV arts producer explained: "I respond emotionally to ballet in all forms, to Paul Taylor, to Martha Graham, but not to a dance form such as this. Here I'm watching the technique, how they put the movement together, how the electronics work. I simply don't enjoy this type of work on an emotional level."

There were also people who had trouble categorizing and expressing what they observed: "The emotions conveyed are too abstract to grasp clearly."

**TABLE 4.** Dunn Concert: How Audience Perceived Emotions

| Clues per person: 3.46<br>N = 113<br>Emotion | Action | | Perceptions through<br>Body<br>Parts | | Quality of<br>Movement | | Nondance<br>Factors |
|---|---|---|---|---|---|---|---|
| Playfulness | Locomotion | 19 | Arms | 4 | Dancers' | | Music 1 |
| | Gesture | 3 | Feet | 3 | Relations | 15 | |
| | | | Hands | 2 | Energy | 7 | |
| | | | Legs | 2 | Time | 5 | |
| | | | Face | 1 | Space | 5 | |
| | | | Shld | 1 | Other | 17 | |
| | | | Other | 5 | | | |
| Perceived clues | | 22 | | 18 | | 49 | 1 |
| % of total | | | | | | | |
| (91) clues | | 24% | | 22% | | 54% | 1% |
| No Emotion | Gesture | 4 | Face | 8 | Dancers' | | 0 |
| | Locomotion | 4 | Other | 3 | Relations | 8 | |
| | Posture | 2 | | | Energy | 6 | |
| | | | | | Space | 5 | |
| | | | | | Time | 3 | |
| | | | | | Other | 28 | |
| Perceived clues | | 10 | | 11 | | 50 | 0 |
| % of total | | | | | | | |
| (71) clues | | 14% | | 15% | | 70% | |
| Eroticism | Locomotion | 11 | Pelvis | 16 | Dancers' | | 0 |
| | Posture | 11 | Arms | 3 | Relations | 11 | |
| | Gesture | 10 | Legs | 3 | Soul/ | | |
| | | | Face | 1 | Charisma | 4 | |
| | | | Eyes | 1 | Energy | 4 | |
| | | | Abdo- | | Space | 1 | |
| | | | men | 1 | Other | 10 | |
| | | | Other | 4 | | | |
| Perceived clues | | 32 | | 28 | | 30 | 0 |
| % of total | | | | | | | |
| (90) clues | | 36% | | 31% | | 33% | |
| Caring | Gesture | 3 | Arms | 8 | Dancers' | | 0 |
| | Locomotion | 1 | Hands | 3 | Relations | 15 | |
| | Posture | 1 | Face | 2 | Space | 3 | |
| | | | Legs | 2 | Energy | 2 | |
| | | | Other | 1 | Time | 2 | |
| | | | | | Other | 6 | |
| Perceived clues | | 5 | | 16 | | 31 | 0 |
| % of total | | | | | | | |
| (52) clues | | 10% | | 31% | | 58% | |

*Table 4, cont.*

| Clues per person: 3.46 N = 113 Emotion | Action | | Body Parts | | Quality of Movement | | Nondance Factors |
|---|---|---|---|---|---|---|---|
| | | | | | *Perceptions through* | | |
| Vitality | Locomotion | 5 | Arms | 4 | Soul/ | | 0 |
| | Gesture | 3 | Legs | 3 | Charisma | 7 | |
| | | | Feet | 1 | Energy | 6 | |
| | | | Other | 6 | Time | 4 | |
| | | | | | Space | 4 | |
| | | | | | Dancers' | | |
| | | | | | Relations | 2 | |
| | | | | | Other | 8 | |
| Perceived clues | | 8 | | 14 | | 31 | 0 |
| % of total (53) clues | | 15% | | 26% | | 58% | |
| Competitiveness | Locomotion | 3 | Arms | 4 | Dancers' | | 0 |
| | Gesture | 2 | Face | 2 | Relations | 9 | |
| | | | Eyes | 1 | Space | 3 | |
| | | | Hands | 1 | Time | 2 | |
| | | | Legs | 1 | Soul/ | | |
| | | | Other | 1 | Charisma | 2 | |
| | | | | | Energy | 1 | |
| | | | | | Other | 4 | |
| Perceived clues | | 5 | | 10 | | 21 | 0 |
| % of total (36) clues | | 14% | | 28% | | 58% | |

*Note: Percentages have been rounded off. For this concert only, Body Parts "other" refers mostly to whole body or all body parts, occasionally to the neck or head.*

Let us now turn to how respondents thought the emotions were conveyed.[8] For the sake of convenience, I shall address the six emotions which were seen by 30 percent or more of the respondents. In table 4 we find that respondents perceived the same emotion through different means. So, too, some spectators perceived an emotion in more than one way, that is, across categories of clues. On the assumption that dancers draw upon the everyday offstage to convey messages, we can assume that social interaction in daily life is also diversely interpreted and with different means.

An outstanding pattern is that perception of emotion is primarily identified through the dimension of Quality of Movement, especially in dancers' interaction. Eroticism, however, is an exception; more people identified this emotion through Action (gesture, locomotion, and posture). Communication is by more than "word of foot."

Is there a relationship between perception of emotions, identification of clues to them, and a perceiver's background characteristics? Respondents professing the Jewish faith (67 percent of 24) were more likely to perceive playfulness than those identifying themselves as Christians (51 percent of 61).[9] Folklorists have documented that minority groups, including Jews, put a premium on humor as a way to cope with life's tribulations. Dunn plays with form as he manipulates the elements of time, space, effort, body parts, and sex roles.

High school students (71 percent of 7) noticed eroticism more than those with more education (43 percent of 47 postgraduates; 31 percent of 29 college graduates; and 39 percent of 18 with some college). Experiencing puberty, the young respondents may have been projecting juvenile fantasies.

Perhaps because those knowledgeable about dance (38 percent of 8 very; and 60 percent of 20 somewhat) are more aware of dance language possibilities, they saw caring through dancer interaction, whereas those not at all knowledgeable (9) did not.

Those who considered themselves very knowledgeable about dance did not perceive eroticism through locomotion, posture, or the pelvis. By contrast, of respondents somewhat knowledgeable about dance, 48 percent identified locomotion; 38 percent posture; and 52 percent the pelvis as erotic clues. Spectators who described themselves as not at all knowledgeable about dance did not find locomotion as a clue; 11 percent noted posture; and 33 percent the pelvis. It may be that the people very knowledgeable about dance concentrated on form and those without any dance knowledge did not perceive these clues because the Dunn duet was generally understated. Lower and higher income groups (20 percent of 20 under $20,000; 8 percent of 13 over $40,000) saw eroticism through locomotion less than other groups. Those in the $31,000–$40,000 group (60 percent of 25) and $21,000–$30,000 (33 percent of 12) did see locomotion as a clue to eroticism. Perhaps the income distribution coincides with age, suggesting a difference between the extremes and the middle groups.

Now we come to the matter of the congruence of dancer intention and audience perception. Is there a good connection or a short-circuit? Dunn had said that he assumed audience members would respond on the basis of their individuality. He wanted the spectators to participate in creating meaning in response to his message of danced visual images.

As we have seen, the audience did not respond to the nonverbal communication in a universal way. Some audience members fulfilled Dunn's expectations for his performance. The receptive "modernists" were willing to be creative and fill in part of the meaning of act 1 from their own life experiences. Thus a lawyer said, "I received the impression I was seeing the span of life of two people between the ages of 16 to 40. But no children were involved. Each had own career." A newsperson said his "main impression was the dancers' alienation broken fitfully by desperate gropings for love." Spectators in the same ritual watching the same performance got diverse messages ranging from many emotions to none; clues to identifying emotions also varied, as did spectator responses to the emotions.

While there was a good human connection between performer and spectator, there was also a short-circuit. The hostile "traditionalists" balked, as I have noted. Some refused to participate in this kind of theatrical experience and left before it ended. Some were negative about the dancing. Although some spectators liked the music ("It was dynamic and added a sense of detachment to the performance"), others found that "it caused static": "I would prefer to hear the New York Philharmonic 'warm up.' The sound man is rudely exploiting a captive audience causing me to feel like a prisoner thus preventing full concentration on dance."

The avant-garde "Foot Rules" was provocative. There was both harmony and discord between performer's hopes and audience members' expectations. The favorable/unfavorable dichotomy between newspaper dance critics in Washington's major newspapers reverberated in the theatre. Audience perceptions about what feelings the dancers conveyed onstage (and how) were controversial. Dunn has ardent admirers and supporters; he also has die-hard opponents. People boo, catcall, and exit noisily from avant-garde concerts in New York City (e.g., John Cage music at Avery Fisher Hall); Washington detractors make no such manifest demonstration but merely depart in relative silence.

THE CHALLENGE
So, in light of the difficulties posed by the avant-garde, how do performers and audience members connect? Where does the responsibility or possibility lie? Sometimes series organizers or performers write notes for programs. Introductory remarks may precede a performance. Discussions may take place afterward. Indeed, the Smithsonian offers a host of opportunities for spectators to gain an understanding of each concert. Thus there are lecture-demonstrations, seminars, films, workshops, and articles in the *Smithsonian* magazine and the Performing Arts Division publication *Notes*. This bimonthly even has a section where the staff sug-

gests appropriate background reading for each concert. However, not all theatregoers avail themselves of these avenues to enlightenment.

For Dunn's concert, the January–February 1981 issue of *Notes* listed Sally Banes's book *Terpsichore in Sneakers* as background reading.[10] A Saturday night lecture-demonstration preceded the Monday evening performance. The demonstration, which *Washington Post* critic Alan M. Kriegsman called "droll and dadaistic," illuminated the dancer-musician approach to collaboration.[11] Dunn and Driscoll showed how each did his own thing independently. After the demonstration, Dunn invited the audience to ask any questions they wished.

Following the Saturday event, on Sunday the Smithsonian offered a free showing of Michael Blackwood's "Making Dances." This ninety-minute color production, narrated by choreographers with interviews by critic Marcia Siegel, presented insights into the post-modern movement. Seven post-modern choreographers—David Gordon, Trisha Brown, Douglas Dunn, Lucinda Childs, Meredith Monk, Sara Rudner, and Kenneth King—are shown (ten minutes each) at work in lofts, studios, or parks, in concert, and in conversation about their future plans for choreography. These avant-garde choreographers all said they want to be taken seriously by larger audiences. They did not elaborate on how this would come about.

Dancers and audiences (including critics and researchers) need each other. This challenging, symbolic sender-receiver relationship also exists between teachers/ students, doctors/patients, and lawyers/clients. Few performers (perhaps those who are independently wealthy) can avoid catering to the public by providing some guidance for understanding the unfamiliar. Ignoring the living traditions and ghosts of the past that shape audience expectations, such performers for a small elite can video or film their work for posterity, although losing the immediacy of live performance, in hope of eventually gaining recognition from a wider audience.

"But I do have a question," wrote a respondent on the audience survey form after act 1 at the Dunn concert. "What was going on?? Could the inexperienced audience be prepared with an introduction so we could appreciate the artistic efforts and nuances of a dance that was obviously carefully prepared? The program notes are helpful." On the same form, this person wrote later on in the evening: "Part 3. Program notes and time have eased culture shock." Another respondent remarked: "The performance is a series of exercises but not an entire system of expression. But perhaps this is because I do not understand this branch of the art (an announced introduction would have helped to appreciate it)." Dunn, however, did not want an announcement of any sort to precede the performance and to set up audience expectations. And some spectators would agree with him. Controversy certainly inheres in the avant-garde. With the burgeoning dance audience and offerings, most performers are likely to find an audience somewhere, sometime. On and offstage people want attention, understanding, and human connection. A wide performer-audience connection yields box office receipts, without question helpful to a dancer's survival and new creativity. In the last moments of our first lengthy interview, Dunn concluded, "I want the audience to see whatever occurs. It's great if they come. It's great if they get something. It would be wonderful if it's useful to them."

Many great, lasting achievements are preceded by experimentation and even failure. Without support for the avant-garde's daring affront to established traditions, there can be little growth in any endeavor—science, business, or the arts. Of course, this is not an argument for casting traditional forms onto the trash heap. Without the living traditions, there are few directions for the future. Humans do crave both security and arousal. Much that was once considered outrageous or bizarre when first performed is now part of the vernacular. If people do not try something new, they will not know if they like it. Occasionally more than one try is called for—some things grow on people. The comfort of the familiar occurs only with exposure.

Choices are part of artistic production, programming, processes, and audience selection. James R. Morris, director of Smithsonian Performing Arts, writes, "The exercise of critical faculties is an intrinsic element of the artistic process, and is implicitly in the public presentation of any art form, in any medium. When any art goes on display, someone—or several someones—have taken responsibility for [in I. A. Richards's words] 'an account of value and an account of communication,' and have arrived at a decision that the work is worthy of public examination."[12] Morris continues, "In practical application, the strengths and talents of the performing unit and the tastes of the prospective audience must be addressed, but the primary concern of producer and performer, each in . . . turn, is that art be well and truly served. Such complex balances are . . . delicate." The test of time will tell. Perhaps the abyss is bridgeable.

## CHAPTER 7

# Men Usurp Women's Public Kabuki: Sachiyo Ito Renews Women's Performance

A woman created Kabuki dance, which evolved into a theatrical form that included other arts. However, its associations with prostitution led to disorderly conduct among warriors fighting over their favorites. The political leadership consequently banned the women's public performance of Kabuki and men took over the art form. Male supremacy reigned. But Sachiyo Ito is one of the contemporary Japanese women to follow in the steps of the first creator and to wrest exclusive public concert performance from men. The cultural context of Kabuki is critical to understanding Sachiyo Ito's intent in a dance at the Smithsonian concert as well as the performer-audience connection.

## THE LEGENDARY PAST AND CURRENT HISTORY

Rich in costume, melodramatic action, and emotion, Kabuki was the key popular theatre of Japan during the feudal Tokugawa or Edo premodernization era (1615–1868). A mercantile, urban society evolved, and it had the resources to support and control a plebian theatre. The eighteenth-century prototype persists in Tokyo today. Kabuki themes dealt with heroic and legendary figures as well as shopkeepers, artisans, prostitutes, and farmers and the tragic-mundane problems they faced. Current events in the city—murder, vendettas, or scandals in elite families—got sensational treatment onstage.

Japanese scholar Masakatsu Gunji tells us that the concept of *yatsushi* runs through the whole of Kabuki. This concept is an attempt to "modernize or translate into terms of contemporary society or to parody the old. . . . *Mitate* refers to the up-dating of famous characters or episodes from . . . history."[1]

In the Japanese dance tradition, feeling is conveyed through the combination of heart, mind, and spirit. Performers must seek meanings of emotions through learned people and remember the cause of an emotion.

Sachiyo Ito, Kabuki dancer. *Photograph by David Fullard, courtesy of the Performing Arts Department of the Asia Society.*

*Kokoro* is the concept that describes the resulting inner tension. Kabuki gave full play to a performer's individuality.

Theatre in the past was more intimate because the audience had greater familiarity with the performer; the interaction between them was freer. Highly sensual, Kabuki had deep ties first to female and then to male prostitution. The government repeatedly attempted to separate Kabuki from prostitution by banning women from the stage and concentrating houses of prostitution in quarters apart from theatres and actors' residences. Female dancers, however, continued their Kabuki performances at private parties, and actors continued to offer sexual services. Men considered dance outside the theatre to be the province of women.

As was the case in the West, officials classified prostitutes and actors as pariahs and denied them privileges given to other city residents. But Donald H. Shively found that "while regarding these members of the demimonde as somewhat disreputable," commoners found them endlessly fascinating in their beauty, splendid clothing, social poise, and savoir faire. "In a society in which there was an easy acceptance of homosexual relations, the presence of actors on the stage who deliciously exploited sexual nuance occasioned far more excitement than it does today."[2] The atmosphere had a more erotic charge.

Legend places the origin of Kabuki with Okuni's appearance in the city of Kyoto in 1596 or 1603. An itinerant dancer claiming relationship to the great Shinto Izumo Shrine as a *miko*, or sacred ritual *kagura* dancer, Okuni had wandered through several provinces where she danced and solicited contributions to repair the oldest and one of the most sacred shrines. When she reached Kyoto, she apparently was fascinated by the lively capital and was diverted from her responsibilities to the shrine. Okuni supposedly embellished the religious dance that celebrates the pleasure of the god and divine spirits with suggestive erotic movements and skits. She performed in the dry riverbed of the Kamo River by Gojo Bridge, the eastern part of the city, where amusements and sideshows flourished.

Her dance occurred at the end of the era of incessant and virtually meaningless civil war between rival fiefs. Weary of fighting and destruction, people naturally sought diversion. At this time, No theatre was the court entertainment. No interludes, *kyōgen* farces about daily irritations and joys, were also popular. These *kyōgen* were given for the public, which had its folk dances or *odori*. Women had apparently performed *kyōgen* and *odori* as well as prayer dances (*nembutsu odori*). *Nembutsu* refers to chanting in adoration of the name Amitabha Buddha. The dances are said to have been devised in the tenth century to draw people into the Buddhist fold and to pray for the repose of those fallen in battle. *Kabuki* was a word that meant crazy, strange, or eccentric. So after more than one hundred years of ravaging warfare, when Okuni performed Kabuki, it magnetized the commoners. It also drew bored aristocrats and samurai who were seeking amusement.

There are conflicting statements about early Kabuki in the ancient records. Years ago Zoe Kincaid reported the following story.[3] Okuni, the founder of Kabuki, sometimes wore a priest's black silk robe with a small metal Buddhist gong suspended from her neck by a vermilion silk cord. As she danced and chanted a Buddhist *sutra* (discourse), she struck the gong with a mallet. The Great Temples at this time combined elements of Shinto and Buddhist religions. Buddhist priests had been prominent at Izumo, and a bronze image of Buddha was located before the Shrine, where incense was burned. Okuni began performing with a prayer dance and priestly incantation. "Man is mortal. Money is nothing. Believe in Buddha." She soon, however, included erotic movements. At the conclusion of a performance, she held a general large group dance performance, *so-odori*.

Okuni attracted people who wanted to join her troupe. Some people believe that her dance was transformed under the influence of Nagoya Sanzaburo, a renowned samurai who married Okuni and joined her in public appearances. Coming from a military family and associating with a celebrated feudal lord, he became acquainted with the best in literature and art. Familiar with the No stage, especially the *kyōgen* comic interludes, he taught Okuni elements of these as well as popular songs and composed pieces for her. She won the greatest popular favor when she tranformed herself into a man, sporting two swords and covering her head with an odd headdress, and depicted a scene of making impassioned love to a courtesan in a teahouse or public bathhouse, newly developed places that had become popular. People then flocked to see her. Sanzaburo called her performances *Kabuki*, a word that had long signified something "far out" or avant-garde. It came to refer to the popular stage performance of song, dance, and skill. Faubion Bowers, supported by recent scholars, disagrees with this account of Sanzaburo's role.[4] He claims that Okuni's dance story came upon the heels of this well-known samurai's death: "It was natural for rumor to wed them."

The word for theatre, *shibai* (meaning to sit on the lawn or grass), got its impetus from Okuni's performances. She danced on a temporary platform, and the audience sat on the ground.

Okuni was highly popular with the masses; she also intrigued the nobility who patronized her. She even appeared before the Tokugawa Shogun. Okuni's performances were romantic if not erotic. These excerpts from three Okuni-Kabuki songs suggest the general tenor:

Abandoning ourselves to the urgency of Nature,
We sing and dance.

There is no past, no future,
But only the present.
The world is a dream;
Let us lose ourselves in it.
The reality of thunder
Cannot destroy the dream between us.
How lonely it is to sleep alone!
I have not even anyone to talk to.
Come, my dear pillow,
I will talk to you.
My pillow is silent.[5]

In imitation of the Okuni Kabuki, other women formed companies (Onna Kabuki) that performed in Kyoto as well as in distant parts of Japan. Their popularity was so widespread that a man called Sadoshima Yosanji taught women recruited from the ranks of prostitutes. *Yujo*, or prostitute kabuki, gained popularity. Other training schools appeared, and talented dancers developed who competed with each other for the public's favor. What was a woman's theatre soon had the two sexes playing together, with each sex taking the role of the other. Men played the musical accompaniment.

> Had the women companies remained exemplary in conduct and kept their ranks free from the other sex, the history of the Japanese theatre might have been quite different. But the leading actresses were prostitutes; their art was a means to an end, and they abused their privileges as entertainers. . . . The degradation of the Onna Kabuki was due in no small degree, however, to the playing of men and women together. The public very soon came to look down upon these players, and they were referred to as Kawara Kojiki, or Riverside Beggars.[6]

However, more than morality was a concern. During the performances, fights frequently occurred among the hotblooded samurai or foot soldiers in the audience. Unemployed samurai who had drifted to the cities in search of new masters, work, or merely excitement were a disorderly element. The brawls ignited by rivalries over the performers led to sanctions against female players. The Shogun's government, less concerned with immorality than with curbing disorder, limited the Kabuki to the city's outskirts in 1608. The climax was the 1629 order forbidding female public performances. Exiling women was an attempt to create greater social order and stability and also to recognize various trades and to afford them security and protection from competitors.

Successors to Women's Kabuki were troupes of Young Men's (*wakashū*) Kabuki. The boys had been performing alongside women's troupes. The suppression of *onna* brought them into prominence. Leonard Pronko points out that their major contribution to dance was the amalgamation of *odori*, a lively dance style, with *mai*, a more contained style.[7] Beautiful faces and voices were important, and performances served as preludes to prostitution. As happened with Women's Kabuki, quarrels over favorites broke out among samurai, and government intervention then prohibited young boys from the stage in 1653. Thereafter only mature men whose front locks had been shorn were permitted to perform Kabuki onstage. No longer able to rely upon physical attributes, the performers required acting skill for success.

Strict laws regarding the appearance of women onstage remained in effect until the last days of the Tokugawa shogunate, when its grip on moral and democratic tendencies loosened. The succeeding Meiji Era (1868–1912) brought about changes. About 100 women began to perform on stage with men.

The revival of women's performance onstage was in part related to Japanese receptiveness to imported ideas from Europe and China. Kabuki's openness to absorbing material created outside the theatre and Japan manifested itself when Okuni and her successors wore rosaries to decorate their costumes. An illustrated scroll called "Kabuki Zōshi" shows Okuni in Portuguese trousers and a lacquered "coolie hat." The Portuguese were the first Europeans to begin calling at Japanese ports in the 1540s. During the Meiji period, Western influences inundated Japan. Actresses and realism were both features of the Western stage. A famous Kabuki actor, Danjuro the ninth, eager to experiment, introduced his own daughters onstage. Kumehachi (1845–1913) was among his pupils and took his family name, Ichikawa. She was even called "Woman Danjuro." The male dominance in Japan, however, proved a stumbling block to her advancement. However, she did head a woman's theatre in which women took both male and female roles. Upon Kumehachi's death, the company disbanded.

Because women dancers were excluded from prestigious theatre positions, they were consequently freed from restrictive, conservative traditions. Fujima Shizue decided to become a professional dancer after seeing Kumehachi. Unsuccessful in this endeavor, she became a geisha. However, in 1917 she organized the Fujikage-kai dance troupe. When she staged her ninth performance, her "Shibon" (Everyday Thoughts) piece caused a sensation among critics and actors. Nevertheless, conservatism reigned, and women were refused the right to use the names of the established schools. So were men if they were too independent.

In a movement toward realism in theatre, Kawakami Otojiro (1864–1911) used actresses. His dramas became the New School Theatre (*shimpa*). He married Saddo Yakko, who became a gifted actress. Since the appearance of the *shimpa* drama, strictures against men and women appearing together onstage have loosened. Yakko had a prominent role in the theatre company. Because she recognized her handicap in training, she founded a school for actresses. The Imperial Theatre, opened in 1911, took over the school when it established a department to train women.

Nakamura Kasen, a successor to Kumehachi, achieved influence and popularity in her own crowded Tokyo theatre.

Although actresses returned to Kabuki with the opening of the Imperial Theatre, the Western custom of mixed sexes onstage did not prove successful. Having lost their artistic public performance heritage, women imitated the male technique. But they were unable to compete with the actors. The women players then performed new pieces in their own company.

Ritsu-ko Mori was the first educated woman from what the Japanese consider a good, respectable family to go on the stage. Her father was a member of the Imperial Diet. Her associates and rivals included Murata Kaku-ko, Hatsuse Namiko, Kawamura Kikuye, and Fujima Fusa-ko.

Sachiyo Ito pointed out that females had been learning to dance as they had been learning to perform the tea ceremony, arrange flowers, and play a musical instrument. However, they did not appear publicly in a concert until the early twentieth century, under the influence of the West. Anna Pavlova's 1922 visit to Japan drew throngs to see her dance, and it had a stimulating effect on Japanese women's public dancing. As noted earlier, this ballerina also stimulated the revival of Indian dance forms.

In the 1920s a rift developed between the world of dancers and that of actors.[8] Actors changed choreography for dramatic purposes in order to add to the atmosphere of role and situation. In contrast, dancers (*buyoka*) believed that traditional choreography was sacred and should be preserved at all costs. One became a superior dancer by performing correctly.

World War II destroyed the momentum of the performing arts in Japan. Many young actors were drafted into the military; certain plays were forbidden because they were too luxurious and incompatible with the austere times. In 1944 all large Kabuki theatres were closed because they were said to represent frivolous activity. The following year most of the great theatres of Tokyo were destroyed. After the war the occupation and new Japanese government recognized the cultural significance of Kabuki. The Western influence continued to encourage women's public performance.

The National Theatre of Japan opened in 1966 across the moat from the Imperial Palace. It was built to revive and maintain art which was in decline. Kabuki's vocabulary of nonrealistic expression had lost popularity with the advent of Western realism, especially in the cinema and television. When geisha districts decreased in importance in social life, the vocabulary of gestures depicting their manners became unfamiliar.[9] Formerly drawing all classes, Kabuki had become expensive and thus exclusive. It no longer drew a lively people's crowd.

Classical Japanese dance changed from a salon art to public concert hall performance. The Tokyo Department Store began sponsoring an annual festival of new pieces for classical Japanese dance in 1968. New patronage from middle-class families has made dance independent of the pleasure districts. Many families believe that dance lessons are a moral exemplar and provide their youngsters with discipline and inner strength. A million or so students of classical Japanese dance disperse among more than two hundred schools, reports historian Thomas R. Havens. Teaching is the bedrock of classical dancing and it is lucrative for the top headmasters. "The pupil who studies classical Japanese dance for six or seven years, almost regardless of talent, can expect to take a stage name (*natori*) for a fee of $5,000 or more and enjoy the right to teach."[10] Amateurs and professional teachers with stage names are expected to perform and pay for the privilege. A professional pays nearly $10,000 to put on a single ten- or fifteen-minute number. The headmaster receives one-third of this amount. Teaching subsidizes stage performance in each dance genre (ballet, classical, and contemporary). Most classical Japanese dance concerts are private and accept untaxed honoraria rather than selling tickets to nonstudent families.

KABUKI FORM

Kabuki is a cumulative genre incorporating other art idioms over three hundred years. It has several play forms: everyday life (*sewa-mono*), historical drama (*jidai-mono*), music-posture (*shosagoto*), and high imaginary improvisations (*aragoto*) from centuries ago that have become set. Closely allied with these forms is *odori*, the descriptive dance. This quick and lively people's dance has rhythm, leaping, stamping, jumping, and free use of the upper limbs.

*Buyō*, coined in the twentieth century, is the general term for dance. Kabuki *buyō* belongs to the *furyū odori* category. The *furyū* prototype of Kabuki is a form deriving from dances to avert pestilence during the Muromachi period (1392–1568). Characterized by "wild" movement and bright costumes, *furyū* are often performed with hats, poles, and umbrellas. Kabuki includes pantomimic gestures of real life movement. These include the use of the fan, towel, and hat props. A dancer depicts the form of a mountain by a hand gesture or opened fan held upside-down; if the words of a song are about writing a letter, the dancer pretends to hold a scroll of letter paper in the left hand and to write on it, with the writing brush held in the right hand, in the vertical rows from right to left. From the No, aristocratic theatre, Kabuki adopted the *mai* dance. This was a slower, refined, graceful dance that emphasized many turning movements and earthward-oriented steps in which the feet rarely leave the floor. The original circling *mai* dance was probably a solo about the sacred abode of a divinity or holy water or before an altar. The early vertiginous quality could lead the performer to a state of ecstasy. The popular folk dance *zokkyoku* and the movement of the dolls in puppet theatre also influenced Kabuki dance. Because the popularity of the marionettes outstripped that of living actors, actors incorporated some of the puppet mannerisms, pantomime, and repertoire. The puppets motivated the *ningyo buri*, imitating the movement of a Bunraku puppet while being visibly "manipulated" by several stage assistants, and *michiyuki*, a travel dance.

Another form of Kabuki dance especially relevant to Sachiyo Ito's performance is the *fuzoku mitate mono*, a solo dance that acts out moods and depicts manners, customs, and personalities (e.g., "Wisteria Maiden"), first produced in 1826. The solo dances of today are largely survivals of the first thirty or forty years of the nineteenth century, the Bunka-Bunsei era. An actor in what were called *hengemono* rapidly changed roles and would perform as many as nine dances one after the other.[11] This pattern led to nonprofessionals studying dance and to the establishment of dance schools. Impersonations of townspeople, babysitters, and country folk in dance brought new lyrical movement and a simplified costume.

Tamura Nariyoshi, a theatre manager during the Meiji period, said, "Dancing, like acting, should have a meaning, and the performer must keep steadfastly to the central idea, otherwise interest would be lost." Dance training gives complete body control. Every gesture has significance—nothing is left to chance. Kabuki reflects situation, character, and role. The dance begins with a song text for which music is then composed, or the rhythm of accompaniment when there are no words. The elements of Kabuki—movements, colors, costumes, words, music, and props—convey meaning in themselves and also symbolize something else, although some may be merely decorative or a kind of punctuation. The knowledgeable Japanese audience can understand the meaning of the dance through gesture and by the words of the accompanying song.

Earle Ernst describes Kabuki dance as rhythmically ordered movement that is taken from actuality and presented to the audience in a series of clearly defined, specific, nonrepresentational images.

> Movement from real life is its point of departure, and Kabuki dance reduces the multiple movements of human existence to their essential forms by narrowing, and thus intensifying, the visual impression of the movement, not by broadening it so that it no longer has precise meaning. . . . The Kabuki dancer distinguishes three degrees of literalness . . . *shinsho*, the "precise" style which the student of dance is first taught. In *gyosho*,

details of the gesture are contracted, while *sosho* is a cursive style, the least literal of the three.[12]

In Kabuki dance movement, although there is considerable vigor, the general impression is one of a series of concrete visual images. This contrasts with the continuing progression of movement in time and space that characterizes Western dance. It is noteworthy that Japanese dance students are not taught movements or steps which are then later put together in dances. Rather, in a one-to-one relation of teacher to student, they are taught the complete dance from beginning to end.

Women's Kabuki movement tends to be centripetal; the knees bend and draw together, the arms turn toward the body. Women walk by moving the knees close together with feet somewhat pigeon-toed. As the body slithers across the floor, it sways delicately as the shoulders gracefully undulate. The chin moves slightly away from the direction of the advanced foot. The opening of the kimono down the front of the body to the floor should not be disturbed by the walking. Heavy wigs force the head to move gently from side to side. The elbows are held at the hips, the fingers close together. Sometimes, to break the monotony, the fourth and fifth fingers of each hand are held slightly crooked and bent to give an asymmetrical contour. The thumb is sometimes curved under and held close to the palm.

Male characters move with turned-out feet. The men's movement tends to be expansive. In strong roles (mostly actors and not dancers) they project intense stress by crossing the eyes, grimacing, and sticking out the tongue.

Kabuki has many stylized conventions. The fan has been a symbol in dance for thousands of years. Opening and shutting the fan causes flowers to bloom and rain to fall. Waving it outstretched, the dancer makes butterflies flutter, a boat toss on the waves. The fan can disclose shyness, affection, disapproval, and consent. A falling leaf, tea cup, letter, moon rising behind a hill, flute, and sword are within the descriptive vocabulary of fan movement.

Kabuki movement is centered, *koshi o ireru*, which means that the hips are "set" and serve as the pivotal point from which all other movement flows. To set the hips the dancer lowers the spine, thus causing the knees to bend slightly.

Gunji pointed out that although Kabuki had originated as a celebration of the sensual new liberation of the human body, this freedom was exchanged for the beauty of the costume.[13] The Kabuki costume is a complicated, gorgeous attire that may weigh about thirty pounds and in rare cases as much as fifty or sixty. It consists of several layers of kimono. Men developed the long sleeve and special techniques of sleeve and hem movements in order to disguise the male physique when they impersonated women. The colors are often blazing. Bowers remarked, "In Japan the feeling for color is almost a lust."[14] Makeup, too, is lavish.

The music derives from and underlines and sharpens the effect of the movement. Commonly used instruments are the Nō drums and flute and the more recent samisen, a three-stringed instrument played with strident rhythms. Certain rhythms of particular instruments convey the meaning of natural elements or humanly created places.

### THE HUMAN CONNECTION: JAPANESE AESTHETICS

The Japanese audience has a deep love of nature that originated in pre-Buddhist and Shinto nature worship. Since Buddhism allows no sense of opposition, the Japanese make no distinction between humans and nature. The human aesthetic, too, merges with the world of nature. Japanese people appreciate the asymmetry of nature and the human designs imposed upon it, as in bonsai (creating a miniature tree in which design through pruning triumphs over the natural growth) or flower arranging. Art aims to isolate the simple, significant visual moment. The highest point of interest occurs as movement resolves into a static attitude. The audience, Ernst said, does not go to Kabuki "to be moved by images made to resemble those occurring in actuality, but by images clearly distinguished from reality by the precision of their design."[15]

> The audience comes to the Kabuki not for a sustained comment on life, either tragic or comic, nor to witness the erection of a complex dramatic structure in time. It comes to the theatre to see a succession of striking images. . . . the colorful images of the Kabuki remain chiefly those of the world of sensation and pleasure.[16]

> The Kabuki runs the gamut of Japanese taste. On one hand there is restraint, austerity, economy of statement, strict design; on the other, lavishness, sumptuousness, luxuriance. Both these extremes are equally admired by the audience. Kabuki gestures and movements, though broader and less hieratic than those of the Nō, are, by the nature of their precise design and technique polish, restrained and austere. Although they have the power of immediate communication of emotion to the audience, they avoid representing the full, detailed reproduction of actual movement and gesture. . . . But at the same time, the audience requires that the Kabuki be an eye-filling spectacle. . . . Visual opulence provides at least half the pleasure of the theatre-goer.[17]

"Art is that which lies between the shadow and substance" (Chikamatsu Monzaemon).

In his treatise *Kadensho*, Zeami (1364–1443) articulated some key principles of Japanese aesthetics which underlie Kabuki dance. As Gunji explained, "Without the body there is no dance beauty, but also there is no dance beauty unless one transcends the body. Dance, which is a symbol of life, expressed through the rhythmic movement of the body, is a world of beauty built on the premise that life disappears little by little with the passing of time." [18] Zeami considered the changing aspect of flowers the very life of dance. Like a flower which falls, dance is gone as soon as it is performed, yet it is constantly reborn and lives forever.

The Japanese view living things in nature as flowing and changing and seek to capture this quality in dance. Sachiyo Ito has written, "Unfolding the emotional flow fluidly, as in the ripples of a river, is a vital dance technique." [19]

In appreciation of nature, Japanese dance confirms the existence of the earth, as the performer hovers above, pressing the hips downward "to make the body appear shorter and in close contact with the ground," along with sliding feet and strong foot beats. Gunji further noted that "Japanese dance makes the world we live in a paradise closely related to everyday life and expresses the two as a sort of double exposure." [20]

Achieving *kakucho*, or going above and beyond one's humanness to reach a high spiritual level, is another aesthetic goal. An element in reaching this level and style of performance is *okisa*, a kind of largeness.

> *Okisa* is a breadth of expression and a depth of content. This is not a matter of stretching the arms an additional foot, jumping several feet higher into the air, or whirling around in a wider circle. . . . when a hand is to be extended forward, it is first pulled back in a preparatory gesture; when the right hand is to be extended to the right, it is first brought slightly toward the left side and then extended to the right with a graceful twist of the wrist; when the head is to be turned to the right, first the chin is pointed to the left, the head is dropped forward, and the face is lifted to the right in a three-part movement. The preparatory movements create a slight pause which draws attention to the final gesture and makes it seem larger in scope. [21]

Of course, technique alone does not create the ideal performance. The Japanese call the spiritual state and artistic presence that enliven the technique *iki*. The concept of *ma* is the space or time between poses and movements that is artistically transported. This quality is achieved only after many years of study and stage experience. So too is *utsuri*, expressing transition from one kind of movement to the next, from foot to hand or head, for example.

How does the Japanese audience respond to Kabuki? Ernst noted: "The emotions aroused in the audience do not have a very wide range. At the base of Japanese artistic thought lies the Buddhist concept that all things pass, that glory is evanescent, that all bright quick things come to confusion, and this notion constitutes almost the whole intellectual content of Japanese art."[22] The audience shows its approval or disapproval during the performance immediately and spontaneously through applause or shouts. Theatregoing in the traditional Kabuki context was a hubbub of voices, the din and clatter of tea cups and sake bottles, the cries of vendors selling hot tea, rice-cakes, and oranges, and children moving back and forth. Kabuki performances were long affairs with frequent, lengthy intermissions. In 1868 a government regulation fixed the time of performances at a maximum of eight hours a day.

## A PERFORMER-AUDIENCE CONNECTION

Sachiyo Ito was born in Tokyo. Excited by seeing her first Kabuki performance at the age of six, she began her dance study the following year. In the Japanese system of dance and theatre education, a pupil studies at one school and succeeds to the family name of the head of the school when he or she achieves mastery and receives a diploma. The student pays a considerable sum of money to the school master/mistress for the privilege of receiving the coveted licensed name. When Ito was eighteen, she received the professional name of the Hanayagi School, the largest of about 150 dance guilds. The school derives from a lineage of choreographers founded in 1849. *Hanayagi* means flower and willow tree. While in college, Ito began to teach in the Tokyo American Club. The students were mostly foreign. She wished to convey the characteristics of Japanese people's lives through dancing. Foreigners in Tokyo "may have difficulty understanding the way the Japanese are. The expression is different, not so outspoken. We don't say black and white clearly. . . . Even we see the dance, not straightforward, but more making an understatement. And through learning about dance, we would know about music, costume, poems, literature, religion. Because certain dances came from religious ceremony, Buddhist or Shinto, or just a mystic or folk belief."

At the Smithsonian concert, Ito demonstrated and explained some meanings of the gestures and movements of each dance before she performed it. Most Japanese do not know these ancient symbols, and from her work in Japan, she was aware of even greater difficulty in reaching a foreign audience.

The subject of the performer-audience connection was the 1930s Kabuki dance "Wisteria Melody," an excerpt from "Wisteria Maiden Dance" (Fuji Musume), which is 150 years old. Wisteria flowers refer to a woman, the pine tree to a man. These are favorite motifs among the Japanese. Ito explained that this dance "is about a girl, and also at the same time a spirit of a wisteria tree. She pours out her emotions of love to the pine tree because always in Japanese literature the pine tree and wisteria flowers appear together. So it's like a dainty beauty of a woman in those dances of the seventeenth or eighteenth centuries expressed through the beauty of wisteria flowers." Ito danced this poem:

As the blossoms of wisteria are so beautiful
The wine was brought to her.
She enjoys the wine and expresses her feeling to the pine tree.
Please don't go away from me.
Please don't pretend that you don't know my feelings though
    flowers are said to have no speech.

*Performer Intention.* "In this dance, what feelings do you want to convey to the audience?" I asked. Ito replied, "I wish they would understand the delicate expression of a woman who is in love and in a good mood, and at the same time, there is some pathos just as in love you have a sadness and happiness. So it's the showing of the sad part because he hasn't responded. In this case, the pine tree; it's human being and spirits together."

In response to the question "How do you think you get that across?" Ito explained that she relied on her traditional training. Her teacher was a woman. Although there are many male master teachers, there are more women. "In most of the concerts, what I like is to forget myself. I don't want to appear Sachiyo Ito in a concert. If I am dancing Wisteria Maiden, I like to be a Wisteria Maiden. If I am dancing Dojoji, a person who is trying to repent her feeling, appearing sad, I try to be her character. When I do babysitter's dance, I try to amuse the baby with masks. I'd like to be a good babysitter. In Ayako Mai dance, I try to forget myself and dance with the music."

To get across the notion of the dilemmas of a delicate woman in love, Ito draws on her acting education to become the Wisteria Maiden. "Training is not how you can move the leg and how many degrees. We are concerned with how you express that character, how you become that particular woman. Our training basically consists of imitating teacher's dancing, teacher's acting, also seeing many dances so that you will know various other teachers too, how they project. Of course, we repeat the dancing, many hours of the week." Ito explained that the Japanese usually begin such work at five or six years of age and continue for a decade. Then students take an audition in front of headmasters. If a student passes, the individual receives the school name as a family name. In Japan, this is very important.

Besides drawing upon her training to get across certain feelings, Ito said she had to be in a good mood when she performed the "Wisteria Melody" dance. "I don't drink, but she drinks wine and gets in a good mood. But also, she becomes sad in one part of the song; her loved one is going back home or doesn't answer to her feelings."

"Does the feeling of happiness lead to the movement or does the move-ment lead to the feeling?" I asked. "The feelings have to come first. . . . You have to have the feelings inside." The music and the poetry help. The poems use wordplay. "In one part she would feel like crying because she is talking to the pine tree; *matsu* in Japanese means 'pine tree'; it also means 'to wait.'"

Ito explained that delicacy is conveyed through facial expressions and the graceful hand rotations. "I have sleeves, and I show my face and hid-ing; hiding face with hands, that means, I am shy." The eyes open and close and move in arcs. Each little finger linking with the other means you and I together.

*Audience Perception.* How did the audience react to Ito's performance? Critics, of course, are members of the audience. They do have special roles—their reactions get broader recognition than do those of most au-dience members. "Sachiyo Ito," wrote George Jackson in the *Washington Post*, "is a small, delicate dancer of resolute movement. She was dressed, coiffed, painted and befanned elaborately as she swung through the ele-gant curves of a princess' gait, skipped like a young lass or thrust her foot forward for masculine battle. Common to all her characterizations was a stolidity from hips to calves. This secure stance made many of the selec-tions seem more like animated poses than dances."[23]

What were the background characteristics of the 121 Kabuki concert audience survey respondents?[24] Twice as many women as men (61 per-cent to 29 percent) participated in the study. Thirty percent were between 21 and 30 years of age; 27 percent, 31–40; and 25 percent, 41–62. Whites comprised 72 percent, Japanese only 3 percent. Respondents were highly educated; 42 percent postgraduate, 37 percent college graduates, 4 percent had some college, 9 percent high school education. Thirty per-cent reported family income between $21,000 and $30,000; 25 percent under $20,000; 24 percent over $40,000 and 9 percent between $31,000 and $40,000. Nearly half of the respondents were professionals, 11 per-cent students, and other groups less than 10 percent. According to their own categorization, 44 percent were somewhat knowledgeable about dance, 37 percent not at all, and 9 percent very.

Many respondents admired the beauty and grace of Ito in "Wisteria Melody." A student remarked, "It was intellectually stimulating, ex-citing. It was also groovy and out-of-sight."

The audience at this concert, as at most of the other performances, raised the issues of the influence of program notes and explanations upon perception, ethnocentricity, and familiarity with a dance form. Another recurring theme was whether a dance can or should be analyzed.

A news producer from the United Kingdom with a postgraduate educa-tion thought that "the interpretation of what you see is affected by the verbal introduction and program notes, and that affected the validity of people's perceptions." Yet it is important to point out that people's perceptions are always conditioned by the situation in which an exchange takes place.

An opera singer called attention to ethnocentricity: "The concept of this study is quite interesting, but I found my comments and comprehension were limited to certain body areas due to Western cultural 'blinders.' That is, I found myself focusing on facial expression, which is probably typically Western. Style of walk would also probably be difficult to misinterpret both from an Eastern *or* Western point of view."

The foreignness of Kabuki gave some respondents difficulty. A retired man who had been in personnel could not fill out the questionnaire: "Not possible. The dance form is too unknown to interpret." In agreement with this spectator's view, a teacher explained: "It is difficult to know where you are in a dance and dance form you are not familiar with. . . . A moving body expressing emotions is a very complex visual; also most impossible to analyze at the moment it is happening as to which parts are involved. Indeed, it is hard to believe any *part not* contributing." A retired teacher said, "I am not sophisticated enough with this kind of dance to recognize emotions and gestures that evoke these but I felt great pleasure in watching and trying to become more able to appreciate." A jazz dance/exercise instructor, very familiar with dance "but not at all familiar with this [dance] form," said, "It is difficult to assess the dance as I am totally unfamiliar with the Kabuki. As a first experience, I am somewhat confused at times, but find the performance aesthetically interesting if not totally enjoyable." "I would love to see the dance sixteen times to sort out the parts," remarked an antique dealer. In a cooperative survey report two respondents wrote: "We are two Anglo-Americans. We cannot fill out the form, for from our Western viewpoint the symbols and gestures are too abstract and obscure, and we would rather not know the story but just take pleasure in the beauty of gesture and costume. And we also very much enjoy the music. Absolutely no emotions have been aroused in either of us." A librarian found a monotone of feeling. "Sorry —I can't answer this form. She [Ito] only changed expression twice. I believe this survey could be interesting with American-European dancing." An educator echoed her sentiment: "Idea—try this with some American dancer—without knowing what the music means and being unable to remember the fifty basic movements shown at the beginning, it is impossible to help you. Sorry."

A female lawyer who filled out the form in detail nevertheless raised the issue of whether dance can and should be "analyzed" or intellectualized: "Maybe a Kabuki should *be* not mean." However, as noted earlier, from the traditional Japanese perspective, everything has a meaning. A housewife, who checked the emotions conveyed onstage as "happiness, playfulness, vitality," put the anti-interpretation perspective rather strongly: "Just quit bugging us about our feelings and just let us enjoy the performance." The questionnaire, it should be noted, has the following statement: "Note: Information furnished by you on this survey is purely voluntary."

Some people view wholes; others see parts. There are also people who see both. A Japanese-American graphic designer expressed a gestalt perspective: "I enjoyed the entire formal emotional acts totally expressed." Reacting to "each emotion just lessens the beauty. Please forgive." A sculptor referred me to Sullivan's *Beethoven, His Spiritual Development*: "It may be that our reaction to a work of art is a synthesis of relatively simple emotions . . . effect exists as a whole." [25]

Other respondents had no difficulty in sharing their views on emotion. Which emotions were most frequently identified onstage? As noted in appendix table 1, playfulness ranked high, seen by 89 percent of the respondents. Next came sadness (64 percent), happiness (63 percent), caring (61 percent), nostalgia (35 percent), and vitality (35 percent). People seemed to perceive what Ito described as the delicate expression of a woman who is in love and in a good mood, and, at the same time, sad with longing or fear of being deserted.

Table 5 shows how spectators identified these emotions. [26] Body parts, most notably the face, comprised 50 percent of the clues to playfulness. The action of gesture and locomotion also helped. Throughout the piece, hands and arms, use of the fan, face, and especially blinking eyes and lowering lids captured this feeling. For sadness, body parts and notably the face were prominent, with gesture, locomotion, and posture contributing. In the middle of the dance, the face and the eyes blinking and tearing depicted sadness. The pattern for playfulness was similar to that for happiness. Gesture was the key clue to caring. The different body parts and gesture tended to indicate nostalgia. Vitality was seen through hands, all parts of the body, and various actions. Facial expressions, use of the face, and sinuous movements of the limbs indicated eroticism. Fatigue was conveyed at the end of the dance through facial expression and sitting and kneeling.

A fishery biologist was sensitive to the subtleties of expression. She saw Ito create anger through holding her hand vertically, making facial expressions, or turning her head away. Moving the arms together to the face or bosom conveyed caring. Ecstasy was seen through the horizontal and vertical fluttering of the hands. The slow weaving of the body and facial gestures imparted eroticism. Irregular movements of the body suggested fatigue; movements opening the body and smiles, happiness; tilt-

## TABLE 5. Kabuki Concert: How Audience Perceived Emotions

Clues per person: 7.65
N = 121

| Emotion | Action | | Perceptions through Body Parts | | Quality of Movement | | Nondance Factors |
|---|---|---|---|---|---|---|---|
| Playfulness | Gesture | 47 | Face | 42 | Energy | 10 | 10 |
| | Locomotion | 39 | All | 24 | Time | 6 | |
| | Other | 7 | Hands | 19 | Space | 4 | |
| | | | Eyes | 14 | Other | 2 | |
| | | | Shld/Arms | 12 | | | |
| | | | Other | 14 | | | |
| Perceived clues | | 93 | | 125 | | 22 | 10 |
| % of total (250) clues | | 37% | | 50% | | 9% | 4% |
| Sadness | Gesture | 32 | Face | 46 | Space | 4 | 7 |
| | Locomotion | 14 | Eyes | 18 | Other | 2 | |
| | Posture | 8 | Hands | 14 | | | |
| | | | Shld/Arms | 13 | | | |
| | | | Other | 13 | | | |
| Perceived clues | | 54 | | 104 | | 6 | 7 |
| % of total (171) clues | | 32% | | 61% | | 4% | 4% |
| Happiness | Gesture | 39 | Face | 37 | Energy | 6 | 7 |
| | Locomotion | 31 | Hands | 21 | Space | 6 | |
| | Other | 8 | All | 14 | Time | 5 | |
| | | | Eyes | 11 | Other | 1 | |
| | | | Other | 16 | | | |
| Perceived clues | | 78 | | 99 | | 18 | 7 |
| % of total (202) clues | | 39% | | 49% | | 9% | 3% |
| Caring | Gesture | 32 | Face | 5 | Energy | 8 | 4 |
| | Locomotion | 10 | Feet | 5 | Time | 4 | |
| | Posture | 10 | Other | 8 | Space | 4 | |
| | Other | 6 | | | Other | 2 | |
| Perceived clues | | 58 | | 18 | | 18 | 4 |
| % of total (100) clues | | 58% | | 18% | | 18% | 4% |

Table 5, cont.

| Clues per person: 7.65<br>N = 121<br>Emotion | Action | | Body<br>Parts | | Quality of<br>Movement | | Nondance<br>Factors |
|---|---|---|---|---|---|---|---|
| | | | Perceptions through | | | | |
| Nostalgia | Gesture | 18 | Face | 23 | Space | 3 | 2 |
| | Other | 11 | Eyes | 10 | Time | 1 | |
| | | | Other | 17 | Energy | 1 | |
| Perceived clues | | 29 | | 50 | | 5 | 2 |
| % of total<br>(86) clues | | 34% | | 58% | | 6% | 2% |
| Vitality | Locomotion | 17 | Hands | 14 | Energy | 3 | 2 |
| | Gesture | 16 | All | 14 | Time | 3 | |
| | Other | 5 | Shld/ | | Space | 1 | |
| | | | Arms | 9 | Other | 2 | |
| | | | Feet | 8 | | | |
| | | | Other | 23 | | | |
| Perceived clues | | 38 | | 68 | | 9 | 2 |
| % of total<br>(117) clues | | 32% | | 58% | | 8% | 2% |

Note: Percentages have been rounded off.

ing down of the mouth and head, nostalgia; clapping hands, stomping feet, and teasing hand movements, playfulness; whirling motion, waving arms, and fluttering fan, vitality.

How did the audience respond to the emotions they perceived on stage? Most individuals felt the same or similar emotions. There were, however, diverse reactions. A woman said, "The portrayal of emotion is fairly subtle and low key. The emotional response to such dance is a quiet pleasure. There is not an erotic or other 'cathartic' participatory response, although this may be because these dances were performed solo outside of their dramatic context." A gunsmith felt fascinated by the caring eroticism Ito conveyed through "the movement of the feet and the sweep and fluidity of the arms, back, and neck."

A teacher felt happy in response to the perceived emotions of ecstasy and eroticism. Nostalgia and sadness on stage evoked the same feelings in her. An artist/teacher experienced involvement and empathy in reaction to the emotions of caring, ecstasy, eroticism, fatigue, happiness, nostalgia, playfulness, pride, sadness, shame, surprise, and vitality. A government employee felt entertained in answer to the emotions of caring, eroticism, and playfulness that Ito conveyed to her. "Excited" was a designer's reply to the emotion of vitality conveyed through body parts. A teacher was touched by the caring emotion he perceived, made tingly by playfulness, hopeful for change by sadness, and fresh by vitality. He felt good about the deep pleasure (aesthetic) that Ito imparted. A Japanese-American statistician said she sensed the emotions of caring, happiness, sadness, and surprise that were being demonstrated but "did not feel or sense them deeply, only lightly." A student felt no memorable emotion in response to the several emotions depicted, but "simply a flowing interest."

Several respondents commented that they did not react to the emotions they identified on stage. A man who is an artist/matter-framer with postgraduate education saw the emotions of anger, caring, eroticism, fatigue, playfulness, and sadness. He said, "My reactions did not come in response to the emotive behavior of the artist but rather in response to the human movement and kinesthetic elements. As the feelings I got from the performer were theatre emotions and no more real than those being conveyed, no meaningful correlation can be made without an elaborate explanation of the context." An editor with postgraduate education perceived the emotions of anger, caring, eroticism, fatigue, happiness, nostalgia, playfulness, and sadness. She remarked, "The emotions registered in the dancing movements. Movements played across my imagination—but I responded to the grace and excitement of the dance illusions, not to the emotions portrayed." Perhaps some Americans are too accustomed to the reality of TV and cinema to be aroused by the stylized movements of Kabuki dance. But scholar and dancer Leonard Pronko believes that when Americans become familiar with Kabuki, the movements will seem less "stylized" and more understandable and "rousing."

Were there any associations between audience respondents' perceptions and their background characteristics? Because there were only three Japanese respondents, it was not possible to find out if the members of the dancer's ethnic group viewed the dance differently than members of other groups. There was an association between age and vitality. Younger people (78 percent of 9 under 20 years) were more likely to see vitality than older people (39 percent of 36 in the 21−30 age group, 30 percent of 33 between 31 and 40, and 23 percent of 30 between 41 and 65).

While many people enjoyed the performance, others found the subtlety and understatement detracted from their enjoyment. Ito had noticed that these Japanese qualities disturbed the foreigners who lived in Japan. A speech pathologist at the concert who perceived the emotions of caring, happiness, sadness, and loneliness conveyed through the positions of the body and eye and hand movements said, "Emotion was so subtle that I had no specific response to it. I was a bit disappointed—bored by it. All too much the same."

The performer-audience connection exemplified the problem of cross-cultural communication. In spite of our familiarity with Datsun, Toyota, and Sony, there is another sphere of Japanese productivity that remains alien—the dance. Although many people understood Ito's intentions, others were puzzled. Missing the meaning, however, was not a deterrent to admiring the performer's gracefulness for some audience members. In a culture where dance gesture is less codified semantically than in the Orient, Americans seem to need to understand the story before they feel they understand the meaning of movement. Hence, audiences respond to "meaning" through exposure to program notes or broad stage action or else focus on "gracefulness," only one of the many facets of artistry.

Rooted in Japan's national consciousness for almost three centuries, the popular Kabuki dance that Okuni created, and men then dominated, has once again become a vehicle for women's public performance. Kabuki dance for men and for women is now accepted in Japan and elsewhere, and it is performed as a classical form outside the drama. Because Japan and its scholarship have been male-dominated, there is still a woman's story to be told about Japanese dance. Furthermore, there is yet to be a better human connection between Japan and the United States.

## CHAPTER 8

# Shifting Illusions—
# Does the Emperor Wear Clothes?
# Sage Cowles and Molly Davies

The last performance of the American Dance Experience Series was a 1980s avant-garde event. Acclaimed by cognoscenti who found only "trifling" problems, the "Dance and the Camera" event with dancer Sage Cowles and filmmaker Molly Davies was as controversial, if not more so, than the post-modern Douglas Dunn concert.

Cowles's background includes study of dance at the University of Wisconsin with Margaret H'Doubler and Louise Kloepper, at the School of American Ballet, and with Louis Horst and Hanya Holm. Although Cowles has performed on Broadway and with companies in the Midwest, she currently specializes in teaching dance to nondancers of all ages. Davies trained in filmmaking in New York City in the late 1960s. She has produced Super 8 and 16mm films since moving to St. Paul, Minnesota, in 1973. Her work has been exhibited at the Kitchen Center and Cunningham Dance Studio in New York, the Cabrillo Music Festival, the San Francisco Museum of Art, the Minneapolis Institute of Arts, MIT, the Anthropology Film Archives, and the Walker Art Center.

John Cage, the musician who collaborated with dancer Merce Cunningham, was a mutual friend of Cowles and Davies and introduced them to each other. They began to work together in 1976. Sharing a curiosity about the North Dakota wheat field, they explored this space as part of their collaborative work with dance and film.

Both Cowles and Dunn had studied with Cunningham and were interested in movement for its own sake. However, whereas Dunn was fascinated by the working out and complexity of self-imposed problems and by relying upon the rules of the "game" that he set up, Cowles was more intrigued by the beauty of simple, everyday common movement and calling attention to it. Each performer wanted the audience to see a performance and view movement in a different way. "What interested me more and more," said Cowles, "was thinking about how to describe real movement, just movement, what we do all the time but never stop and look at." To realize this interest, Cowles, in collaboration with Davies, uses the layering and interchange of real and film images of Cowles alone, with other dancers, or other dancers alone. The dance-film collaborators juxtapose, shift, and interweave illusions.

Davies wanted to make a film portrait of Cowles and confronted the question of what can be revealed. She wanted to know which has more presence—the real person or the image of the person?

Film and dance share visual imagery. They both can highlight, expand, and embellish movement, or they can abstract it. Both media of communication play with time, space, and rhythm. Bringing the two forms together combines each form's distinct characteristics. Film has two-dimensional flatness. It has the capacity to bring a range of scenes and fantasies to our vision, to show defiance of gravity, to distort time, and to project a larger-than-life illusion of space. Excluding technical projection failure, film is predictable in that it shows the same performance over and over. Live dance, in contrast, has a three-dimensional quality of softness, smell, gravity, immediacy, and the risk and uncertainty of the outcomes of performance.

The Smithsonian program notes for the performance gave the audience members suggestions of earlier attempts to combine film and dance in live performance. In 1924, for example, filmmaker René Clair, artist Francis Picabia, choreographer Jean Borlin, and composer Erik Satie offered the ballet "Relâche" in which film images were used to evoke a mood appropriate to the movement. In 1967 Robert Joffrey and Gardner Compton collaborated on the multimedia ballet "Asarte," inspired by the light-music-movement era of the Electric Circus type of nightclubs and discos. I vividly remember the images of Joffrey's dancers that were projected enlarged during their live performance. Fred Astaire's dancing on film with silhouettes of himself is another noteworthy example of the combination of film and dance in live performance.

FLESH-FILM CONNECTION
The Cowles/Davies (CODA) collaboration jars preconceptions of film as larger-than-life historical reality. The performance also challenges prejudices about dance being like ballet or modern dance with its various techniques. Here everyday movement falls under the rubric of dance. CODA gives us visually real propositions through live dancing at the same time that it offers visually metaphorical statements through filmed dancing. In certain sections the performers onstage and those on film become interchangeable. At other times the live dancers and their projected images are confounded. The live figures on stage mirror the movement of their celluloid selves. They prefigure or step behind the film image, or they act

Sage Cowles and Molly Davies on performance set. *Photograph by Rick Weise, courtesy of CODA.*

in counterpoint to their cinematic selves, and they create interwoven patterns.

The film provided the stage setting and scenery. It also structured objects and ideas and intensified the image of self. We all have diverse roles in different social situations as well as self-images that relate to them. In addition, other people have various images of us. As roles and relationships shift with illusionary quality in everyday life, so the performance continually shifts. When Cowles dances with her filmed self, is it a dream? An anticipation? A reminiscence? Is it her spirit or conscience? Herself as seen by the filmmaker? The interplay of live and film imagery evokes the uncertainties of life. The ultimate scene with only a live image onstage suggests a certainty.

An understanding and appreciation of Cowles and Davies's work is most fully realized if the viewer knows about post-modern tenets. "I think that all movement is important," said Cowles. Familiarity with Hindu philosophical tenets of life cycles, reincarnation, and the merging of the individual and here-and-now with the universal is also helpful.

The program notes explain that "Small Circles Great Planes" is a seventy-minute performance involving three performers and three screens onstage with projections in black and white and color film. Indian concepts of the divisions of a person's life determine the theme and form of the piece. "The first section explores 'preparation, play, dependence, and experimentation.' The second deals with 'a treadmill of activity, repetition, and accumulation.' And in the last, 'the direction is away from group activity toward the individual who pares away, simplifies, and finally alone, prepares for death.'"

At the Smithsonian performance there was some confusion about what part of the evening was the specific focus of the audience-performer connection, creating ambiguity about what the audience was invited to respond to. Originally the schedule called for the presentation of "Small Circles Great Planes" as listed in the program. It was to be presented without intermission at the Hirshhorn Museum and Sculpture Garden, which was supposed to be cleared of people immediately after the performance. Instead of the usual procedure of inviting people to reply to the dance before the first intermission and collecting the survey forms as they left, the audience was given addressed, stamped envelopes in which to mail the forms. However, on the day of the performance, a decision was made to show part of the "Sage Cycle," an earlier collaborative work. It was followed by an intermission and then the originally scheduled piece. Consequently, some audience members reacted to the last dance in "Sage Cycle" or to the entire film and then turned in their survey forms to ushers at the intermission as they had at other performances in the concert series. Other people reacted to the second piece, "Small Circles Great Planes," and mailed in their answers. Because audience members responded to different dances, a description of the highlights of the entire program follows.

One of the three portions of the "Sage Cycle" was presented at the beginning of the evening performance. In "Grasslands and Sage," created in 1977, there is one uninterrupted telephoto shot of Cowles running a mile on a dirt road in South Dakota. The running lasts about eight minutes. Cowles comes from a distance into the foreground, where we see her increasingly larger image and hear her louder panting. The running is combined with the live Cowles who sits on the stage to the lower right corner of the screen. In a cross-legged lotus-like position she makes tranquil, meditative gestures. Her arms slowly rise and her hands outstretch. Later her arms and hands wrap around her waist. Then she places her hands on her knees. Her head slowly tilts backward. The filmed image of Cowles runs off the screen; the flesh and blood figure walks offstage. While the celluloid Cowles portrays physical endurance, the live figure depicts an internal, spiritual strength. These opposite qualities are juxtaposed, and yet similar because both running and meditation lead to altered states of consciousness.

Another portion of the film also contrasts the internal and external. Cowles is shown in relation to a prairie environment. The filmed image of her face and torso appears on a field. The live Cowles, dressed in the same pale blue leotard with dark blue warm-up pants, appears in front of the screen. With her film double, she stands, stretches, and bounces. The camera captures up, down, and sideways views of the movements. Onstage Cowles moves her torso in counterpoint to the screen image, and we hear her count out the exercise. No sound comes from her filmed figure. Cowles then runs offstage and the film ends.

In the third portion we see two film images of Cowles in a wheat field, from different camera angles. She runs, picks up rolls of string, and methodically unwinds them from the camera location to a more distant place. At the same time, the live Cowles appears onstage. In a mirroring action, she unwinds masking tape and puts it on the floor.

"Small Circles Great Planes" has three sections. In the first, three dancers—Cowles (in her fifties) and the younger Patricia Gorman and Mark Stanley—perform onstage with three simultaneous projections of themselves to composer Alvin Curran's live music. The piece begins with abstract images of vertical bands of light that expand and contract to a clanging, gong-like accompaniment. The first section explores the early years of "preparation, play, dependence, and experimentation." Cowles sets the stage by preparing for the ensuing duet between a young man and woman who walk and dance with a tango-like stylized control. They face away from each other. Then they move their torsos forward and backward and face each other.

Later we see film images of silvery clumps—St. Paul grain elevators. The center screen dissolves to a long shot of birch tree trunks. In the film dancers disappear and reappear among the trees, walking, running, circling. Onstage a dancer peels off a removable panel of the center screen to walk through the opening and join in the game. The dancers mingle with their filmed selves. The trees are projected behind the screen. The live dancers weave in and out of sections of the film screen that are placed at different distances from the audience, three at the front, two in back.

In another scene we see a film of a storefront called "Ice-Dancing Groceries." It is named for a sign Cowles once spotted while driving in northern Minnesota.

The trio cavorts in the light-hearted spirit of Fred Astaire. However, the movement is folk-social and reveals no evidence of technical training in dance. We see the filmed dancers before the store, while onstage the dancers mimic their film performance. Cowles assumes plaintive poses to watch the young couple. A synthesizer provides the musical accompaniment for this scene.

A scene from Sand Lake Wildlife Refuge, South Dakota, is a transition between the first and middle sections of the Indian life scheme. Three people appear on the right film screen. In reed-filled marshland the filmed performers go wading off into the distance in a three-screen spread. The horizon-to-horizon expansion creates a glowing Cinemascope-like panorama. Gorman carries long poles which she plants in the shallow water. Stanley dreamily starts his work and does T'ai Chi movements. With her skirt hitched up to her waist, Cowles leaves them moving on a diagonal through the middle screen and then to the left off in the distance, where she stands on one leg while holding a pole. We hear birds. Then we see the screen filled with wild geese in flight.

The second section of "Small Circles Great Planes" deals with another aspect of the life cycle, the middle years of "a treadmill of activity, repetition, and accumulation." Thus we see revolving doors of Bloomingdale's Manhattan department store. Live dancers urgently sweep past the three projection screens onstage and past each other to Curran's pulsating, throbbing music as people in the film enter and exit at the store. Then, while we view a New York City subway scene, the performers onstage appear to move about the subway cars. "Moving Chords" is the transition between the middle and last sections of the Indian life cycle. The dancers, dressed in long white robes with baggy pants, appear upon a white background. Like gurus or monks they bend forward and back and spin about.

The third and final section portrays the ultimate phase of the life cycle—movement "away from group activity toward the individual who pares away, simplifies, and finally alone, prepares for death." The two young dancers have exited from the stage. Cowles is alone, preparing for the end. Not only is there no other human presence onstage, there is no film image either. After Cowles takes down the scrims in the screens, leaving the frames and their shadows on the wall, she prepares a sacred space onstage. Here she walks counterclockwise and then spins, one hand held behind her back, the other outstretched. Dressed in white, she performs repetitive, ritualistic movements in the blank, stark white light of the projector. All movement ends abruptly. When the film runs out, so does the life of the performance.

PERFORMER-AUDIENCE CONNECTIONS
AND PEOPLE'S PERCEPTIONS
The questions Cowles had in her mind before completing the "Small Circles Great Planes" piece were: "How is seeing affected by habit and expectation? How does one's perception of what is real change when confronted by a live performer juxtaposed on a series of dots of himself?"

Although I did not have the opportunity to talk with Davies, the filmmaker, she had earlier prepared a narrative for *Avant Scene* (published in Paris, France, 1980). In this nine-page statement, she said, "Hopefully, there is something felt and understood that goes beyond the literal explanations and sequence of events. I suppose I surprised myself at how far from structuralism we've come." She did not say what feeling should be conveyed and evoked.

I asked Cowles what feelings she wanted to get across in her last dance, the ritual scene in which she prepares for her own death. This dance was supposed to be the focus of discussion about the performer-audience connection. Cowles referred to the program note that "the whole idea, the large concept of that dance came from the concepts of the Hindu philosophy and had to do with various stages and cycles of life. . . . The underlying idea of the piece . . . [was] the final phase after you have been very dependent, learning, playful, and then the middle years of accruing relationships, working. The final stage of life is then shedding your worldly possessions or relationships and so forth, and you really seek a more solitary pursuit to prepare for death." Implicit were the feelings of acceptance and resignation, not anxiety, pain, fear, anguish, or grief.
*Performer Intention.* I asked, "How do you get that feeling across?" Cowles said, "I don't know if I do. And I don't care if I do. I really have no wish to have a literal translation. I can only say that it was important that the other dancers leave the stage, that I be left alone and I want to create my own space and pin it down in a very specific place onstage and

try to get a sense that this was the continuing circle, that this was my circle, whether you want to think it was life or death or my own place." "Do you have to have a particular feeling to do that?" I wondered aloud. Cowles replied,

> Every time? No. I find that always I am more involved when I am very centered, and I am very aware of my breath. And there's something about being very aware of breath that brings me instantly back to myself—just in case my attention has gotten onto some other preoccupation. It could be an audience thing or something else that is going on. It's a wonderful thing to just get aware of the breath and come back. And soon as that happens, my attention comes to right wherever I am. . . . I know the part, and I do have a feeling about it and the film image. I begin to turn independently and then my film image begins to leave the stage. It disappears, and then I am alone. And in that first series of turns I want to feel very floating.

I asked Cowles about the reciprocity of emotion and movement. She said that the movement evokes the feeling in performance. No movement is more important than any other in her view. "Each thing gets full value in terms of concentration and the way you do things. It's not important that I get a feeling from it."

*Audience Perception.* What was the audience reaction? The avant-garde, as discussed in chapter 6, is by definition controversial. The critics, the most articulate component of the audience, offered opposing perspectives. In writing about the earlier Walker Art Center premiere of "Small Circles Great Planes," Allen Robertson, in the *Minneapolis Star*, described the work as "often brimming with gentle images of quiet beauty. . . . The most elaborate and didactic piece that the twosome has yet produced. . . . [which] exploits the audience's visual perceptions of time and space. Melding film footage with simultaneous live performance, Davies and Cowles create a hybrid art form that is neither dance nor film but an amalgam that uses both arts to comment on and expand each other."[1]

Critic Richard Dyer of the *Boston Globe* spoke of the "authenticity of the highly-wrought."[2] Of the narrative, Donald Hutera of the *Twin Cities Reader* remarked, "None of this is explicit in Circles/Planes, yet all of it is selectively suggested in the brilliant marriage between Davies' imagery, Curran's music, and Cowles's lithe 'everyday' movement."[3]

Robertson described the creation as "a celebratory affair composed of bucolic landscapes that glow with a positive and regenerative spirit. This is not art composed from pain or deprivation but art that is awestruck by the glories of everyday existence. In a complex technological fashion these two women create a small intuitive and interior art that speaks of serenity in the midst of the hustle of our world."[4] In a similar vein, Donald Hutera notes, "It's important to stress that CODA's work is not the esoteric pretentious navel contemplation of the privileged. Obviously neither woman falls into the struggling artist category." He observed that Cowles, 54, and Davies, 36, are both married to prominent men. John Cowles, Jr., is president of the Minneapolis Star and Tribune Company, and Dennis Russel Davies is the former conductor of the St. Paul Chamber Orchestra and now music director of the Stuttgart Opera.

The critics who praised the performance also found some shortcomings which other critics considered more than "trifling." Robertson pointed out that "Small Circles Great Planes" is more complex than CODA's earlier collaborations. "It is more diverse and not as concentrated as the shorter works. At times, it seems almost a catalogue of the techniques they discovered in their first pieces and some of the scenes are overextended. But when it works—which is most of the time—it is a visual treat that both intrigues and feeds the mind's eye."[5] Hutera refers to the scene of a South Dakota marshland: "Here is where we most forget whether we are watching filmed or live performances. All three live performers seem secondary to their screen selves. The pace is daringly contemplative. Risking our impatience, CODA mesmerizes us instead. . . ." He praises a scene of wild geese "so big and beautiful and mysterious that it hurts and transports us to watch them. The effect is exhilarating and wondrously graceful. It's also just a trifle overextended. So is the next section, on location shots of the revolving doors of Bloomingdale's department store in Manhattan."[6]

In addition to the problem of being "overextended," there is the issue of projecting feeling. Hutera puts it this way: "Although our involvement in Circles/Planes is less emotional than intellectual and aesthetic, the polarity of moods the piece evokes, and the challenging images CODA creates, take up a permanent residence in an audience's consciousness."

Writing in the *Washington Dance View*, Julie Van Camp is less sanguine about the success of the film-dancing collaboration. "Combining a film of dancers with live performance is an interesting experiment when it jars our preconceptions about the reality of both film and performance and when it exploits the sharp contrasts between the media, especially the differences in methods for entering and exiting from the visual range. Too often, however, the Cowles-Davies experiment is nothing but the exhibit of interesting footage with no significant role for human bodies, either filmed or live."[7]

Overextension was excessive, according to Van Camp. In "Grasslands," she notes, "Sometimes . . . [Cowles] runs out of camera view in one of the screens, showing the ease of exit on film, but the sequence goes on too long, repeating variations on the same point, without much added insight." Of "Small Circles Great Planes," Van Camp writes, "the work goes far beyond the primitive insights of 'Grasslands,' yet loses much impact with excessive length and repetitiveness. The preoccupation with capturing the visual reality of film seems to have overshadowed the importance of distillation in artworks of all genre." Of the birch tree segment, she says, "The hide-and-go-seek games between live and filmed dancers are quite engaging, although they go on too long after making the point. . . . Another too-long segment shows three scenes of a boarded-up grocery store." She continues: "Almost every segment in this piece needs shortening. Additional media do not necessarily need more time to make their point. The movement designs are singularly unimaginative and unmemorable, a disappointment accentuated by the innovative interactions. Original music by Alvin Curran provides an appropriately plunky modernistic background."

Some audience members were enthusiastic about the evening's offerings. Several of Cowles's classmates from the University of Wisconsin in the 1940s came backstage to praise her performance. The son of one, who works in a bank which closes at three and thus has daylight hours to work on his four-tape-deck music, was fascinated with the synthesizer accompaniment. He remarked that each time he saw the performance, he saw something new. An Afro-American herbologist commented: "A very unique performance. I found the concept of live performance intertwined with recorded performance very stimulating. Would like to see more." A woman artist who had studied at Bennington College and was a friend of Cowles represented a viewpoint that recognized the CODA contribution as well as some faults: She wrote on the survey form, "Cowles and Davies are original and interesting. But they should be edited—some areas *too* long and repetitive." A travel agent thought the "concept is very good, that is, combining film and dance so they intermingle very closely." But she added that CODA needs "to *condense* the material to keep the viewers' attention. Perhaps more variables which are not so subtle." Another respondent remarked, "Music was slow, movement slow; this type of dance would be more effective with fast-moving motifs."

Other members of the audience saw little redeeming value in the concert. In fact, 37 percent of the audience left before the end. Some of them shared their concerns with me. My constant presence during the 1980/81 performance series put me in the position of a friendly sounding board and information source. Upon entering the Hirshhorn, two couples with whom I had spoken at other series events greeted me: "Would it be like last time? Will I like it?" I told them it would be different but I had not seen the presentation. "It will be new for me too." The two couples mentioned in chapter 6 who were angry about the Dunn Concert and expressed their displeasure to me at one of the intermissions and on the survey form were somewhat skeptical at this concert. The most verbal of the group told me it was his mother's seventieth birthday and he postponed going to Florida he explained, for a day to come to this evening's performance. As the couples left about a quarter of the way into the performance, he said, "Ruby Keeler dancing in the film *42nd Street* it is not." He noticed my puzzled look. I had not seen the 1933 film, or if I had seen a rerun, I did not remember it. "Oh, that's before your time." Ruby Keeler, of course—an apple-cheeked, sweet, ladylike hometown girl with charming, innocent youth—was a tap dancer.

Another seriesgoer joked with me at each concert. He always refused to fill out the survey form offered at the concerts. But this evening at intermission, he stridently walked up to me and requested a survey form. Later, as he walked out during some very contemporary music, he said to me, "That synthesizer doth make cowards of us all!" Another person walking out remarked, "the film is too jerky." Other disappointed audience members on their way out said, "They should pay us to educate us, not the reverse." One man told my assistant Teresa Ankney, "First it was very amateurish, second, the ideas were interesting but carried too far . . . over and over again. The music was horrible . . . the dance was painful to watch and listen to, aggravating! It raised anger in me."

Audience members also shared their views on the survey forms. A woman in public television management noted: "The soundtrack and film completely overwhelmed Cowles. She, in my opinion, was entirely irrelevant to the experience in the first piece. Twenty minutes of a heavily breathing person running toward you on film was interesting for approximately five minutes. I was disappointed and felt no emotions were conveyed." About the second piece she said, "Sitting half way back in the Hirshhorn Theatre, the live dancer[s] were completely overwhelmed by the screened images. It wasn't until half the audience left when I could actually see the performers below their waists."

In "Grasslands" a retired man saw feelings of happiness conveyed through arms, legs, head, face, and torso; playfulness through the masking tape and sounds. He responded with feelings of quiet interest. A public school teacher saw happiness and playfulness captured through the whole body. In addition, the faster speed of the background created the feeling of vitality. She felt as if she "wanted to be up there moving also." Another respondent experienced calm, tranquillity, in response to the total body portraying feelings of happiness, playfulness, and vitality. A travel agent saw boredom, which evoked a feeling of boredom in her. She felt tired in response to the fatigue presented through the dancers' breathing.

A museum professional perceived feelings of boredom, nostalgia, and playfulness throughout. She said, "I had a hard time determining what emotions they were trying to convey." A Spanish physician observed ecstasy in the sitting, eroticism in the breast, fatigue in the heavy breathing, happiness in the smile, playfulness and vitality in movement, and pride in the facial expression.

An attorney identified boredom through the lack of movement and competitiveness and vitality through the arms, legs, and torso. In response, he felt bored. About the evening he commented: "This is either over my head or it's a case of 'the emperor has no clothes.'"

Jarred expectations characterized the reaction to the concert. The performer-audience connection was not explored as systematically (quantitatively) as at other events in the series because of the last-minute program changes, audience exodus, and low mail-in response.

The performance typified the avant-garde: some strong enthusiasm and some strong disappointment, with more of the latter than the former. Part of the difficulty was that the American Dance Experience Series did not offer dance in the usual sense of tap, ballet, modern dance, or a Fred Astaire/Gene Kelly presentation. The CODA performance combines movement-acting, mime, and film. I had sympathy for the difficulty that some audience members experienced in trying to understand what was going on because I did not have an opportunity to see the program notes prior to the performance. As a result, I had little to rely upon in interpreting what I saw, only my "making sense mechanisms" based on general experience.

It later became obvious to me that reviewers who see previews and receive promotional press packets that describe the performers' intentions, techniques, metaphors, and reception elsewhere are at an advantage in understanding and (possibly) appreciating this type of performance. Cowles and Davies wanted the audience to view in a new light the movement we see all the time and never stop to look at. Some people do not stop to do this because they find it boring. They associate dance with movement transformed within a special technique and performed by trained individuals who transcend the ordinary. Cowles posed the question about how seeing is affected by habit and expectation. Her concern was with the impact of the live and celluloid images—which has more presence? However, the audience expectation, rooted in cultural biases, centered on what dance is. The concert was, after all, in a "dance" series. Many spectators did not accept Cowles's conceptualization of dance as "movement we do all the time but never stop to look at."

## CHAPTER 9

# Cultural Cross-Currents and Creative Identity: The Philippine Dance Company of New York

Dance reconstruction is not merely an American phenomenon. It is occurring in many parts of the world, where indigenous cultural life was suppressed or repressed by colonial impact. Sometimes the people themselves sought the foreign and in the search forgot or neglected their former traditional ways. Philippine history is rife with waves of foreigners, including Americans, coming to the shores of its islands and introducing different life styles and cultural forms. Some of these expressive forms underwent transformations in the Philippine environment and emerged with a distinctly national character. Over time, these expressions often became traditions.

## LOOKING BACK TO REACH ONE'S DESTINATION

Francisca Reyes Aquino had a vision. She devoted her life to the research and documentation of the rapidly disappearing traditional indigenous and later colonial-Filipino forms of dance in her country. Known as "Mother of Philippine Dance," she received various honors from her country, including the Ramon Magsaysay Award, the Republic Cultural Heritage Award, and the National Artists' Award. Aquino pioneered the development of dance in the 1920s. As a student assistant instructor in the University of the Philippines' Physical Education Department, she was asked by the president of the university to present a program of folk dances. However, she soon discovered that there was little recorded source material to draw upon. American ethnologists after the Philippine-American war had recorded some dances of the mountain tribes and other cultural minorities, but the dances of the lowland peoples had been neglected. In remedy Aquino traveled throughout the archipelago collecting material wherever she found it. Part of this research became her master's thesis. Aquino subsequently revised this project and published it as *Philippine Folk Dances and Games.* She continued her work and with Tolentino published *Philippine National Dances* in 1946.[1] This book contains instructions for fifty-four folk dances and music, a brief history, and illustrations. Aquino visited New York in the 1950s and at that time taught some of the pieces she had annotated (more than 200 of which are published in her ten books) to the Philippine Dance Company of New York.

The company follows this definitive source in presenting Philippine dance to Philippine and American audiences in the United States. The performers' keynote is the Filipino aphorism "ang hindi marunong lumingon sa pinanggalingan ay hindi makakarating sa paroroonon" (if one does not look back where one comes from, one will not reach one's destination).

The Smithsonian Institution World Explorer Series featured Reynaldo Alejandro and the Philippine Dance Company of New York. Alejandro not only has choreographed and directed but has also written books and articles on dance and theatre for various journals and has worked as a librarian and caterer of Filipino food. Author of *Philippine Dance: Mainstream and Crosscurrents*,[2] he founded and directed the Reynaldo Alejandro Dance Theater, Inc., and from 1969 to 1980 was the artistic director–choreographer of the Philippine Dance Company of New York. In addition, he founded the Dance Pantomime Theater of the Philippines and choreographed for Allnations Dance Company.

Alejandro won awards for the best choreography in the Philippine National Songfest of 1967 and 1968. In the 1960s he toured with Filipinescas Dance Company in Europe, the Middle East, North and Central America, and China. On Manila's channel 13, he staged, produced, and directed the "Mystika" cultural series. Alejandro received an Asia Foundation Fellowship to study mime movement and dance in New York (1969), a Creative Artist's Public Service (CAPS) Fellowship in choreography (1973), and a grant from the New York State Council on the Arts to bring Philippine dance to the boroughs of New York City (1979). Recipient of the Philippines' Outstanding Filipino Overseas in the Arts Award (1978), he was named Outstanding Young Man of America (1980).

Performing at the Smithsonian under Alejandro's direction, the Philippine Dance Company of New York, founded in 1943 by Bruna P. Seril, was formed to promote Philippine culture abroad. In "a quest for identity in other lands," Filipinos, Alejandro tells us in his beautifully illustrated book, are the second largest ethnic group entering the United States (second to Mexicans). About 30,000 Filipinos arrive annually and settle in Hawaii, California, New York, the Washington, D.C., metropolitan area, and Chicago. Because dance is a signature medium to express cultural identity, it can be a showcase to Americans and a focus for ethnic social solidarity. In pursuit of its goals, the Philippine Dance Company has performed extensively in the United States and other countries. Thirteen of

Reynaldo Alejandro and Allnations dancers. *Photograph by Richard Lindner, courtesy of Reynaldo Alejandro.*

the current twenty-five dancers appeared at the Smithsonian: Ramon de Luna, Nester Laxina, Ray Tadio, Charles Quintos, Jaime Santiago, Martin Danao, Rebecca Estepa (also artistic director), Elizabeth Roxas, Loida Mendoza (also the singer), Maya Evangelista, Mimi Toral, and Joyce Toral. All but two members of the company are engaged in non-dance jobs or school. One dances with the Joyce Trisler Company, and the other studies at the Alvin Ailey School of Dance in New York.

THE PERFORMER-AUDIENCE CONNECTION

At the Smithsonian performance, the focus of the sender-receiver exchange was the *pandanggo/wasiwas*, a combination of *pandanggo sa llaw* and *wasiwas* or *oasioas*, which reflect the important Spanish imprint on the Philippines. During three and a half centuries of Spanish colonization, high-ranking church and government officials were instrumental in propagating European social dances. Among the dances to flourish in a modified form and become a Philippine dance was the fandango. This dance came from southern Spain but probably originated elsewhere. Fandangos are said to derive from the Arab/Egyptian Ghawazees (dancing girls). First mentioned in Spanish literature in the eighteenth century, the fandango developed a number of local variations. It may be danced in the spirit of religious homage on the threshold of the Catholic church, or it may be danced in flirtatious charm in the theatre and cabaret. Skill with quick, intricate footwork characterizes the Basque fandango.

The Spanish fandango is generally for two people and is in quick 3/4 or 6/8 time. When the feet are still, the wrists move undulatingly with the arms and hips. The dance combines an earthy quality through foot and pelvic action and a traveling-into-space kind of movement through the upper limbs. Of key importance are the eye actions, the "dance of the eyes."

Filipinos who were receptive to the Spanish *conquistadores*, their Christian religion, and their dances adapted the fandango to suit the Filipino cultural temperament and regional orientations. Out of the fandango thus evolved the *pandanggo* and the *pandanggo sa llaw*. The steps, rhythm, and harmony of European music remain. Yet the Filipinos express their gracefulness and charm through many different regional versions. The dance has a lively spirit. Steps, figures, and directions depend on the skill and choice of the dancer.

The *pandanggo sa llaw*, popularized in Mindoro Province, is performed with oil lamps.[3] The female dancer balances three lighted *tinghoy* (oil lamps), one on her head, the other two in each of her palms. *Oasioas* means "to fling" or "to swing" and originated in Pangansinan Province— the dancer's hands reach out horizontally and diagonally into space as she spins about in place, exhibiting restraint and virtuosity. The male dancer also moves lights enclosed in handkerchiefs under his legs. *Performer Intention.* At the Smithsonian concert, Alejandro introduced the combination *pandanggo/wasiwas* dance. He explained that gracious hospitality and skill are the hallmark of the *pandanggo sa llaw* from the province of Mindoro. *Wasiwas* is from the province of Pangasinan, where the people recognize the precariousness of the sea. The dancer's lights are supposed to guide fishermen safely to the shore. The lights are also symbolic of the fireflies ablaze in the night.

In our conversation about performer intentions, Alejandro said that the dancers tried to get across two kinds of feeling. Because the dance is festive and performed after a successful fishing harvest, joy is projected. The feeling of expertise and confidence also should be conveyed. "Of course, originally, it is a skill dance . . . the audience is thrilled to see these lights, balanced on the head and the hands, so there is more or less a communication. Sometimes they applaud and then sometimes they don't when there are difficult step movements. It's skill." The dancers have to see to it that these glass lights do not fall. Beginners feel anxiety at first. Alejandro recalled that this was especially true when he taught this skill to an American and Korean for the Allnations Dance Company European tour. "What we do is to get them to walk around the room to get the balance, to walk and to balance, to walk and to balance. Once they get the feeling that they're secure, that they're confident, they won't fall anymore, then we teach them other steps."

I asked about the relationship of the movement to feeling. Alejandro thought that the movement did motivate feeling, especially the feeling of security and accomplishment for the duration of the dance. "The turning, for example, when you're turning with the glass on, doing a turn in place, it conveys the very message of the dance." About feeling in Philippine dances generally, Alejandro thought that all Filipinos can dance. "They are one of the more graceful people I've encountered. Also, American dancers and choreographers say the same. Filipinos dance with feeling . . . maybe because of the Hispanic influence, more than 300 years of the Spanish domination. There is all this emotionalism in dance. It becomes part of our dance. Hispanics are very sentimental. The Hispanic influence has had the major impact for the Christian dances. For the non-Christians, there is an inner absorption, a mysticism, a subdued feeling in their dance, to quote my mentor, Leonor Orosa Goquingco."

Alejandro compared the Filipino and American approach to dance. "For Americans, the movement is the thing." In contrast, where he comes from, the movement and the feeling are intertwined. "In courtship dances, you have to feel that you are courting somebody. That is the only way to convey to the audience. . . . You feel it to yourself and to your partner, and that's the only way you can convey your feeling to the audience. If you don't communicate anything, you can't get a response. It's a confrontation between the audience and the performers."

I wondered which came first, the emotion or the movement. "You have the idea first and then the feeling. The movement has some feedback. What you try to express is conveyed through the movement, which had already a feeling beforehand. . . . Before you do anything first you have to learn the steps. There's no feeling. But eventually, you tell them to read this, you tell them what it's all about . . . the feeling comes out."

After talking with Alejandro, I had the opportunity to speak with Loida Mendoza, who performed in the dance that was the subject of the performer-audience connection. She said she wanted to convey the feeling of joy to the audience. "How do you do it?"

"In our dances, the swaying, through our movements, I guess. When we move, we smile, and we look at the audience, and they'll know it's joyous. So you're opening up the chest and arms." She demonstrated the sway and balance in which the arms and torso gently undulated.

"Do you have to have a particular feeling to dance the *pandanggo/ wasiwas*?"

Loida explained, "Yes, you should feel it, while you're dancing. You know it's a happy, joyous dance." The movement also affects the feeling once the dance is underway. Three pairs of dancers performed it. "There's also a part where some people are dancing, and others are in the background. We interact, we look at each other, we smile at each other. So when the audience would see us smiling at our partners, they would know it's a happy dance."

Alejandro has performed for Filipinos in the Philippines and United States and for Americans. "Is there a difference in audience response?" I asked. "A slight difference," he replied. "But the final test is the Filipinos themselves. They know what to expect. They know better. You can feel it. You can get the feel or vibration from the audience as a whole. There are some portions that if the audience doesn't respond, either you are not projecting enough or they don't like it. This is my experience from dancing it so many times."

*Audience Reception.*    Critic Deborah Jowitt recognizes the difficulty of preserving cultural roots and trying to be scrupulous about details of style: "Most difficult of all is putting up for exhibition folk or social dances customarily done for the dancers' pleasure and at an event where almost all the watchers have been, or will be, dancing. How do you entertain sedentary spectators and yet not betray the style by too much theatricalizing? How do you recreate the ambience of a community or particular occasion on a limited budget?"[4] Jowitt reviewed the Asian Dance

Festival in New York, in September 1980. About the Philippine Dance Company of New York she wrote: "Director Reynaldo Alejandro and co-choreographer Rebecca Estepa present the dances gravely, as little exhibition pieces. . . . The problem is that the dances are all very gentle and sweet; they suffer from being presented as 'numbers.' Most of them lilt along in three-four rhythms; most are couple dances, with men and women advancing and retreating, turning now back-to-back, now face-to-face, exchanging partners, dipping and bending in the maneuvers of courtship. . . . the dancers are animated in a becomingly modest way." Yet for Jowitt "the dances seem adrift in time and space."

How did the audience respond to the company's Smithsonian performance? First we will consider the 87 respondents.[5] There was a fairly even distribution of men and women (47 percent and 45 percent, respectively), some spectators not indicating gender. Most people (44 percent) were in the 41–65 year age group; 20 percent, 31–40; 17 percent, 21–30; and 6 percent, under 20. Of those individuals who indicated ethnicity, 59 percent were white, 12 percent Philippine, and 6 percent other. The respondents were a highly educated group, 51 percent with postgraduate training, 23 percent college graduation, 9 percent some college, and 9 percent high school education. The latter were likely to be young students. Family income level data showed that 38 percent earned over $40,000; 17 percent $21,000–$30,000; and 17 percent, $31,000–$40,000. Occupationally most of the respondents were professionals (48 percent), the next largest group being sales and clerical (10 percent). Students were 7 percent, managerial-administrators 5 percent, skilled labor 4 percent, housewives 4 percent, dancers 2 percent, and other creative artists 1 percent.

About half (48 percent) of the audience members who filled out the survey form considered themselves somewhat knowledgeable about dancing, 31 percent not at all, and 12 percent very.

What emotions did spectators perceive on stage? As indicated in appendix table 1, most of the audience respondents perceived the feelings of playfulness (90 percent). Other emotions identified were happiness (85 percent), vitality (62 percent), pride (48 percent), caring (48 percent), and eroticism (22 percent). Some spectators even saw competition. There was more recognition of nighttime gaiety and fireflies ablaze than aid to seafarers, judging from the comments on the survey forms.

Let us now turn to how respondents thought the six most frequently seen emotions were conveyed.[6] Gesture was the most common clue. Locomotion, face, hands, and energy were the other clues which led respondents to identify emotions onstage. Playfulness was identified through action and body parts (see table 6). A respondent noted with amazement that the dancers' feet moved while candles perched precariously on their

TABLE 6. Philippine Concert: How Audience Perceived Emotions

| Clues per person: 7.23 N = 87 Emotion | Action | | Perceptions through Body Parts | | Quality of Movement | | Nondance Factors |
|---|---|---|---|---|---|---|---|
| Playfulness | Gesture | 33 | Face | 22 | Energy | 4 | 5 |
| | Locomotion | 20 | Hands | 17 | Space | 2 | |
| | Other | 5 | All | 13 | Time | 1 | |
| | | | Shld/ | | Other | 1 | |
| | | | Arms | 9 | | | |
| | | | Feet | 8 | | | |
| | | | Pelvis | 6 | | | |
| | | | Eyes | 6 | | | |
| | | | Upper | | | | |
| | | | Torso | 5 | | | |
| | | | Other | 9 | | | |
| Perceived clues | | 58 | | 89 | | 8 | 5 |
| % of total (160) clues | | 36% | | 55% | | 5% | 3% |
| Happiness | Gesture | 41 | Face | 36 | Energy | 6 | 4 |
| | Locomotion | 19 | Hands | 10 | Time | 4 | |
| | Other | 6 | Feet | 7 | Other | 1 | |
| | | | All | 7 | | | |
| | | | Shld/ | | | | |
| | | | Arms | 6 | | | |
| | | | Other | 13 | | | |
| Perceived clues | | 66 | | 79 | | 11 | 4 |
| % of total (160) clues | | 41% | | 49% | | 7% | 3% |
| Vitality | Gesture | 24 | All | 14 | Energy | 10 | 2 |
| | Locomotion | 19 | Shld/ | | Time | 1 | |
| | Other | 5 | Arms | 7 | Space | 1 | |
| | | | Hands | 7 | | | |
| | | | Face | 6 | | | |
| | | | Feet | 5 | | | |
| | | | Other | 14 | | | |
| Perceived clues | | 48 | | 53 | | 12 | 2 |
| % of total (115) clues | | 42% | | 46% | | 10% | 2% |

*Table 6, cont.*

|  |  |  | Perceptions through | | | | |
|---|---|---|---|---|---|---|---|
| *Clues per person: 7.23*<br>N = 87<br>*Emotion* | *Action* | | *Body*<br>*Parts* | | *Quality of*<br>*Movement* | | *Nondance*<br>*Factors* |
| *Pride* | Gesture | 15 | Face | 11 | Energy | 3 | 2 |
|  | Locomotion | 12 | All | 8 | Time | 1 |  |
|  | Other | 12 | Other | 18 | Space | 1 |  |
| Perceived clues | | 39 | | 37 | | 5 | 2 |
| % of total |  |  |  |  |  |  |  |
| (83) clues | | 47% | | 45% | | 6% | 2% |
| *Caring* | Gesture | 18 | Face | 15 | Energy | 11 | 2 |
|  | Locomotion | 5 | Hands | 7 | Space | 1 |  |
|  | Dancers' |  | Shld/ |  |  |  |  |
|  | Interpret | 5 | Arms | 6 |  |  |  |
|  | Other | 1 | All | 5 |  |  |  |
|  |  |  | Other | 6 |  |  |  |
| Perceived clues | | 29 | | 39 | | 12 | 2 |
| % of total |  |  |  |  |  |  |  |
| (82) clues | | 35% | | 48% | | 15% | 2% |
| *Eroticism* | Gesture | 6 | Face | 4 | Energy | 2 | 2 |
|  | Other | 4 | All | 3 |  |  |  |
|  |  |  | Other | 8 |  |  |  |
| Perceived clues | | 10 | | 15 | | 2 | 2 |
| % of total |  |  |  |  |  |  |  |
| (29) clues | | 34% | | 52% | | 7% | 7% |

*Note: Percentages have been rounded off.*

heads. Happiness was seen in body parts (49 percent of the total clues mentioned). The face was prominent, although not the only clue. In terms of action, gesture was most notable, the prop of the hand-held lighted candle figuring heavily in audience perception.

Vitality was seen mostly through action, especially gesture (53 percent of the total clues to this emotion). The total body or all body parts category was also prominent (31 percent of total clues).

Respondents generally looked at action and body parts to identify pride. Nearly half of the clues to mark caring were body parts. Gestures were also helpful. About half of the total clues to distinguish eroticism were body parts.

Nearly all the respondents who reported their responses to the emotions perceived in the dancers felt the same or similar emotion. Thus there was a high degree of empathy between performers and audience. Audience member perceptions did generally coincide with the performers' intentions of getting across feelings of joy.

Is there a relationship between perception of emotions, identification of clues to them, and a perceiver's background characteristics? Analyzing the cross tabulations of background characteristics with the most frequently mentioned clues to the most frequently mentioned emotions revealed an association between occupation and caring. Whereas 26 percent of the professionals perceived caring, none of the sales and clerical people identified this emotion.

There were also some distinct patterns between responses of Filipinos (members of the performers' ethnic group) and other audience members. Whereas Filipinos generally perceived happiness through gesture (80 percent of 10), only 43 percent of the other 77 respondents did. Another difference lies in the Filipinos' perception of happiness through the hands: 60 percent in contrast to only 5 percent of people who belonged to other ethnic groups. Filipinos differed in perception of playfulness through the hands: 50 percent as opposed to 16 percent who did not identify this feeling. A similar result appeared in the perception of pride. Half of the Filipinos noticed this emotion through the face, whereas only 8 percent of other ethnic group members recognized it. Clearly, shared cultural background and understanding of gestural and facial semantics between the performers and their compatriots accounted for the difference between Filipino and other audience members' perceptions.

Following are some illustrative survey comments from people affiliated with the Philippines. The company did earn its ethnic group's stamp of approval, what Alejandro said was the supreme test of performance success: "Filipinos know what should be." An elementary grade teacher from the Philippines saw caring through movement, happiness through smiling, playfulness through movements of the body, and vitality through liveliness. In response she felt "great, happy, and proud of my fellow Filipinos." She wrote, "I know the feeling. I'm a dancer, too." A Filipino male registered nurse felt entertained and "nostalgia for my country" in reaction to the feelings of caring, happiness, playfulness, pride, and vitality he perceived through movements of the hands, smile, chin and swaying. A Filipino woman who is a federal employee testified to the success of the program: "I enjoyed the performance because the dances were not modified. They were performed as they were in Mrs. Aquino's book. . . . I was carried away, all the way. They gave me feelings of nostalgia." She did have some suggestions: "the sway balance could be improved. I thought the Ilocano a Nasudi had castanets?" Obviously, there are regional variations.

An American who lives in the Philippines can gain knowledge of the "native aesthetic." A sixty-five-year-old man who had been an educator with the Naval Military Personnel Command's Overseas Duty Support Program in the islands identified feelings of caring, happiness, nostalgia, playfulness, pride, and vitality through technical accuracy and gracefulness. In response he felt elated and respectful of the authenticity. "I knew and worked with Mr. and Mrs. Aquino in the Republic of the Philippines and assisted her on her tour of the United States. It was a great honor and privilege and this young company is totally worthy of her great work." One Filipino demurred about the performance. Born in a rural area, this physician saw no emotion depicted and stated the reason: "no facial expression." This made him indifferent.

Here are some non-Filipino reflections. A student who saw happiness through hand movements and smiles felt good in response. She perceived pride throughout the dance conveyed in the head being immobile in order to balance the lights. She was amazed. Another student found "lightness of step" a clue to happiness. A researcher who was not knowledgeable about dance saw happiness through flowing motion and the music, and vitality through moving lights. She remarked that little dramatic emotion was conveyed. "Dance not intended to. . . . Unlike Martha Graham dances . . . these appear in general to be happy, sociable, and not intended to convey deep, varied emotions."

Caring is often associated with joy. A young woman perceived feelings of caring through the eyes, happiness in the face. She also identified playfulness and flirtatiousness. What was her response to the emotions conveyed? "Everyone seems to be enjoying themselves—it is a very good performance and I am in a happy mood." Another individual noticed the feeling of caring and thought it was captured through interaction with other dancers. Pride was seen in the use of hips and arms, vitality in flexibility and suppleness. She felt the messages were well expressed and conveyed. "The emotions the dancers felt, were reflected upon me." Caring was also seen through the proximity of the partners, and playfulness in the formation of lights. A geologist recognized the feeling of nostalgia through the costumes. A violinist/teacher said, "I was nervous throughout that someone would be burned." A teacher commented that the stage was too small to allow much movement of the groups of dancers. She liked the costumes. However, she found fault: "The youth of the artists is responsible for the lack of polish. There is too much concentration on the dance routines to allow for relaxed, fluid movement." She identified caring, ecstasy, eroticism, happiness, playfulness, pride, surprise, and vitality and felt "amused, happy, and entertained." A university professor was not too sanguine about the performance. He felt "faintly entertained—somewhat apprehensive that my guests may be bored. . . . not of professional caliber, introduction at very beginning silly. Many of the dances are designed more to make the dancers attractive to the partner . . . and not express emotion." He elaborated this latter point, although he identified flirtation and affection: "Narrow range of emotions by our standard of expression."

In spite of a few audience members' reservations, the performer-audience connection was generally mutually rewarding. The young Filipino dancers, most of whom are not usually professional performers, had driven from New York City the morning of the performance. They arrived just in time for Alejandro's 3 P.M. lecture-demonstration. By 4 o'clock, the two vanloads, and myself as their guest, headed out to Oxon Hill, where a Filipino couple customarily hosts compatriots when they come to Washington. A sumptuous, ample Filipino feast was spread. The dance event brought coethnics together. The performers, their gracious hosts, and the numerous Filipinos who attended the concert obviously took pride in their native culture and the opportunity to celebrate its showcasing in their new homeland. Filipino dancers successfully conveyed their cultural identity and artistry to Filipinos and Americans alike.

## CHAPTER 10

# Good versus Evil: Kathakali Dance-Drama from the Kerala Kalamandalam

Kathakali dance-drama appeared in the Smithsonian's World Explorer Series six hundred years after its beginnings in the state of Kerala on India's southwest Malabar coast. With a blend of popular theatre and technical virtuosity, a seventeen-member all male troupe from Kerala Kalamandalam, the most famous Kathakali theatre arts training and performing center, moves in the realm of imagination and fantasy. The stylized renderings of Hindu epics and legends create a world of the supernatural that humans cannot know with certainty. The following cultural history provides the backdrop for the discussion of the performer-audience connection.

PASSING THROUGH HISTORY
Moving through time and across the seas, the sixteenth-century Kathakali genre has retained some continuity and undergone some change. The performance setting, which in the past was an open courtyard within or near temples and village compounds of patron families, now also includes the stages of the world's major cities. The Kerala Kalamandalam troupe made its United States debut in 1971 and was on its third North American tour in 1981. Whereas in traditional Kerala, performances are in the open air with the audiences seated on mats spread on the ground, in Washington, the performance was in the Smithsonian Baird Auditorium with the audience seated in fixed seats. Missing were the booths for coffee and tea and the vendors of sweets that appear when there is to be a Kathakali drama in the Kerala villages or city suburbs. As befits the performance conventions of contemporary Western theatre, the traditional four-day sequence from dusk to rising sun for a Kathakali dance-drama was modified to fit a one-night sequence of one hour and forty-five minutes, including an intermission. Recruitment to the performance group has changed from members of related Nayar warrior caste families to individuals competing for places in a contemporary school. The training regime, too, has altered. Students who graduate from Kalamandalam

often open their own schools and receive invitations from abroad to teach and perform.

Kathakali was and continues to be performed for religious and domestic celebration. An occasional, cost-free offering to the Kerala people of the surrounding countryside from temple authorities or wealthy families, Kathakali is still a gift to an audience. However, in many towns and cities of Kerala, clubs now arrange performances that are supported by ticket sales and club member donations. Abroad, foundations and ticket sales back performances. Some of the stories are the same, some have changed, and some are new.

When I asked the actors of Kalamandalam, with the translation and commentary of P. C. Nambudripad, secretary and administrative head of the academy, if there is any religious experience involved in Kathakali, I was told, "No. It is just storytelling. . . . There are a few rituals that perhaps in the olden days had some religious background, we don't deny that, like the burning of the lamp before the beginning of the performance. That's a sign of light. That still continues. And when they come to the stage they pray behind the held curtain [as I observed from a seat at the side of the auditorium]. But the performers pray to whatever god or deity they wish. One may be thinking of Christ or Krishna. We have mixed, though mostly Hindus. One of our best musicians is a Muslim." In their book *Kathakali*, Clifford R. Jones and Betty True Jones note that scenes of symbolic death or destruction of agents of evil by the gods and heroes in the dance-drama parallel folk rituals that are integral to religious festivals as well as priestly *mudra* and Tantric ritual notions. "The magical symbols of the initial evocation, cycles of progressive action, strength, endurance, perfection in execution, and the final resolution are ritual concepts common to both the tradition of the temple and that of the theatre." [1]

In spite of the changes, traditions predominate. For example, there is the large oil and wick lamp of burnished bronze. This symbol of Shiva is placed downstage center as in the past. Because this lamp was the single light source, floor patterns of movement were confined to a small area; this use of space continues. In keeping with tradition, there are two singers standing upstage, and two drummers at stage right, a wooden stool upon which characters may sit or stand, and the curtain or *tirassila*, hand-held by two assistants. The curtain divides one scene from the next and reveals the characters at the appropriate moment. The few other stage properties are swords, bows and arrows, and maces. The acting, dancing, costume, and makeup follow classical rules laid out for all forms of theatre as well as the regional Kathakali code of conduct that evolved.

Kathakali draws heavily upon the classical art of Kutiyattam. It is the

Kathakali male actors. *Courtesy of the Performing Arts Department of the Asia Society.*

only surviving tradition for presenting Sanskrit drama extant in India. Dating from at least the ninth century, with origins perhaps in the second century, Kutiyattam is found only in Kerala. In addition to drawing upon this tradition's structure, choreography, makeup and costume, and aspects of acting technique, Kathakali also utilizes the physical training techniques from Kerala's military tradition. Added to these main sources is a synthesis of the many arts of the indigenous Dravidian culture in Kerala.

The style, structure, and intent of the classical tradition of Kutiyattam and the more recent Kathakali dance-drama, are guided by the *Natya Shastra*. As actor M. S. Pillai (with Nambudripad translating and interpreting) put it, "The entire Indian theatrical manner of dance form is based generally on the science of theatre, *Natya Shastra*. It's a very famous book written by a great sage. Bharata was a great scholar and seer, and he wrote on the theory and practice of dance. . . . *Natya Shastra* literally means science of dancing. . . . Kathakali has also taken very much from *Natya Shastra*, very much. . . . But each form of dancing has its own individual style and detailed emphasis in the application." As noted, the Kerala language and military life contributed to the evolution of Kathakali.

Kathakali, which means "story-play," received a major impetus from developments in the language of Kerala. Malayalam, the vernacular, began to develop before the thirteenth century. However, Sanskrit continued to be the major literary language. Between the thirteenth and fifteenth centuries, poets of Kerala began to write in Manipravalam, a Sanskritized form of the local language. When Tancattu Ramanujan Ezhuttacchan wrote a version of the *Ramayana*, one of India's great epic poems, mostly in Malayalam but stylistically related to earlier Manipravalam literary compositions, his work gained great popularity. The *Ramayana* plays of Kutiyattam Sanskrit drama also enjoyed great recognition. Thus the prince of Kottarakkara in South Kerala (1555–1605) was inspired to compose eight plays on the same theme in Malayalam and Manipravalam. The plays were called the *Ramanattam*. When a member of the royal family of Kottayam in North Kerala (1645–1716) composed four plays on themes from the *Mahabharata*, the other great Indian epic, these "Kottayam stories" further created interest in this dramatic art, which became known as Kathakali. Because of its high quality of poetry, portrayal of epic characters as having many human qualities rather than as stereotyped legendary figures, and wide range of emotional mood, Kathakali gained great popularity.

In its early life, Kathakali patronage came from the rajas of the few powerful kingdoms of Kerala, rulers of smaller principalities, and Nayar chieftains. The patrons all belonged to the upper classes of the ruling aristocracy. The Nambutiri Brahmanas of Kerala, upper-class families, gained prestige and merit for maintaining their own private Kathakali troupes. Current aficionados of Kathakali are the descendants of the traditional patrons. Not only did they materially support the Kathakali, but they contributed leading stories to the repertoire.

The performing artists came from a variety of castes and communities. However, the actors were principally Nayars. They were dependents of ruling families or wealthy landowners, who also tilled their fields and formed their armies. The Nayar warrior class was famous for its prowess in battle. Its military ethos found a new expression, not in the themes of the historic past, but in the stories from the *Mahabharata*, the mythical past. In supernatural, violent, blood-chilling scenes, the hero courageously and nobly triumphs in subjugating evil to climax the performance. Heroism (*vira rasa*), a pervading emotional mood of Kathakali, and incredible stamina that sustains an actor through lengthy performances are part of the military ethos.

Kathakali superseded the ancient Sanskrit dramas, whose erudition and obtrusiveness as well as performance in temple confines or royal courts from which many castes were excluded made them the special preserve of learned castes. Manjusri Chaki-Sircar and Parbati K. Sircar suggest why the Nayar heroic warriors, under the supervision of the Brahmin caste, created such powerful and spectacular drama and staged it as a public ritual for the entire community: Kathakali was a reaction to foreign aggression and a reaffirmation of Nayar-Nambutiri social status. Furthermore, in a society where descent and residence are on the maternal side, masculine pride, perhaps, needed to be affirmed.[2]

More texts for Kathakali plays were written, and performance techniques developed. Kaplinatu Nambutiri, a performer, teacher, and artistic director of his own troupe in the eighteenth century, established canons of perfection which continue to be observed today.

Kathakali suffered a decline in the early years of the twentieth century, British colonialism, Westernization, and industrialization took their toll on arts throughout the world. Indigenous forms were ignored or publicly discredited.

The revival of Kathakali was led by Kerala's famous poet, Mahakavi Vallattol Narayana Menon, together with Manakkulam Mukunda Raja Tamburan, in 1930. Beset by a growing deafness, Vallattol found Kathakali a sign language for the intellectual artist and also for the deaf. With his poetic talent he wrote new plays, thereby enriching the repertoire.[3] With great effort and expense he and his colleague established the Kerala Kalamandalam, a school to preserve and maintain the traditional arts. They engaged the finest teachers available. Financial pressures made it necessary to turn the school over to the raja of Choci. Kalamandalam now receives grants from the Indian government through the Sangeet

Natak Akademi and from the Kerala government. Other Kathakali schools followed, many headed by former Kalamandalam students. As Nambudripad put it, "We can't take everybody."

Because the Kerala Kalamandalam is an organization dedicated to the preservation and presentation of Kathakali, it is engaging many of the same issues debated by American dance groups and individuals concerned with reconstructing dance. For example, the Repertory Dance Theatre and the tap movement share concerns with their counterparts in India. The questions of the renaissance in classical forms of art, what to change and how to train participants, are alive in Kerala. Nambudripad was keenly aware that there has been a "great movement toward living history" in the United States. "I understand it is the new 'wave' to reconstruct. Structuring, restructuring, and preservation are important questions." He admitted that he did not know what was the right form. "Kathakali, it's been so meticulously structured. It's very difficult to touch anywhere. Where to improve, what has to be improved, the costumes, the dance sequences? We tried new stories. We tried one experiment with living people. During the Second World War we wrote a story about Hitler, Roosevelt, this man, that man. Hitler was a demon character and all that. The story was developed. The demon descended from someplace, killing people. Chiang Kai-Shek and Stalin were among the green [good] characters. They went about asking support and people came to support them. There was a fight and ultimately Hitler was killed." But Nambudripad said these stories did not survive because of their short-term value and familiar characters. "We have seen them. They are real human beings you have seen either in motion pictures or in photos. But you don't know what Shiva is. People can only imagine what is his exact nature. The costumes fit only such characters. So realism that way is not appropriate to a dance-drama like Kathakali." The sage Bharata, mentioned in chapter 4, had proclaimed the importance of abstraction in the arts so that godlike and unlimited ideals may be expressed by the performer and imagined by the spectator.

There is a problem of recruitment to the dance-drama training and the training itself. Because of the decline of the form, traditional recruitment from certain related families ceased. Furthermore, Nambudripad explained,

> People are not able to appreciate. How do you get interested unless you see? Some boy about twelve tells his father, I want to apply to Kalamandalam; this means art center. See, that may be out of some impulse which may not survive. Having come there, we find a good face. We try him. See, the examination for admitting a boy is superficial. Many people have been asking us, how do you select your students? What are the criteria? I ask them back the same question. Well, how do you do it? They have certain

standards, but very often they fail. I say that is our own experience. We have been trying to be very, very accurate in thinking a lot about it. We consider whether the boy has a rhythmic sense, whether he can sing at least some folk songs, whether he can walk correctly, whether his body movements are correct, his face, his eyes, the shape of his body. This is all at the age of eleven, twelve, or thirteen. He defeats everything after some years.

As an illustration Nambudripad remarked that one of the actors I had talked to briefly had been a very small boy with a very good face. "We thought he would grow up as a woman character. He would have the body shape for a woman character. He would be medium height. We didn't want a very tall man to take a woman's character, especially in India. Women are not as tall as here. So we wanted a medium, five foot five inches or five foot six inches. But then he shot up. He's a six footer with a face neither fitting for a woman's character nor for a man's character. Otherwise he's all right. You see, sometimes we fail in these things."

The training traditionally began at 3 A.M. Nambudripad explained that "3 is too early for us now. The bell goes off at 4:45, and they must be ready by 5 A.M. for their early classes."

## METAMORPHOSIS TO THE IMAGINED WORLD
Kathakali has an other-world quality. It achieves supernatural spectacle and grandeur through the dance-drama themes and the symbolic stylization of its many facets of production: acting, dance, sequence, costume, makeup, and code of conduct. The use of these various components of Kathakali creates a metamorphosis of the human and everyday and yet retains ties to human behavior.

The themes are stories dear to the heart of the people of India for centuries. They come from the Hindu epics and Puranas, or legends. The *Mahabharata*, the longest epic poem in any language, tells about wars and offers discourses on religion, government, and philosophy. The *Ramayana*, the story of Rama, an incarnation of Vishnu who was born a man to save the world from the dangerous and powerful Ravana, is the other major epic. The story of Daksha that the Kerala Kalamandalam presented appears in the *Mahabharata*. "But," said Nambudripad, "it's not very important there; it's just a mention. The story comes from Shiva Purana."

The timeless legends and myths of cosmic activities are the central motif. The performance unfolds messages of good and evil, virtue, duty, and devotion; Kathakali envelops the audience in an experience of wonderment. Like life itself, Kathakali is a mixture of the terrific and auspicious.

The counterpart to the message of the story is the stylized expression of feeling. In chapter 4 I briefly discussed the Indian theory of aesthetics with the *bhava*, or situations and acts that evoke sentiments the performer expresses, and the corresponding *rasa*, or emotion that the performer attempts to evoke in the spectator. The ultimate performer-audience connection is the blissful state of savoring aesthetic delight through the emotions.

The dramatic production has a strict code of conduct that draws from the *Natya Shastra* and the local Kerala codification that became infused with a military ethos. Kathakali performers are male. The roles available fall into three main ranked categories of mythological characters. The major parts are *sattvika*, or virtuous characters such as divine beings, kings, and heroes. *Rajasika*, also included in this category, have vices such as greed, vanity, and lust. Medium parts are *tamasika*, destructive characters who appear in the form of demons. The minor parts include such characters as assistants and servants.

Nambudripad explained that a man can play a male and a female role. However, the male role is more prestigious. Women are not even classified in the ranking system for character roles. Women are different. "Traditionally taught actors thought that the type of woman doesn't give adequate scope for acting. See, the woman's usual characteristics are love or grief, nothing else." When we were talking about this, Nambudripad's Indian friend, a dentist, explained that Indian women were not as athletic as Americans. They did not have swimming and other physical exercise. "They were more modest, they didn't come out."

Of all the Indian classical dances, Kathakali is most stylized, has a greater preponderance of *tandava*, masculine feeling, and requires more alteration of the body, augmented *mudras*, gestures, *aharya*, costumes and props, and *abhinaya*, acting using the entire body. Kathakali requires a unique training and body conditioning in order for performers to become the gods and demons they present.

The basic stance is with feet spread wide apart, a distance of not more than three times the length of the actor's foot. The weight falls on an unnatural position—the outside of the "cupped" foot—or curved outer sole—as the toes point forward. The knees are bent. The legs rotate outward from the pelvis, ideally in a 180-degree turn-out. Training for the hyperflexible, vigorous, demanding movements involves the periodic use of medicinal oil rubbed on the body; teachers, *asans*, complete the massage by using their weight and feet as hands upon the student's body. After vigorous movement the pupil lies face downward, legs spread with knees bent at right angles. The guru's pressure on the back stimulates the nervous system. Actors receive the massage once a year during the rainy season.

The footwork is emphasized with vigorous floor contact. The feet lift and maintain the unusual outward rotation. There are jumps, spinning turns, and square, circular, or diagonal patterns across the floor.

The chest lifts and opens as the abdomen relaxes. The basic arm position is extended outward from the shoulder with bent elbows. Forearms extend forward and slightly to each side, while hands lift at the wrists with palms facing forward and fingers pointing upward.

A curving circular movement of the upper torso, *cuzhippu*, is common. There are six varieties of this movement, in which the body bends not from the waist but from the ribcage.

The face is choreographed stylistically. Each of the nine basic emotional moods is learned and practiced in an ideal form. Controlled breathing renders the more intense sentiments. For example, in the erotic mood the breath moves in and out with equal effort. However, in sudden fury the breath is temporarily suspended as the ribs expand and fix. The diaphragm pulsates to convey sorrow, sobbing, and laughter.

The movements, although highly stylized with symbolic content, are nevertheless related to ordinary life. In what the performers call *kalasa*, a "pure" dance sequence between two interpretations of a text, the movements of a woman differ from those of a man. "You will find women doing it slower. Their steps are much slower. Men, when they do it, have different forms, vigorous, very vigorous; and there is a lot of fight and battle, slow movement, and lovemaking. All movements in Kathakali have very much to do with actual life, whether it is the natural movements of the humans or the natural movements of the wind. They show it through the hands." Cultured people, and deities, do not open their mouths. Nor do women characters or saints.

The female sometimes puts a hand across the front of the body to rest by the waist. Sidelong glances, gliding neck movements, and inclined head express modesty. It should be noted that demons also differ in movements according to gender. Women demons undulate when they walk except when they are very angry.

The discipline and technique of body movement in Kathakali derive from the *kalari*, the military gymnasium practices of the medieval period. This heritage incorporates qualities of unquestionable honesty, loyalty, respect, pride, and belief in one's tradition. The spartan training is physical, moral, and intellectual. Performers must commit to memory an enormous amount of literary material and interpret it. The training of musicians is equally demanding.

Music has a specific stylized format. The melody modes of *ragas* and the rhythmic patterns or *talas* in Kathakali come from the Karnatic classical music but developed in their own unique way. Kathakali has six *talas*. It has as many as six tempos or *kalas*. Each is exactly twice as fast as the preceding one. The selection of musical elements depends upon the dramatic situation and emphasizes a change in emotional mood.

The lead singer plays a gong, *cennalam*, and sets the tempo. The second singer plays three-inch hand cymbals and reinforces the beat. The singers usually alternate in singing the lines of the text. One percussionist plays a barrel-shaped drum, *suddha maddalam*, and accompanies all *padams* (verse written in the first person as if the actor were speaking). The *itekka* drum replaces the *centa* to accompany *padams* by female characters, demons excepted. At dramatic or portentous moments of the drama, the *sankha* or conch shell sounds.

Metamorphosis to the imagined world occurs when the performers enlarge their human proportions in width and height and with dazzling, rich, multicolored adornment. The costume contrasts markedly with the traditional Malabari everyday dress, a sari without blouse or petticoat for women, a strip of thin muslin tied at the waist and hanging to the knees for men. When the dance-drama company members arrived at the Baird Auditorium, I was there to greet them. They asked me about the dressing room. From the theatre stage we entered the backstage area. The senior actor looked at the doorway in utter disbelief. A narrow, two-foot passageway! The Kathakali costumes are more than three feet wide. "What will the performer do?" I asked. "They'll squeeze the costume," replied the administrative head of the Kerala art center.

Colors, patterns, and materials communicate ideas and transformations. Most major male characters wear the same dress as the hero. The villainous and evil characters differ from the hero in wearing an oversized crown and shaggy red jacket.

The costume has many parts that must be tied or pushed on in an elaborate tying of the "one hundred knots." Actors wear two stiff, bunchy petticoats, not as stiff as in India because of the starch they use there; these billowing knee-length underskirts support eye-catching, voluminous, bright overskirts. Performers wear jackets, black wigs with three-foot-long false hair, girdles, epaulets, scarves with ruffled or mirrored ends, leg bells, bracelets, and large lower ear ornaments. Long talons adorn each finger of an elite male character's left hand. In addition, a turban cushions a curved, jeweled, silver-inlaid and gilded towering wood crown. At intermission some Indian audience members were talking with one of the major characters. An Indian man told me, translating rupees into dollars, that a hero's costume cost about $1,000.

Female characters are distinctly costumed. The dress and makeup are more naturalistic. They wear brilliant head scarves, jeweled nose rings, necklaces, ear ornaments, armlets, and hair knotted on top. Women carry loops of holy beads.

Makeup is unique in Kathakali. This quality aids in creating a super-natural aura. The makeup process is both lengthy and ritualistic. The company requires a place in which the actors can lie down on the ground while master makeup artists work their craft. The area is called the "green room" after the color of the hero's makeup. At the Smithsonian an area for makeup and dressing was roped off in the entryway to offices adjacent to the auditorium. Along the walls stood about eight trunks and the makeup case with its sixteen jars and eleven vials. Makeup for the major characters began about 3 P.M. for the 8 o'clock performance. Some of the other company members curled up in a corner of the area and caught an afternoon nap until they had to get ready. The makeup artist, who now requires a two-year training course, works on the face of a major or medium-ranked actor who lies on a mat on top of a large sheet spread out on the floor. Two makeup people sit cross-legged, each with an actor's head between his knees.

The face serves as an index of emotion, and the facial colorings correspond to the moods and psychological temperament of the character. For example, the erotic mood is allied with the color of light green, the terrible with black, and the furious with red. The colors—primarily white, green, vermilion, red, black, and yellow—are ground into a fine paste and mixed with coconut oil in coconut shell bowls. Applied to the face, the mixture creates a smooth, varnished effect in the mellow light of the oil lamp.

Characters fall into key mask types. They are classified as *pacca* (green), *katti* (knife, from the shape of the red and white design over each eyebrow), *tati* (beard), *kari* (black), *teppu* (special characters), and *minukku* (smooth).

The *pacca* green makeup apperas on *sattvika*, heroic or divine person-ages and kings, such as Shiva and Daksha. A light pea-green pigment is spread on the face. A stylized velvet black design exaggerates the ap-pearance of the eyes and eyebrows. The lips are colored red-orange. The *cutti*, a one- to three-inch curved extension applied along the sides of the face and over the chin from the cheek bones along the jaw, further alters the typography of the face and transforms the actor. A thick, viscous rice and lime paste holds the graduated layers or ridges cut out of white stiff paper that flare out most broadly at the cheeks.

The *katti* personality appears similar to the *pacca* type but in keeping with demonic and noble traits has a red and white pattern and white knob attached to the nose superimposed upon the *pacca*. Villainous, evil characters wear *tati*; red beards and predominantly red makeup with black and white designs, with fringes of paper attached to the face and protuberances on the nose and forehead. Black and white beards distin-guish specific characters. *Kari* is for the demons. Upon the black are crescents with red and white dots. The *minukku* makeup is smooth light buff that distinguishes women, Brahmans, sages, and messengers. Sati, in buff makeup, has eyes outlined in a petal pattern and eyebrows shaped in a curve.

The final step in makeup is the insertion of *cuntappuvu* seeds under the lower eyelids. I watched the character Daksha insert the seed and rotate his eyeballs until they reached the proper shade of rose. The demons' eyes get inflamed to a ruby-red color. After performing, the actors remove the seeds and their eyes return to normal.

The sequence of Kathakali is part of its stylization. In addition to the aspects already described, the structure also sets the performance apart from everyday life. (Some of the traditional structural components are eliminated when the company tours outside its home area.) The *keli* is a musical announcement of the program. Drums call the audience to attention. Following is the *purappatu*, a dance invocation performed by a male and female character. It is a composition of abstract dance representing Krishna and Balabhadra. Then the drama is performed. Before a major character appears, there is usually an anticipated suggestion of the personality, who performs hidden in full or in part behind the curtain or *tirassila*, about six feet by nine feet. The curtain lowers part of the way, and the actor grasps, vibrates, and billows it. This prelude arouses the audience's curiosity. The character gradually appears as the curtain is slowly lowered.

The performance is regulated by the poetic text. Sung texts further the transcendence to the imaginary. At the Smithsonian performance, all of the narrative of each scene described in the program was not visually portrayed because the program was shortened. Each scene in the drama begins with a sung verse or *slokam* in the third person to set the stage for the *padam* (in the first person) to follow. The stylized gestures or *mudras*, coordinated with the movements of the feet, legs, torso, head, eyes, eyebrows, and facial expressions, closely follow the words of the text. The *kalasam* passage of dance, not fully pure dance since the emotional mood or *bhava* continues, punctuates sections of the *padam*. There are also interpolated passages of movement which are performed to percussion alone. The range of movement is from complete improvisations of gesture to traditionally set passages of choreography.

AN EVENING'S STORY

To place the discussion of the human connection in context, it is important to present the specific story that the audience was told in the program notes:

> Daksha Yagam (The Sacrifice of King Daksha). Daksha, the son of Brahma, the Supreme Creator, and his wife, Prasuti, have adopted a child,

Sati, who is given in marriage to the God Shiva. Daksha, unimpressed by Shiva's spiritual standing, persists in treating him as an ordinary son-in-law, and relations between Daksha and the newly married couple have become strained.

Scene 1. Sati, the consort of Shiva, wants to go to the palace of her father, King Daksha, in order to participate in a sacrifice which he is arranging. The purpose of the sacrifice is to obtain a male child for Daksha. But Shiva, Sati's husband, urges her not to go, pointing out that they have not been invited and that they will surely be insulted if they go. She, however, insists and finally Shiva lets her go, sending attendants to accompany her for protection.

Scene 2. Sati enters the Sacrificial Hall. Daksha, who is sitting there, says, "Leave the Sacrificial Hall at once. You were not invited, and I am no longer your father." Sati says: "Why do you insult me? This enmity between you and us is bad. Please listen to what I have to say." But he refuses to listen. Sati then warns him that his insult to Shiva will be avenged, and she leaves.

Scene 3. Sati returns to Shiva and tells him about her experience, complaining that Daksha insulted not only her but Shiva as well, and that he must be punished.

Scene 4. Shiva creates two demons, Virabhadra and Bhadrakali, and orders them to destroy Daksha. [This scene was the focus of the performer-audience discussion. As the music is loud and persistent, Shiva pulls his four-foot-long black hair to the side in what I thought was a gesture of anger. Nambudripad clarified the act: it was from his hair that Shiva created the demons.]

Scene 5. At the Sacrificial Hall: A *puja* (ritual) is being performed. The two demons destroy everything and behead Daksha.

Scene 6. Believing that an uncompleted sacrifice will do great evil to the whole universe, Brahma, the Supreme Creator, urges Shiva to forgive Daksha and bring him back to life in order that he may finish the sacrifice. As Virabhadra has already burnt Daksha's head, a goat's head is placed on his body, and Daksha is then restored to life. He is repentant, and prays to Shiva for pardon. The sacrifice is soon completed, and all ends well.

THE PERFORMER-AUDIENCE CONNECTION

I asked Monkombu Sivasankara Pillai (with Nambudripad's translation and interpretation), the actor who played Lord Shiva, what feeling(s) he wanted to convey to the audience in scene 4 when Shiva creates two demons. Pillai replied, "It is mostly anger mixed with a feeling of retribution." "How do you get that across?" I asked. Nambudripad explained that he does it through action in the face and through the vigorous movements of his body and footwork. I probed, and Pillai demonstrated eye twitches, vibrating hands, and trembling hands with one arm extended stiffly and the other bent.

"What feeling do you have to have to do that dance?" I wondered. The translator said, "At that particular time he tries to merge with the character he plays—to be that person." I sat on the floor cross-legged before an older man, who was subdued and quiet-spoken. He had a kindly demeanor and warm smile. "How do you do that? You're very gentle now; what makes you angry?" I was told, "He lives through the story, tries to understand, tries to live the feeling of Shiva at that time."

When I raised the issue of the relationship between feeling and movement, which comes first and how they interact, the actor was explicit. The movements of the vigorous dance emanate from the feelings and not the other way.

M. P. Vasudeva Pisharoty played the demon. I asked him what feeling(s) he wanted to get across to the audience. He mainly wished to convey anger. He wanted retribution—to take action against King Daksha for having humiliated his master Shiva. Pisharoty showed how he gets the feeling across. I saw strong, tense, angular movement. The hands, eyelids, and eye twitching convey anger. Nambudripad added, "Also, he has a roar." I asked what feeling he has to have to create the demon. "The actor gets excited through the feeling of the character. It is the feeling that must come first. It is out of the anger and feeling of excitement that vigorous movements of the body and leg come." I was curious about how the actor got the feeling. Nambudripad explained that when a performer learns the stylized facial expressions for each of the nine *bhavas*, he is supposed to learn to feel each *bhava* he portrays.[4] "Through long experience and learning from the gurus, masters. And also reading the books. He first imitates what his guru has taught him, and for some time he has been doing that. And then he learns from the experience of acting this character, and also from his reading and thinking about the character he tries to improvise."

Knowing about the formalized system of Kathakali, I was interested in the range of improvisation. Nambudripad put it this way:

In a classical dance all the four walls have been very much structured and built. It is within this structure that has been very firmly built over the years; the scope is limited. but, suppose one man acts as Daksha. Another day someone else acts as Daksha. Two people interpreting the same character will have some differences. In "The Sacrifice of King Daksha," Sati was an adopted child of Daksha. One day he was wading in the river, and then he found a conch. He took the big conch in his hands, and when he broke it a small child came out. It was a beautiful child, a girl. You see the acting was clear. He embraces her. It is this adopted girl, the twenty-eighth or twenty-ninth girl, who was married to Shiva. They lost friendship; they became almost enemies. And so, Sati was not permitted in the sacrificial hall. And she was sent out. In sending her out, Daksha had two feelings. One was anger against Shiva; the other was love for his adopted child. He was not happy. He did it out of what he thought was his duty to humiliate

Shiva, but at the same time, he was very unhappy. And when she left, this man acting as Daksha started to cry. A lot of tears came down. The other actor did not cry. You see, that is an improvisation which only those who watch Kathakali very carefully can understand. The range of improvisation is not very wide but it is subtle. Good actors try to imagine and have their own interpretations.

Western actors often call on their own personal experience for specific roles. So I asked if personal experience apart from theatre was integral to acting in the Kathakali dance-drama. "No. It's esoteric. The stories are not real." Yet, the movements, as noted earlier, are very much related to life. Women's movements, of course, are observed and outside the actor's own experience.

The other major character in scene 4 was the demoness played by K. M. John. "What kind of feeling do you want to get across in this scene?" I asked. John replied, "It is very difficult to answer. You see, this demoness is very much attached to Sati, who was humiliated by Daksha. So the demoness was all the more angry. She wants to retaliate—the feeling of retaliation is the main thing." "How do you get the feeling across?" I wondered. John said, "I try to make the expression. The eyes make it big. I open the mouth and show teeth; the eyebrows go up." The demon roars. But the demoness, said John, "She screeches; the sound comes from the chest."

In response to the question about the feeling he had to have to dance the demoness, John said, "I try to assimilate with the character. If I am the demoness, I try to be the ogress."

About whether feeling leads to movement or the reverse, John explained: "In Kathakali, it is not like that. We have movement, we are not free. It is the emotions that lead to the movements."

There are differences in audiences in Kerala and in the United States. I was curious about how the actors perceived the differences. The actor who played Shiva said:

> The people of Kerala really know much more about Kathakali and the stories, whereas the American audience does not know that much. But there is more interest and attention about Kathakali from a Western audience—the story and the emphases of the movements, of the face, and the *mudras*. For example, the American audience does not know wholly the meaning of the *mudras*, the hand gestures, but in the third scene when Sati comes back from her father's sacrificial palace insulted and humiliated, Shiva gestures like this [he points his finger at the woman]. There is no *mudra*. It's an international gesture of the hand, and then, immediately, the American audience, wherever I have performed, goes into laughter as if they have understood the whole. Shiva says, "See, I have advised you not to go and now that you have gone you have suffered."

"Do most of the people in Kerala know the *mudras?*" I asked. Nambudripad noted, "You have in Kerala one set of people who know these
things very well. You will find in every audience one or two dozen people,
usually sitting in the front, very well versed indeed. But by and large,
other people do not know very well the details of the *mudras.* They know
the story and that will be enough for an understanding and appreciation
of the dance form."

I asked Pillai what he would like the ideal audience member to feel. He
explained that he would like the audience seeing a Kathakali performance to understand the very delicate aspects of Kathakali dancing, including the emphasis on expressions, the *rasas*, the ritual movements to
suit each expression, as well as the costumes.

The Joneses speak of Kathakali *bhrantan*, those who have "Kathakali
madness." Mesmerized by the performance marathon in Kerala, they engage in detailed commentary on the actors' interpretation and technique.
Attention to nuances of performance varies, and the unique interpretations provide one of the aesthetic delights of Kathakali.

Nambudripad added further comment.

You see mostly there are two aspects in every theatrical movement. One is
a question of message, the other is communicating the *rasa*, the feeling of
the sensitiveness of it. You see, you have a symphony. There's no language.
What do you communicate to the audience? To the ear? To the eye? You
see? Flute music? Or a violin concert? You convey the joy of hearing the
ritual harmonious sound, the feelings created out of it. Just so, you see,
there is not always any message in the story but there are messages also in
certain stories wherein there is a fight between the right and the wrong.
The evil kings are always killed by the right ones.

"Through the Puranic story known to all Indians, the memorized literary text, the familiar music, the symbolic make-up, the stylized costuming and head-gear, the Kathakali dance-drama seeks to evoke a particular
emotional state and sentiment," Vatsyayan wrote.[5] Not only were the
masses entertained, but they were also acquainted with the stories of the
gods and the principles of philosophy, the value of virtue and dangers
of vice. The bible of the poor illiterate, the theatrical splendor transports
the people to the world of gods and heroes. People of Kerala are also familiar with the visual images of the characters. They bear strong similarity to the medieval images carved and painted in the major temples of
Kerala. A pervading philosophy divided reality into pure, divine, and active rajas, and the contrasting impure, inert, and base. There is also the
aspect of *alankara*, or ornamentation for its own sake. The artificiality of
the actors' transformation distances the audience sufficiently from the realistic so that it can deal comfortably with the intensity of strong emotions and sensitive issues of betrayal, violence, and other human failings.

When we spoke about audience reaction and whether it was different in India and the United States, John said, "During the performance I do not care about the audience." Nambudripad laughed. "That is a good answer you got!" "I care about my character," John said. He was referring to the obliteration of the individual personality of the actor in the metamorphosis and transcendence into the world of the imagination. Nambudripad explained, "That is the way that they have been taught." He continued, "People have been more vocal and demonstrative here, applauding. Even though those who appreciated the story, sat through the whole night, even though they may come to the dressing room and hug and pat and all that in Kerala, they do not applaud so much." In another conversation, he said that he had seen audiences in Kerala with the feeling of the movement conveyed in the dance-drama. Some have cried with sorrow, love, and grief. Some people even ran about with fright from the violent staccato movement, piercing, sputtering high-pitched drums, insistent tattoo, and intense heroic themes. "They feel the fear; they feel the anger."

*The American Critics.* Deborah Jowitt saw the performance of "The Sacrifice of King Daksha" in the new Asia House building in New York City. After providing her readers with a vivid and insightful description and analysis, she concluded, "I wish I could have seen more. The Kerala Kalamandalam hasn't been here since 1973, and this was like an hors d'oeuvre that only served to increase my appetite."[6] Speaking of Kathakali as "one of India's richest classical art forms," Anna Kisselgoff wrote in the *New York Times*: "As usual, the artists and musicians were excellent. T. T. Ramankutty Nair was ferocious in his arbitrariness as Daksha, and Mankombu Sivansankara Pillai was a contrasting portrait in serenity as Shiva, transforming himself into a warrior on the spot. In the female role of Sati, C. M. Balasubramanian was able impressively to depict two characters at once in recalling the encounter with Daksha." She continued, "Yet, this was an excerpt that showed none of the psychological depth of Kathakali pieces from epics such as the *Ramayana*. The intricate range of Kathakali's dances was barely evident as these artists, younger than those in the past, relied more on mime. Subtlety was played down in favor of broadness. Nonetheless, any glimpse of Kathakali is worth a trip."[7]

At the Baird performance of "The Sacrifice of King Daksha" Alan M. Kriegsman of the *Washington Post* remarked: "What was revealed was a fascinating blend of theatrical arts, marked on the one hand by the most exquisite subtleties of craft and expression, and on the other by bursts of rough, earthy vigor. The vigor comes partly from the strong martial background of the form. . . . the ample costumes and masks bedazzle with color and fantasy." Kriegsman noted a problem found both in India and abroad: "The exotic stylization and such features as the complex hand signs make the symbolism of Kathakali difficult to penetrate. But the visual enticements, the liveliness of the characterizations, the rhythmic vitality and the expressive intensity transcend all barriers to communication."[8] Anne Marie Welsh of the *Washington Star* put it this way: "Though much in the Kalamandalam's performance failed to cross the cultural divide, other scenes—especially the comic moments—were as easy to understand as spoken English. T. T. Ramankutty Nair as Daksha and C. M. Balasubramanian, a male playing the female role of Sati, were especially memorable for one eyebrow duet and a later scene in which Daksha, in a single gesture, indicated that he knew worlds about his wife's recent adventure."[9]

In short, the critics appreciated the virtuosity of an ancient tradition. They recognized the variety of types of performances and wanted either more or different ones. The combination of the esoteric and commonplace led one critic to imply that there was something for everyone and that the more one knew, the greater the feast.

*Other Members of the Audience.*   What emotions did the actors convey to the audience and how? What did audience members feel in response? Audiences can vary markedly. This became evident in the differences between the two evening performances that were part of the Smithsonian World Explorer Series. The first night was part of the series subscription. This concert included welcomes and introductions by the secretary of the Smithsonian and the ambassador of India as well as a reception afterward. The ambassador spoke of the effective suspension of disbelief that Kathakali evokes and the appeal of this dance-drama to foreign cultures not versed in its stories.

The first evening's audience was not as *en rapport* with the performance as the second evening's audience. On opening night about twenty-two people exited before the intermission. By intermission, perhaps two-thirds of the audience had left. Some people found the music, what they called "noise," deafening, especially in the anger scenes. Kathakali is traditionally performed outdoors. Inside the Baird Auditorium the sound reverberated with the intensity of a youthful New Year's Eve noisemaker's cacophony or contemporary high-decibel disco—neither of which is acceptable to the many elderly spectators. Another comment centered on the incomprehensibility of the action and its slow pace. If people unfamiliar with the story or the language of the sung poetic texts (this includes most people) did not read the program notes describing the scenes, they found it difficult to know what was happening. The presentation onstage is repetitive. Some of the action described in the program notes was not visualized onstage. One subscriber wrote on the form, perhaps speaking for those who connected poorly with the performers, "Totally bored and disgusted." This Maryland housewife said no more.

Some audience members on opening night were enthralled. A teacher described the evening as "excellent." She identified anger, disgust, happiness, pride, sadness, shame, surprise, and vitality through the eyes, eyebrows, middle body, hands, and feet. She felt the same emotions that were displayed. An international exchange director remarked, "Fabulous, outstanding performance." She saw anger through the facial muscles, eyes and hands, and general body movements. In response she felt awed. "Saw the power." She also recognized vitality interspersed with sarcasm all through the scene. In response to the emotion of disgust she saw onstage, she felt excited. A political scientist identified a variety of emotions. For him, however, the performance was "very cerebral—not an emotional involvement." An arts administrator for whom the performers created anger, playfulness, pride, shame, and vitality through hands, fingers, eyes, feet, and the entire body felt "fascination" in response.

There are moments of "universal" communication, as the actor who played Shiva noted in our conversation. A member of the audience commented on the gesture of the finger pointing the way out of the hall. He also noticed the actions common to Americans such as the double-take, the coquetry of the woman's eyes, and the warrior's fighting movements.

A female economist reacted to both the technical and social aspects. She noted that the "dancers are *very* skilled; they present conflicting and combined emotions." She also went on to remark, "Most vivid is the clear depiction of the relative status of the two sexes. This permeates the entire performance. The female is *always* submissive and even an attempt at anger is subdued." I had spoken earlier with Kerala men about this tradition in India. Yet India has had a female head of state; the United States has not.

The second concert attracted many cognoscenti and people who belong to the Kerala immigrant and temporary resident association in the Washington metropolitan area. At this performance no more than about twenty people left before the end of the dance-drama. A graphic artist said, "I am a student and performer of Bharata Natyam at churches, retreats, and other events. I am very interested in the combination of dance and drama, and the effect of the story upon the audience. I believe the audience is a participant in the performance and can share in the emotions of the dance." Another woman at the second concert was also a student and dancer of Bharata Natyam "for nineteen years. I also have seen this dance form performed here eight years ago." She identified feelings of anger, disgust, and fear through the body, face, and *mudras*. In response she was "mostly interested in the technique." An Indian doctor learned about the performance through the Kerala Association. He remarked that "it was an excellent performance." A New York writer found the performance "brilliant and beautiful."

First-timers also attended the concert. A medical student said, "Though this is my first exposure to Kathakali, the performance is extraordinary in that it is understandable, enjoyable." In spite of the stylized symbolic movement, costume, makeup, music, and philosophy, she noted the universal elements of Kathakali. "It illustrates that emotions and the ability to recognize these emotions are universal. Through facial expressions, body movements, and so forth, a plethora of emotions can be expressed, interpreted. Excellent!"

A teacher of theatre arts and English came to the free lecture-demonstration and "got turned on." She commented that it was "very hot in the auditorium (impairs concentration!). Sat in next to last row (couldn't see facial refinements). Demons—dynamite." She saw Shiva's caring for Sati when he embraced her after Daksha's insult, his boredom through his head "nodding off" as Sati chattered on, disgust in his face, fatigue when he touched his hand to his head—tiredness of his father-in-law, sadness in Sati's head and body, and vitality in Shiva's body and foot movements when preparing for the demons. In response she "felt surprised and pleased to understand so much."

One audience member remarked on the quality of effort in Kathakali. A statistician found "extreme tension almost throughout due to the compulsive nature of the music, even at moments of tenderness, flirtation, and so forth." He identified anger through finger motions and the feet. In response he felt nervous. When he saw pride conveyed through facial expressions, he felt confident. The feeling of revenge conveyed through hand movements made him feel uneasy.

Nearly all the respondents indicated that they felt the same or similar emotion to the one, or more, they perceived onstage. For example, out of twenty reports perceiving anger, only two indicated feeling the opposite emotion, and two, no emotion.

For purposes of analysis, the two Kathakali audience surveys were combined, since it was possible to distinguish the responses of Indians and individuals who were knowledgeable about dance. The forty-eight survey respondents have the following characteristics.[10] Fifty-four percent were women, 40 percent men. A third of the group were in the age category 31–40; 29 percent, 21–30; 27 percent, 41–65. As at all the concerts, whites predominated (56 percent). There were 27 percent Indians. The postgraduate population was high, 67 percent. Twenty-one percent were college graduates. More than a third (38 percent) reported family income over $40,000; 19 percent, under $20,000; 19 percent,

$21,000–$30,000; and 17 percent, $31,000–$40,000. Half of the respondents were professionals, 13 percent students, and under 10 percent
other groups. Two-thirds (67 percent) were somewhat knowledgeable
about dance, 17 percent very, and 13 percent not at all.

What were the most frequently perceived emotions? Nearly everyone
(96 percent) saw anger, as indicated in appendix table 1. Next come pride
(69 percent), caring (65 percent), disgust (65 percent), playfulness (58
percent), and sadness (56 percent). For the most part, cross-cultural and
intra-cultural communication was effective at the Smithsonian Kathakali
concert. The actors who played Shiva and his demon creations wanted to
get across feelings of anger. Over 95 percent of the respondents perceived
this emotion.

Clues to identify anger were mainly body parts, as indicated in table
7.[11] The hands, face, eyes, total body, and other parts were noticed, as
were gestures and locomotion. In fact, body parts were the main clues for
the other emotions as well: the face, hands, eyes, and other components
of the body contributing.

Were there patterns of relationships between perceptions of emotions/
clues and respondent background variables? All of the female respondents perceived anger, 90 percent of the males. The proportion of women
who perceived anger through the clues of gesture (26 percent of 19), face
(37 percent) and hands (42 percent) was greater than the proportion of
men (58 percent of 26). Twice as great a proportion of women (81 percent) as men (42 percent) perceived the emotion of disgust through the
face. It has been suggested in the research literature (cited in chapter 1)
that women, because of their less prestigious position in society and their
general socialization to pleasing others, are more sensitive to signs of
displeasure.

There was a relationship between ethnicity and perception of anger
through the face and the identification of disgust. Proportionately, Indians more frequently perceived these than members of other ethnic
groups. Whereas 62 percent of 13 Indians saw anger through the face,
only 43 percent of 35 others did. Eighty-four percent of the Indians
noticed disgust through the face, to 57 percent of other groups.

There were also relationships between family income group and perceptions of emotions and clues to them. The tendency was for those (18)
with family incomes over $40,000 to see anger through the face (61 per-
cent) and hands (83 percent) and caring (50 percent) and disgust through
the hands (61 percent). Respondents with less family income perceived
these emotions and clues roughly 22 to 40 percent of the time.

A Kathakali performance in traditional Indian life was a gift to the
people of a local area. Some audience members in Washington, and elsewhere in the United States, although they paid for tickets to see the com-

TABLE 7. Kathakali Concert: How Audience Perceived Emotions

| Clues per person: 10.13 N = 48 Emotion | Action | | Perceptions through Body Parts | | Quality of Movement | Nondance Factors |
|---|---|---|---|---|---|---|
| Anger | Gesture | 20 | Hands | 26 | Energy 4 | 4 |
| | Locomotion | 13 | Face | 23 | Time 1 | |
| | Posture | 2 | Eyes | 16 | Space 1 | |
| | | | All | 14 | | |
| | | | Feet | 10 | | |
| | | | Other | 12 | | |
| Perceived clues % of total | | 35 | | 101 | 6 | 4 |
| (146) clues | | 24% | | 69% | 4% | 3% |
| Pride | Gesture | 10 | Face | 13 | Energy 1 | 1 |
| | Locomotion | 6 | Hands | 9 | | |
| | Other | 3 | Eyes | 7 | | |
| | | | Other | 13 | | |
| Perceived clues % of total | | 19 | | 42 | 1 | 1 |
| (63) clues | | 30% | | 67% | 1% | 1% |
| Caring | Gesture | 9 | Hands | 14 | Energy 2 | 2 |
| | Locomotion | 5 | Face | 13 | | |
| | Other | 3 | Eyes | 9 | | |
| | | | Other | 15 | | 2 |
| Perceived clues % of total | | 17 | | 51 | 2 | 2 |
| (72) clues | | 24% | | 71% | 3% | 3% |
| Disgust | Gesture | 10 | Face | 18 | 0 | 2 |
| | Locomotion | 5 | Hands | 16 | | |
| | Posture | 1 | Eyes | 10 | | |
| | | | Other | 18 | | |
| Perceived clues % of total | | 16 | | 62 | 0 | 2 |
| (80) clues | | 20% | | 78% | | 2% |
| Playfulness | Gesture | 9 | Face | 10 | Time 1 | 1 |
| | Locomotion | 5 | Hands | 10 | | |
| | Other | 2 | Eyes | 9 | | |
| | | | All | 8 | | |
| | | | Other | 5 | | |
| Perceived clues % of total | | 16 | | 42 | 1 | 1 |
| (60) clues | | 27% | | 70% | 2% | 2% |

Table 7, *cont.*

| | | | | Perceptions through | | | |
|---|---|---|---|---|---|---|---|
| Clues per person: 10.13 N = 48 Emotion | Action | | | Body Parts | | Quality of Movement | Nondance Factors |
| Sadness | Gesture | 11 | Face | 16 | Space | 1 | 1 |
| | Locomotion | 6 | Eyes | 10 | | | |
| | | | Hands | 10 | | | |
| | | | Other | 10 | | | |
| Perceived clues | | 17 | | 46 | | 1 | 1 |
| % of total (65) clues | | 26% | | 71% | | 2% | 2% |

Note: *Percentages have been rounded off.*

pany, or received review tickets, also considered the performance a gift. Kathakali's offering of everyday life metaphors and its transporting of the audience to the gods of the upper and the demons of the nether worlds reveal the ingenuity of the art form.

There were some newcomers to the form who were alienated and put off by the strangeness. For spectators baffled by the dance-drama, Alan M. Kriegsman's comment is apt. There were certainly obstacles to understanding the complex layers of meaning or merely what was occurring. Someone wanted to know how the actors-dancers can tell where they are in the music. Another spectator thought that providing a translation of the poetry would be helpful. She referred to music concerts that provide translations of lyrics sung in French, German, and Italian.

I spoke earlier of the knowledge of a sophisticated Kerala viewer. Yet the combination of the broad, "universal" [Indian and American] actions and the sensory opulence of Kathakali seduced many of the unsophisticated into the world of fantasy, feelings, and enjoyment. For the most part, the performers' hopes for conveying feelings to the audience were successful. The drama had broadly stroked actions that were easily understood. Most of the spectators who filled out the survey form saw anger through the eyes, eyebrows, middle body, and feet. A few also identified the feeling of retribution that the performers wanted to convey.

The Smithsonian museum Kathakali exhibit, however, detracted from what the performers wanted to convey about their cultural form. Audiences had to enter the performance auditorium by passing through exhibits of headpieces, jewelry, and other parts of the Kathakali costume as well as dolls in complete costumes of Kathakali characters. When the Smithsonian Institution secretary offered remarks on opening night, he commented on the exhibit with pride. However, the Kerala Kalamandaram repertory company thought the life-sized costumed figure placed in the middle of the exhibit hall poorly represented the reality of Kathakali at its best. Indeed, the costumed figure lacked the opulence and grandeur of the heroes, deities, and demons brought to the American stage. The company's Washington performance was indeed a gift (as it was to Indian localities) and a correction of some perceptions about Kathakali.

## CHAPTER 11

# Curtain and Concert Comparisons: Summing Up

This chapter addresses questions raised in the beginnings of the book and explored in the presentation of each concert in the 1980/81 Smithsonian dance series. We shall begin with dancers' views on the reciprocity of emotion and movement, followed by suggestive findings on universal versus culturally patterned communication of emotion; overlapping of performer intention and audience recognition of emotions, clues, and responsive feeling; themes that weave through the dance series; and, lastly, the issue of making a better performer-audience connection.

## PERFORMERS
*Reciprocity of Emotion and Movement.* At the end of *The Expression of the Emotions in Man and Animals,* Darwin commented on intent and the conscious stimulation of emotion.

> The free expression by outward signs of an emotion intensifies it. On the other hand, the repression, as far as this is possible, of all outward signs softens our emotions. He who gives way to violent gestures will increase his rage; he who does not control the signs of fear will experience fear in a greater degree; . . .
> Even the simulation of an emotion tends to arouse it in our minds.[1]

Thus Darwin recognized the reciprocity of movement and emotion.

There has been a tendency for performing arts theorists to view the reciprocity of movement and emotion unidimensionally, as noted in chapter 2. For example, Laban, recognizing that dance begins in a conception of feeling, believed that dance expressed actual emotion, whereas Langer argued the opposite, that the emotion was symbolic. Research suggests that there are several distinct (though sometimes concurrent) relationships between dance and emotion. First, emotion may stimulate dance in the immediate sense. Feeling a particular emotion, the performer expresses it through dancing. Second, emotion may be recollected as a stimulus to dance in the Stanislavski tradition. In this situation the dancer tries to re-create an emotion through remembering earlier situations in which it was felt. Third, the dancer may recollect emotion and express it symbolically, illusionarily not actually. Fourth, dancing may induce emotion.[2] Such energetic physical activity may lead to the dancer's altered state of consciousness through changes in brain wave frequencies, adrenalin, and blood-sugar content. Giddiness may occur through high speed or sensory rhythmic stimulation in more than one sensory mode. Kinesthetic stress, overexertion, and fatigue also increase susceptibility. Fifth, audience reaction to an ongoing performance may evoke the performer's emotions, which, in turn, affect the dancing. For example, modern dancer Erick Hawkins told me at the American Dance Festival that audience laughter at a time when the dancers did not intend to evoke humor or nervousness disrupted the performer's concentration and hurt the "mindset" and consequent performance. Sixth, however the dancer expresses emotion, through immediate or recollected feeling, the dancer attempts to evoke emotion (although not necessarily a specific one) in the audience.

What did the Smithsonian American Dance Experience and World Explorer Series performers think about the relationship between emotion and dancing? Half of the dancers said they had to have the feeling in order to move. A third explained that they had to have an idea of what they wanted to get across to the audience and then they got the feeling, and finally moved. The next most frequent pattern (22 percent of the performers) was to move and then get the feeling. Seventeen percent said they followed the sequence of idea, moving, and then feeling.

The study found some support for Langer's theory that emotion is recollected in tranquillity. However, there was also support for a broader perspective and alternative ways of expressing emotion through dancing. Several dancers reported that they expressed real emotion in successful performances, although during the progression of a dance the expression may vary between being symbolic and real. The relationships between emotion and movement did not follow a universal pattern. Further inquiry is necessary to determine if dancers within a genre with its culture and method of training share emotion-movement patterns. For example, the ancient Indian treatise on classical dance serves as a directive for various regional forms throughout India and beyond its shores.

AUDIENCES

The burden of the performer-audience connection is well put by dancer Murray Louis, who reversed his usual role and joined an audience.

> I found a seat, took off my coat, muffler, hat, gloves, boots, and collapsed. I was exhausted. It was the first chance I had to catch my breath all day, and my energies sagged to the bottom of my wooden chair. (What a way

for a concert to begin! What an unfair handicap I was placing on the artists! They were now faced with lifting me from my own distractions into their world. I was bringing nothing. I was too tired. It took two dances before I could bring my sensibilities to an evaluating level.)[3]

Another problem is the diversity of the audience. Dance critic John Martin explained the situation:

> . . . the general public is not in any sense uniform in taste and background. Those whose experience has been meager, or whose kinesthetic equipment is in defective working order, or both, will be able to take very little in the way of margin; they will find the slightest innovation sufficient to hold them, even if it is only to place the three legs of the eternal triangle in different geographical or social locales. On the other hand, those whose contacts with living have been larger and more intense will be able to respond to substantial margins, provided that they are kinesthetically awake; a considerable proviso, for the two things do not always go together. What pleases one class will never please the other, and since the former far outnumber the latter in the present state of the world, the genuine artist is likely to find himself always with a minority audience in his own day, and through no fault of his own.[4]

To what extent were there universal or culturally patterned perceptions of emotions and clues to them? Humans, as members of a species, are born with capacities to differentiate color, to discriminate background noise from patterned sound, and to recognize the human face and body among competing visual stimuli. These are not learned, but genetically determined capabilities. Patterns that are "hard wired" within the human brain, claim Charles J. Lumsden and Edward O. Wilson in *Genes, Mind and Culture*,[5] lead to certain commonalities among all humans. However, the combined action of many minds in different times and places creates cultural differences. Some individuals because of their strength or personal situation break or expand cultural constraints. Thus both nature and culture predispose us to our responses to performance.

Modern dancer Mary Wigman in 1933 described dance as "a language which all humans understand."[6] Implicit in this statement was the notion of the communication of ideas and feelings through movement. Dance historian and patron Lincoln Kirstein wrote in 1973, "Dance is a universal language transcending every local dialect of Spanish or Portuguese."[7] However, Elizabeth Selden, writing in 1935, modified this assumption.[8] She believed that "national differences" give the universal language of dance "varying localized accents." Modern dance pioneer Doris Humphrey went further: "The strictly patterned gestures of emotional states, those so often occurring as to be easily readable, are not so numerous as one might think."[9]

In the Smithsonian dance concerts, audience responses reflected both common perception and cultural patterns based on some background characteristics. Dance is not a universal but many "languages" and "dialects" with cognate expressions.

*Cross-Concert Perceptions and Background.* By examining the concerts as a whole, considering 598 respondents, we find aggregate patterns that appeared from the analysis of the most frequently mentioned emotions—anger, caring, happiness, playfulness, pride, and vitality—and the most commonly identified categories of clues—actions of gesture and locomotion; body parts of face, eye, shoulder/arm, hand; and energy quality of movement—with the most salient background variables of sex, ethnicity, occupation, and knowledge about dance. It should be noted that the aggregate and within-concert findings may differ. Given the issues explained in the appendix, the associations of perceptions and clues are suggestive rather than conclusive. They point to directions for further inquiry.

Whether a respondent was male or female did not appear to make a difference in the cross-concert perception of emotions and clues to them. This finding runs counter to distributions within some concerts and to research on nonverbal communication. It may be that as a whole men who attend a dance concert are as sensitive as women, who usually are more aware than men in other settings. At the Kathakali concert, for example, the proportion of women who perceived anger through the clues of gesture, face, and hands was greater than the proportion of men. Twice as great a proportion of women as men perceived the emotion of disgust through the face. Research (cited in chapter 1) has shown that women are more sensitive to signs of displeasure because of their socialization to giving to others and their less privileged status as a group. At the Kuchipudi concert, more men than women thought the performer conveyed the emotions of happiness, perhaps reflecting men's greater enjoyment of conflict; women perceived more competition, perhaps empathizing with the goddess's dual aspects of good and evil. At the RDT concert, men, who share a gender orientation to sports, saw vitality through the clue of energy more than women.

Throughout this empirically informed essay I have pointed out that the meaning of movement for participants in a performance depends upon the expectations within which it is embedded. The perception of performance relies on the way the dance "meshes" with existing mental maps. Knowledge of dance and its ecology mediates the relationship in the performer-audience connection. Across concerts, respondents who described themselves as very knowledgeable about dance were less likely to perceive happiness (42 percent of 99) and vitality (45 percent) in dance than those somewhat knowledgeable (52 percent of 301 for happiness and 50 percent for vitality) or not at all (57 percent of 155 and 50 percent of 78). Dancing is commonly associated with celebrations, from school dances to weddings. Therefore spectators less sophisticated about dance may see the more stereotypic emotions in dance. Recall the Dunn concert: respondents very knowledgeable about dance did not perceive the eroticism noted by individuals reporting themselves to be somewhat or not at all knowledgeable. The former may have focused more on form than content.

There were some cross-concert ethnic differences in perception. Distinct cultural patterns appeared for Indians in contrast with members of other groups. Indians overwhelmingly (91 percent of 34) identified anger, whereas less than a third of the United States whites (30 percent of 111) did. The clues of face, eyes, and hand to identify anger differed between Indians and other groups. Sixty-two percent of the Indians saw anger in the face, 47 percent in the eyes, and 47 percent in the hands, whereas the figures for United States whites were 17 percent, 8 percent, and 12 percent, respectively. These clues were far more important for Indians, perhaps because they were more familiar with the mythological stories and personalities of the characters who appear in dance. The classical tradition emphasizes the face and eyes both in gesture and makeup, and the hands articulate distinct signs. In most other dance forms the hands do not convey such precise meaning. The Indians (77 percent) were also more aware of pride, more than twice as often as United States whites (36 percent) and Filipinos (47 percent of 15). At the Kathakali concert, Indian respondents also differed in their greater recognition of disgust manifested in the face compared with other groups.

Filipinos (93 percent) more often perceived the emotion of happiness and (67 percent) gesture as a clue than other groups (50 percent and 23 percent for United States whites, 65 percent and 12 percent for Indians, and 80 percent and 20 percent of 10 United States blacks, respectively). Although respondents within concerts perceived playfulness, there were differences across concerts in how ethnic groups identified it. Filipinos focused on gesture (53 percent) and hand (47 percent). By contrast, only 21 percent of United States whites, 15 percent of Indians, and 30 percent of United States blacks saw playfulness through gesture; 11 percent of whites and 18 percent of Indians saw playfulness through the hand.

Occupation was associated with perception of the emotions of caring and happiness. People in the skilled labor category (71 percent of 17) noticed caring far more frequently than those earning their livelihood in other ways (44 percent and less of other groups). The reason is unclear.

Dancers (11 percent of 18) noticed happiness less often than other occupational groups (47 percent or more of people in these job categories). This finding seems to parallel the relationship between knowledge about dance and the perception of happiness. Those who were very knowledgeable about dance saw happiness and vitality less frequently than those who were somewhat or not at all knowledgeable about dance. Both the second and last chapters of this book call attention to the stereotypes about dance for joy and emotional expression to the exclusion of its potential to convey ideas about form and substance. The cognoscenti are aware of the greater potential of dance.

In the tap and RDT concerts, where there appeared to be little or no association of audience perception and background variables, the dance form did seem to be not layered with complex emotional meaning. Rather, the dance had comparatively broad-stroked visual images. The audiences also tended to be homogeneous. However, in the simple gesture language of the Filipino dance, as well as the complex gesture language of the classical Indian dances, there was ethnic variation.

Comparing clues to emotions within each concert (the tables appear in each performance chapter) to see if there were patterns across the concerts, I found that audience members identified body parts as clues to anger about three times as often as other categories of clues.[10]

At the tap and Philippine concerts, spectators identified action and body parts as clues to perceiving caring. Gesture and face figured twice as often as other dimensions within their respective categories at the Philippine concert. Fifty-eight percent of the clues to caring at the Kabuki performance were in action, especially gesture. By contrast, 71 percent of the clues to caring in Kathakali were body parts. The Dunn concert was distinct from these concerts: spectators noticed the quality of movement in the dancers' relation as clues to caring (58 percent of 52 clues).

Spectators identified happiness by action and body parts in the tap, Kuchipudi, RDT, Kabuki, and Philippine concerts. The face was seen twice as often as other body parts in the Asian performances.

Playfulness clues were in action and body parts at the tap, RDT, Philippine, and Kabuki concerts (gesture and face standing out in the last). Twice as many clues were in body parts as in action at the Kuchipudi and Kathakali concerts. Similar to the case for clues to caring, the Dunn concert was unique, with the movement quality of the dancers' relationship being most notable (54 percent of 91 clues).

At the Philippine concert, audience members saw pride conveyed through action and body parts. However, at the Kuchipudi and Kathakali performances the body parts were clues, 62 percent of the clues at Kuchipudi (twice as many in the face as in other parts) and 67 percent at Kathakali.

Respondents identified vitality at the tap, RDT and Philippine concerts through action and body parts. Quality of movement was also notable at the RDT performance, all body parts at the Philippine. Body parts comprised 60 percent of the clues for Kuchipudi. Kabuki conveyed about twice as many clues through body parts as through action. The Dunn concert diverged here, too, with 86 percent of the clues in quality of movement.

From a limited sample of dances and respondents, we can conclude that there are different clues to identify the same emotion. It may be that a dance genre conveys feelings in a particular way. For example, the Indian Kuchipudi and Kathakali dances, although different, do have roots in a classical heritage and share more than the other concerts. The Dunn avant-garde performance was most different from the others.

The Dunn concert was the most dramatic in illustrating that the same movements may be perceived in diametrically opposite ways. Recall that the audience respondents divided nearly in half about whether emotion was conveyed at all, with 40 percent perceiving eroticism, several respondents reporting feeling sexually aroused in reaction.

On the basis of exploring the spectator identification of emotions and clues to them at eight dance concerts, it is possible to conclude that there is cultural relativism in the perception of emotion in a live interaction. The study findings clearly disprove Sachs's and others' notion that all dance is and gives ecstasy. At the same time there are some internationally recognized feelings and clues to them. Remember the Kathakali actor playing Lord Shiva, who sees his wife Sati return from her father's palace insulted and humiliated. When he points his finger at the woman, audiences East and West understand the feeling and the "I told you so" gesture. An assumption of this odyssey has been that since the dancers draw upon the everyday and special occasions to convey messages, the performer-audience perceptions in concert are likely to exist in the off-stage social interactions of daily life.

## PERFORMER INTENTION AND AUDIENCE RECEPTION

*Emotions and Clues.*   There was a general dovetailing of the emotions the dancers wanted to get across, how they thought they conveyed them, and audience survey respondents' perceptions. Dunn thought he expressed emotions by whatever means the audience perceived them. The RDT dancers' perceptions of how they communicated feeling somewhat paralleled the clues the audience used to recognize the emotions. The same pattern holds for the World Explorer Series. It appears, however, that audience members also perceive emotion through means dancers may not intend. The tappers' thoughts about how they convey feeling did not coincide with audience perception of clues. Spectators saw more clues. Perhaps those audience members who did not "connect" with the performance may have left the concert or did not fill out a survey form. *Feeling in Response to Emotions Perceived.*   The audience survey asked how spectators felt in response to the emotion they perceived onstage.

Their answers were categorized as same/similar, opposite, no emotion, or other. This latter classification included such responses as being interested in the emotions, noting the gracefulness of the dancers, or focusing on the technique of communicating emotion. Illustrative emotions similar to anger were tenseness, excitement; for competition, excitement, arousal, anticipation.

Emotions that occur during the course of everyday social life differ from emotions that occur when one is an observer of others in social interaction. If we are open to vicarious affective experience, and the dancers are effective communicators, we may identify or empathize with them.[11] In the Western world, however, there is distancing, because the audience knows that what happens onstage is pretend and illusionary— play.

Across concerts there was a tendency for dancers and spectators to share feelings in a specific way. Nearly all respondents felt the same or a similar emotion to the one they perceived onstage. The dancers may well have succeeded in meeting esteemed dance critic John Martin's criteria for a good dancer: The dancer's

> movements retain enough of the stuff of common experience to establish an emotional association in the mind of the spectator, but if this were all he accomplished he would have labored vainly as an artist, for he would have conveyed nothing new. It is not the artist's purpose merely to stir up emotional states, but rather by means of this stirring up to lead the receptive mind to an enlarged experience, to a hitherto unrealized truth. This he does by means of his distortion and abstraction; he sets up, along with the familiar patterns, such departures from them as to give them a new cast, a new meaning, in accordance with his original intention.[12]

Illustrative of the "empathy" between emotions the dancers conveyed intentionally or unintentionally and spectator feeling in response was the Philippine concert survey findings. There were 190 responses indicating that spectators felt the same or a similar emotion to the one they perceived in the dance, whereas there was only one reporting an opposite feeling, and three, no emotional feeling. The avant-garde Dunn and Cowles/Davies concerts, in spite of some hostile audience reaction, had similar responses, including respondents perceiving boredom or eroticism onstage and feeling the same.

THEMES

Similar themes appeared in the varied dance series. Accompanying the dance boom is an appetite for every kind of dance. This interest evokes nostalgia for the past. The hoofers who have seen better times for their dancing continue to struggle to do what they believe in. Although they have lost their former black following, new groups have discovered them.

The Utah modern dance company attempted to portray how we came to be where we are in the evolution of an American strain of dance. The dancers acknowledged and paid tribute to the pioneers in the American dance heritage.

The Philippine dancers sought to share their nation's legacy with each other and with Americans as they showcased reconstructed dances. Similarly, Indians are reviving traditions that were stamped out by British colonialists. Japanese women are seeking to regain preeminence in a dance form they originated, but which men usurped and developed.

A second thread running through the concerts was transformation: who dances what, when, where, how, and for whom. In what is called "traditional" dance—traditional to a particular time and place—the ever-present dynamic of change retains its force.[13] We learn how "folk," "social," and "religious" forms become modified in response to or as a prelude to the dynamics of life in nondance spheres. In contemporary forms, such as those of Dunn and Cowles/Davies, there are also modifications of traditions. The RDT comprises young dancers, trained differently from their forebears, who perform reconstructions of ancestral heroic pioneer figures. Kathakali performers are no longer solely from selected families who pass on dance lore from one generation to the next. Now dancers graduate from academies. From village courtyard and temple festival settings, Indian dance performances have become part of series subscriptions in secular clubs at home and in foreign cities. Stages and meanings have also changed for Kabuki and Philippine dance as they moved from village to world urban settings and from devotional, sexual enticement, or folk celebration and contest to artistic presentation and affirmation of gender or ethnic attributes.

For dances labeled traditional, the issue of authenticity is one that performers and critics must struggle with. Just how much transformation is appropriate before the form is considered new? Authenticity is a multimeaning term, usually with vague criteria to judge a particular dance form. The degree of similarity of a dance to a particular time, place, creator, or people is often hotly debated.

Gender role was a third theme in the dance series. The tap, Philippine, and Kathakali concerts presented traditional sex roles. Recall the comment the female economist offered about Kathakali: "Most vivid is the clear depiction of the relative status of the two sexes. This permeates the entire performance. The female is always submissive and even an attempt at anger is subdued." Kabuki, too, presents distinct images for male and female. Men and women have their own patterns in Philippine dance. As they do in other arenas of American life, men compete in tap. Each performer improvises with individual freedom and attempts to win recognition for his achievement. Although men and women had different movements in early American modern dance, women moved in ways they previously had not. These feminists heralded further women's liberation in other areas of social life.

The post-modern dance exemplified by Dunn and Cowles blurs sex role distinctions. We see unisexuality as both men and women move in the same way through time and space and with effort. Another kind of blurring occurs in Kabuki and Kuchipudi dances, where women play both men's and women's roles. In the Kuchipudi performance, Indrani danced the combined qualities of male and female found in an individual deity. Men performed both male and female roles in Kathakali. However, in this genre, "masculinely" built men played male roles and "femininely" built men played female roles.

The presence of contrasting dualities constituted a fourth unintended theme in the two Smithsonian dance series. An audience member wrote insightfully: "A reaction to something as complex as the dance evokes complex responses having to do with classic inner conflicts regarding male/female, good/evil, life/death—also the almost frightening beauty of the complex working out of these conflicts in an artistic form such as dance. There is considerable awe involved in considering the depth of human nature and its manifestations." I have mentioned the conflicts between tradition and innovation, male and female, audience passivity and audience participation. In tap dancing there is also a conflict between the individual's free expression and the need to conform to the music. Kuchipudi portrays not only male versus female, but also conflicting female qualities of good and evil. In RDT preparation for dance performnce there is the history of conflict between working communally and working with an artistic director. In the Cowles/Davies concert, the duality is between the film and live image of the dancer. Kabuki deals with the human/nature duality and solves it by merging the two; wisteria and the pine tree are symbols of human lovers.

MAKING A BETTER CONNECTION
In spite of the size and growth of the arts, and especially dance—the fastest growing art in the United States—the arts are in desperate shape. Financial costs rise more rapidly than revenues. Funds from government, corporations, foundations, and private patrons are scarce. There are many demands on depressed economic sources at the same time that inflation increases. This situation for the dance requires additional revenues, enlarged audiences, and narrow deficits if the health of the arts and opportunities for dancers are to be ensured.

With the arts boom there has also been an arts management need and expansion. There is growing recognition that a marketing program is the bridge between the artist and the audience. The critic cannot perform this role alone. Professional dancers need audiences. Sidney Levy of the Northwestern University Graduate School of Management points out that "enlargement of the audience for the arts requires taking into account the perceptions of the potential audience."[14] In 1852 Gustave Flaubert warned: "Between the crowd and ourselves no bond exists. Alas for the crowd; alas for us, especially."

In the United States, theatre arts are generally the preserve of the elite. Sometimes members of the nonaudience for the arts, especially low-income or fundamentalist religious groups, feel distant and react hostilely. The hope is to create a bond between at least a portion of the crowd and the dancer. Where the bond is weak, some type of marketing or promotion is required, in which the dance is offered to the audience for the price of attention, emotion, and action. The elite, who have many choices, may have to be wooed to attend a dance performance. Dances are not necessarily or easily created to meet the needs and wants of an audience. P. David Searles, formerly of the National Endowment for the Arts, said a principle that has stood the test of time is a dancer doing well what he or she does and telling people what that is.[15]

This study of the eight Smithsonian dance concerts has focused only on a small area of people's perceptions, reasonings, feelings, and, indirectly, the place and meaning that dance has in some of their lives. The audience responses did, however, inadvertently provide insight into some critical problems: attracting spectators and building a loyal following. While dancers come to performances with their training and creative impulses and projection techniques, audiences come to the performances with their expectations shaped by individual and social history. The lifeblood of the performing arts, the audience must overcome the burden of ticket prices, the availability of substitutes, and getting to the concert. Once there, spectators have some notions about the nature of performance, dance, and criteria to measure a performance's adequacy.

Dances from a different culture and the avant-garde require spectator guidance, according to audience respondents at these concerts. In an urban pluralist society, a prospective member of an audience for an "artistic event" may not have the cultural background (whether derived from socialization into a group or formal education). Program notes, demonstrations, lectures, and books substitute for what is assumed in traditional culture—commonality of symbols and familiarity with how they are presented. Dance gestures in American culture have a minimal codification in ballet and are diffuse and semantically individualistic in other dance genres compared to the stylized, bold, and subtle dance forms of the Orient. Hence, the meaning of such dances is inaccessible to Westerners. In the absence of exposure to program information, familiar story line, or broad universal stage action, audience members tend to focus on the "gracefulness" of movement or opulence of costume—simple levels of artistry. Movement metaphors are not perceived by audience members because they do not share a common culture.

Society's avant-garde, both attracting and repelling, is often a cultural group with specific values, orientations, and codes and messages of communication. Such a group poses an apartness between itself and the broader culture that is akin to the distinctiveness of a foreign culture. La Meri, one of the first performers to bring exotic dances to the United States, pointed out that Middle and Far Eastern forms are hard for Americans to understand because "we're a loud people in a hurry. Understanding quiet [also present in some avant-garde performances] is a difficult emotional task."

So, in light of the difficulties posed by the avant-garde as well as the exotic, non-Western performing arts and the public policy/business and arts needs, how do performers and audience members connect? The lack of some intervention for audiences, including Americans and the foreign-born who lose touch with their own cultural heritage, restricts the possible appreciative audience to a very few. Knowledge about the tenets of a particular dance form certainly is a prerequisite to a good performer-audience connection. Unprepared spectators cannot be expected to perceive emotional or other messages the way a knowledgeable audience would.

At the Dance Critics Association Conference on Ethnic Dance, I asked La Meri what she thought was the responsibility of performers to explain their dance. She said that lengthy program notes were read at home, if at all. From her experience, it was important to introduce the dance and "give the audience some inkling of what they were to see onstage or otherwise they would wring their hands. They approach performances from the head and want to know the story." She believes critics need to know the primary reason for a dance and to have more awareness of the emotional dynamics. "They paid too much attention to costume and technique and virtuosity." Perhaps audiences need explanations of how a new or unfamiliar form is the same as or different from what they are accustomed to.

Although Americans have seen many more kinds of dance with the increase in concerts, television programs, and films about the art, there is still a need to amplify awareness of performance ecology. Previews and press packets given to critics assist them in their communication with audiences. However, spatial constraints of newspapers and periodicals limit what the critic can do. The performer may need to go directly to the audience or through the marketing process. Nearly half a century ago John Martin laid the problem on the line:

It is a truism that the creative artists accepted by any generation are already in their tombs, and obviously the reason for this is modernism. A man's life does not last long enough to allow his contemporaries to catch up with him if he is trying to tell them something new. Sheer animal inertia objects to being disturbed; "well enough" resists to the hilt if it is not let alone. The artist who succeeds in winning a quick acceptance is the one who is telling yesterday's truths.[16]

This study has explored the dynamics of theatrical human connections, a reflection of and influence on everyday social relations. I began by questioning what is universal and culturally specific in the communication of emotion, a critical dimension of performance, from the perspective of participants in an exchange. The views of the dancers and spectators suggest that such communication must be seen within the performance ecology and the concerns and controversies in dance and society.

Chapters 1 and 2 prepared the way for exploring the relationship between dancing and dance viewing at the Smithsonian concerts, which were then presented. This chapter has summarized findings and challenges across concerts. I have tried to show performer intention, audience perception of emotions and clues relied upon and response to the emotions, and some of the dynamics that enter into the calculus of the dancer-audience connection.

Dancers perform, perceptions transform the dance into ideas about dance, and these circle back upon it. Although the curtain has fallen on the Smithsonian concerts, memories linger. Perception is the gateway to contemplation. The excitement and impact of performance have not been measured. However, there is evidence that terpsichorean tendrils stimulate beholders' minds to work and to consider a variety of subjects without falling apart or feeling threatened. A literal means of communication about sensitive themes might be paralyzing. Means too abstract may fail to break through defenses. The following chapter explores one aspect of the ferment of dance performance—the union of mentality and matter in dance beyond the stage.[17] These pages prepare the way for new insights in other performer-audience connections.

# POSTSCRIPT

## CHAPTER 12

# The Punch of Performance: Re-Creation

Dancers, as acknowledged earlier, take movements, ideas, and feelings from everyday and special occasions and transform them in some way. Performance is immediate, emotionally charging the performer and audience in sporadic or continuous interchange if both are receptive. Dancing often generates electricity and reflection about it that linger long after a performance in the theatre or informal setting. Dances we do, see in the street, onstage, or on film or television, or read or hear about sometimes haunt us. These dances can reinforce what is in society or spearhead what may be. The pulse of human affairs is action—reaction and interaction. We do not know which dances will ramify in our thoughts and behavior to shape or explain social and personal realities. Humans have the capacity for memory: the intellect often moves nimbly.

Recall that the activity humans choose occurs relative to a knowledge base. The background material on each concert was presented because perception amounts not just to seeing what is there but to apprehending in accordance with previously accumulated experience and established categories.[1] The dancers, we realize, work elements of sensation into meaningful statements. Audience members transform their perceptions into the experience of dance viewing. And then audience members or dancers, who are also spectators to themselves and other dancers, if sufficiently moved emotionally, re-create the experience, real or imagined, in another transformation, another kind of statement. Of concern to us here is the transformation of perceptions and reactions concerning dance performance into words, that is, movement from stage to page. This metamorphosis of the dance experience into vernacular and literary language has power precisely because it exists in a community that can share and react to its meaning. Emotional reactions depend on how a situation is understood and thus constitute ways of knowing. Dance, I have indicated, is embedded in a social context and carries cultural baggage. Just as individuals pack somewhat distinctively—selecting items and arranging them—so, too, they may attribute different meaning to the same dance referent. The same attribution process occurs with many words in the English language. Just as dance-viewing cognoscenti have enriching historical perspectives, individuals with dance and literature backgrounds have a broader and deeper understanding of dance metaphors.

Because our culture emphasizes language as the supreme mode of communication, our use of dance concepts suggests the emotional punch and magic of dance performance. Metaphors, ways of commenting on one kind of experience in terms of another, make the strange familiar and unleash compelling images that generate new insights.[2] We use a specific concept to characterize a system, thing, or process. Because the body is ubiquitous and sentient, its appearance in dance performance taps potent, dramatic, and easy-to-recall sources of images. As human behavior, dance is grounded in our basic spatial, perceptual, environmental, and social experience. Dance as metaphor is a label operating outside its usual range. It occurs in many dominant areas of human interest: political, economic, technological, and social. In figurative speech, the use of dance allows us to focus on different aspects of a phenomenon, even to see something nonhuman as human. Referring to the people who dance, the myriad forms that abound, the preparation, occasion, and performance, the dance metaphor gives form and purpose to other aspects of social life. The introduction cast dance as one node in a performance web in which dance and society mutually influence each other.[3]

Our way of talking and writing ratify or modify our perception of dance. The significance of a dance performance and its context can be reinvented through talking and writing about it.

Given the view of life as theatre or the acceptance that life is theatre, it is not surprising to find that the concept of dance developed from past performances is used figuratively in vernacular and literary language: "Dancers are the dance. After all, what is this art but one long continuing path, its frail thread handed from dancer to dancer, leading us all through the labyrinth. . . . The dance is a fire, fueled by everyone touched with the madness of dance, not by those who are drawn to the light, but by those who go mad from the heat and who burn."[4] Thus spoke renowned choreographer and dancer Murray Louis about the emotional intensity of dance.[5] The audience can empathize with the dancer and feel the energy, time, space, ideas, and feelings of the dance. And after the performance, when the dance remains in some way etched in memory, the replay of the dancing surges forth in our thought to evoke the fire in a new transformation. Alternatively, capping metaphor with metaphor, educator Jean Cunningham pointed out to me that those who are attracted by its light but not touched by its flame may make new connections.

In previous chapters I have described eight Smithsonian concerts. It is difficult to know the impact of the performances upon the participants. I can, however, suggest how dance performances from various times and places emotionally resonate in the English language. It is relevant to note that much dance has been primarily for doing rather than merely for viewing. Many of these folk and social dances, however, end up being performed onstage and in motion pictures. The waltz, for example, became a basic dance in classical ballet: such celebrated choreographers as Marius Petipa of the past and George Balanchine of the present have used the waltz for large ensembles as well as pas de deux.[6] Thus references to dances in the literature are often rich in meaning. Some of the themes that weave through the Smithsonian concerts also resound in the metaphorical use of dance.

You may remember that in the discussion of the history of attitudes toward the body, emotion, and dance, we found that there are conflicting perspectives on dance. I referred to the dance of Salome and the dance of David before the ark, the Greek fear of dance arousing passions, churches railing against dancing excesses, capitalists deprecating its distractions, and rebels reasserting sentient humanity through dance. These and a host of positive-negative contrasts appear in language about dance to reflect upon dancing and to comment metaphorically and emotionally upon other aspects of life.

THE MANY METAPHORS OF DANCE

The poignancy and allure of the dance metaphor lie in the contradictory images of historical heritage and current events. I found the following examples in proverb collections, a year's casual but regular reading of the *New York Times*, the *Washington Post*, the *Village Voice*, and *Newsweek*, and irregular reading of other publications. The inclusion of material, suggestive rather than complete, illustrates how common the dance metaphor has been in popular speech and writing.

Let us look at the use of the term *dance* in general. We find it portraying many aspects of life: negative feelings about foolishness, the anxiety and dangers of courtship and sexuality, the dismay of disorder, and the excitement of fantasy; and positive feelings about creativity, order, proper social relations and hierarchy, seriousness, joy, and respect. References to dance reflect both the low and high esteem with which people view it and the bodily expression of emotion.

Negative emotion about dance, and lack of awareness of its cognitive complexity, appears in the saying "the greater the fool the better the dancer."[7] A derivative is, "Since you piped during the summer, now dance during the winter." The proverb "the dancer must pay the piper" similarly suggests that the improvident must suffer the consequences of their acts. The expression "never was a dancer a good scholar" and "good dancers have mostly better heels than heads" support the assumed erroneous dichotomy between mind and body. Intellectual affairs require a regime that physical divertissement undercuts.

"Sidestepping: The Dance of Two Mayors under Fire" is the headline for an article that describes black leaders who evade sensitive issues. The metaphor of dance alludes to their recoiling from serious engagement.[8]

Proverbs over the years acknowledge dance as courtship behavior, with or without serious intent of finding a marriage partner. Thus the metaphor of "The Legal Mating Dance" is an apt description for the fall ritual of platoons of corporate lawyers visiting prestigious law schools to woo top students. In the hiring halls, connections are made in a stylized manner comparable to the decorum of many social dance occasions.[9]

It is said, "Dancing is the child of Music and of Love" and "In dance the hand hath liberty to touch." Saying "my dancing days are done" refers to feelings of regret or resignation about settling down or getting old. The adage "an old man dancing is a child in mind" describes an elderly person's rousingly youthful attitude and behavior.

The dangers of heterosexual dancing were well known: "When you go to dance, take heed whom you take by the hand." Sixteenth-century moralist John Northbrooke (*Against Dicing*, 1577) remarked, "Through dancing many maidens have been unmaidened, whereby I may say it is the storehouse and nursery of bastardy." Dangers for men appear in the sayings " 'twas surely the devil that taught women to dance" and "refrain from dancing, which was the means that lost John Baptist's head."

In the Renaissance, one gloss for *dance* was "copulation." There was a ribald association between the two in such songs as "The Irish Jigg":

Then nothing but Dancing our Fancy could please.
We lay on the Grass and danc'd at our ease;
I down'd with my Breeches and off with my Whigg,
And we fell a Dancing the Irish Jigg.

The bawdy metaphor follows in the tradition of Aristophanes.[10]

Humanizing the nonhuman by speaking of "Appliances That Dance" in a 1981 article on coping in Argentina (where things do not work as they are supposed to) implies a negative feeling toward dance. The dance metaphor refers to moving disruptively or playfully instead of working productively. In another instance a writer uses the literal human activity of dance in a particular context as both illustrative and symbolic of an inhuman, sad state: one night in Lima, Peru, the observer saw unemployed poor children who "dance in the street for food money."[11] The act refers to the nation's inept economic planning.

The idea of dance as fanciful joy can be juxtaposed dramatically to grim reality: the greediness of the OPEC moguls. "Before visions of bargain fuel begin dancing in your heads, however, two sobering facts should be mentioned. . . ." [12] In the same vein, an article titled "Dancer in the Goodness of Government" discusses the first incumbent United States senator found guilty of a criminal charge since 1905. Responding to Pete Williams's insistence that the government had done it to him, a commentator says: "It was so heady, that dance in the clouds of Camelot, that pirouette in the governmental goodness of the Great Society, those endless Pete Williams bills that drew endless editorials that said good going Pete, for sending federal bucks in to help the coal miners, the Chicanos and the kids he came here to save." [13]

The concept of dance not only illuminates through evocative images unhappiness about foolishness, anxiety about courtship, and disgust with disorderliness and fanciful escape, but it captures the opposite: the emotion of happiness with creativity and order. The phrase "the poetry of the foot" recognizes the processes of human imaginative, symbolic development. Psychologists have shown that human play, which includes imitative and imaginative dance, is essential to orderly growth of the child. At first its movements are clumsy and halting; they then become refined. Later they can be put together in various ways. Referring to the machinations of Chinese politics and the positions of Hu and Hua in 1981, the *Economist* writes, "A remarkable piece of political choreography reached what looked like an effortless climax in Peking. . . ." [14] In a brisk three-day session, China's Central Committee disposed of two party chairmen and installed a third.

"Argentina Dances 'The Process,' a Slow Martial Step" heads an article on the junta's planned deliberations and official announcement of the country's new president. "A schedule . . . has been drummed"—yet there was a postponement. Implicit is the concept of dance as a regularly recurring, orderly façade to hide the diversionary, typical postponement of the junta. [15]

It is said, "A dance is a measured pace." Herein dancing evokes emotions of calm and concepts of a specific time, space, effort, movement, and accompaniment. When the dancing masters became popular among the elite, the dance was indeed ordered.

Social hierarchy is explained through the concept of dance. An elder sister was said to "dance barefoot" when a younger one married before her. The saying emphasized the propriety of the eldest marrying first during Shakespeare's time. Surely the older sister danced with light heels (barefoot) but heavy heart. What is usually joyful in this case is ironically sad. "To dance to [or after] a person's pipe [whistle, etc.]" referred to dancers following the music of one person acting at another's instigation. "Jack shall pipe, and Jill shall dance" reflected the assumed order of male dominance, as did the saying, "That's the dance her husband means to lead her."

The sixteenth-century proverb "they who dance are thought mad by those who hear not the music" refers to the notion that incongruous behavior is not socially acceptable. The proverb about the dependency of dance upon music and the dancer upon the person who pays for the music appears in discussions about big business and presidential politics. Speaking of Reagan's first hundred days, editorialists said that the president had imposed his priorities on American politics. "Even liberals are dancing to Mr. Reagan's tune, struggling to find coherence and promise in his still mystifying combination of economic mirrors." [16] He depends heavily upon the support of business and yet has not always acted to please them: "The White House does not set policy to suit them and certainly does not now dance to their tune," wrote Evans and Novak in 1981. [17]

Dancing for someone is a way to honor the individual sincerely or sardonically. Illustrative is the old expression "to dance attendance," which means to wait obsequiously upon a person. It appears in contemporary guise. Describing the Guardian Angels, the young volunteer crime fighters, Juan Williams writes, "The standoff between the Angels and Capitol police is a version of the little dance the Angels do with many people they meet." [18] The Capitol police feel disgust for the youngsters, who are surrounded by TV cameras and tourists, and feel threatened that they might make them appear to be less than best at fighting crime. The metaphor of the "little dance" refers to the disdainful propriety between two groups that hides their strong resentment of each other.

A piece entitled "Dance of the Ambassadors" describes a gathering of ambassadors from nearly every country and the United States secretary of state at the home of an international lawyer who held "a *command performance*. They could have held a war . . . [that] night and nobody would have gone." [19] The affair, held to honor a senator who was the new chairman of the Senate Foreign Relations Committee, had the stature and esteem of the politically motivated ballets during the era of Catherine de Médicis.

The proverb "all are not merry that dance lightly" alludes to the illusion of theatre and to the ironical deceptiveness of appearances; it also alludes to the serious context of some dance or the seriousness of some dance forms. When the United States government issued RIF (Reduction in Force) job termination notices in the Washington area, the job crunch was a sweeping and complicated employment shake-up affecting many of the 366,000 civil servants. "It ripples through the whole system, and there is a domino effect, but many agencies haven't gone through this dance before," explained Claudia Cooley, who chairs the Office of Personnel Management's task force on personnel reductions in the government. [20] Here, dance is a metaphor for serious recognized steps and anxiety about the unfamiliar, the latter being somewhat reminiscent of a youth's first teenage dance.

In an article about whether Ronald Reagan represents the West, and, if so, which West, we read: "Isolated, economically exploited, culturally ignored and politically impotent, the West always had its nabobs, but even small Westerners felt lucky. Their life was a dance at which the federal government, owning nearly half of the territory west of the 100th meridian, called some of the tunes but also paid the band and tried to police against crashers. It was a good dance, neighborly, strenuous, spacious, democratic, mobile and satisfying."[21] Here the joyous and socially esteemed dance for good interpersonal relations explains the quality of life in the past. Reference to calling tunes and paying the band for a dance echoes the old proverbs about social control. The saying "he dances well to whom fortune pipes" refers to dancing for happiness.

I have examined examples of the use of the concept of dance as it reflects upon many areas of human interest, communicates emotional associations, and creates a climate affecting attitudes of potential dance participants and the performer-audience connection. Old proverbs and current expressions about dance refer to social dancing in general. There are also references to the punch of performance of specific genres of dance. The particular characteristics of these dances denote and connote cognitive and emotional meanings about ideas, activities, and people outside of dance.

The expression "to dance Barnaby" in the seventeenth century meant to dance a quick movement and also to move expeditiously—motivated by any emotion. "To dance the Tyburn jig" meant to be hanged. So did "to dance upon nothing." Emotional associations would vary according to who was being hanged.

What was called the "dance of death" from the twelfth to the sixteenth centuries probably originated in the medieval sermons and dance-plays on death that emphasized its terrors to frighten sinners into repentance. A performer would beckon people to the world beyond during the period of the unprecedented epidemic of Black Death. This terror caught unwilling captives of all social classes. A set pattern of movement evolved with musical accompaniment and processional design. Symptoms of bread and grain ergot poisoning led some of the sickly to seek relief from pain through dance. Ecstatic dancing was considered of curative value and efficacious in warding off death. Dances of death were also connected with wakes for the dead and the rebirth of the soul to everlasting life. At the graves of family, friend, and martyrs, dancing was thought to comfort the dead and to encourage resurrection.

Memories of the idea and emotion of the dance of death linger and assume new forms. For example, modern dancer Mary Wigman choreographed a "Dance of Death" and ballet choreographer Flemming Flindt, a "Triumph of Death" in the twentieth century. The title "The Irish Dance of Death" heads an article about the Irish Republican Army's terrorism and the Protestant killer-squads.[22] This medieval dance metaphor describing the eye-for-an-eye bloodletting that precludes peace alludes to the horrendous history of human suffering. The Soviet government newspaper *Izvestia* said that President Reagan's buildup of the United States nuclear arsenal was "setting the stage for 'dances of death' that would be countered by the Soviet Union."[23] Here the dance metaphor refers to fears for the future. In the *Guardian*, a writer on economics in London is quoted as saying about the newspapers' bingo warfare, "It's part of the very long drawn-out dance of death going on in Fleet Street."[24] A British politician's speech is described as exposing "the ritualised dance of death that the great Conservative debate has now become."[25] The dance imagery creates its associated emotional ambience.

The fandango is a lively Spanish dance in triple time performed to the accompaniment of castanets or tambourines. As a metaphor it describes California's passionate struggle between its pride in not charging tuition to residents who attend the state's public higher education system and the state's low budget allocation of resources to the system. Thus we read in a *Los Angeles Times* editorial: "The financial fandango heated up when the Legislature cut $10.5 million from the UC budget for next year."[26]

In the introduction I mentioned the metaphor of a "mannerly forensic minuet" to describe the emotionally restrained presidential candidate's televised debate between John Anderson and Ronald Reagan. The metaphor refers to the elegant demeanor, style, and pace of this courtly, undramatic, slow, graceful dance with forward balancing and bowing, toe pointing, artifice, and reserve. The minuet was vertical, with the performer's torso still, while the head tilted and turned in theatrical understatement. Forearms, wrists, fingers, lower legs, and feet moved mincingly and decoratively.[27]

From the late seventeenth century to the revolutionary era in France and England, the minuet was a class badge of the elite. The French court tamed for its use what was originally a fast, joyous folk dance from the Poitou region of France. Untutored peasants, indulgently physical, danced with unfettered gusto as their torsos initiated and responded to movements of the arms and legs. In contrast, well-bred gentlemen and ladies danced with refinement as part of their formalized social exchanges. The minuet had restrained classical values of clarity, balance, and regularity. No individual embellishment was permitted; expressiveness was out of bounds. Manuals explained the rules and intricate steps, and dancing masters spent hours with aristocratic students before they could perform in public. The dance protocol reflected the performers' social rank. Hosts for minuets carefully researched the background of each guest to determine who would open the ball and in what order each guest would step out onto the floor. With a highly controlled vitality and disdain for revealing inner feelings, as well as ordered equilibrium and weightlessness, couples moved away and together again and again, usually keeping their focus on each other.

When literary agents called President Carter, the *Washington Post* covered the story under the headline "The Great Post-Election Memoir Minuet." Carla Hall reported, "These are a few of the opening steps in the Memoir Minuet, a post-election tradition danced by publishers and the soon-to-be unemployed government officials. Each step is deftly taken, and both partners are initially coy."[28] In a column titled "The Mitterrand Minuet" about the 1981 French election, Jack Anderson said, "When Vice President Bush expressed the Reagan administration's concern over the inclusion of four Communists in the new French cabinet, and President François Mitterand told the United States to mind its own business, both men were performing a political ritual as formalized and artificial as a minuet."[29]

Earlier I noted how the metaphor of the "podium polka" described the last night of the 1980 Democratic convention when observers were trying to interpret the gesture language of the supposedly friendly candidates. The polka, an informal happy people's recreational dance, was used to characterize the Democratic party as the common person's party.

Contrary to what is often assumed, the polka is not the national dance of Poland.[30] The most popular dance there today is the tango, which I will discuss later. Danced in Poland and all over Europe, the polka originated in Bohemia (Czechoslovakia) about 1830. This peasant dance with its hop and skip was in 2/4 time and usually ended with a fast gallop. It reached the fashionable ballrooms of Prague, Vienna, and Paris in the mid-nineteenth century. For many mid-European ethnic groups in the United States today, the polka is a symbolic and emotional link with the "old country." Polish immigrants who became workers in coal mining, steel, tanning, and meat-packing identified with the dance. Today polka clubs exist throughout the United States. The relatively small Polish-American middle class, however, seeks a different image associated with the aristocracy and intelligentsia.[31] It prefers the polonaise. (This dance originated about the mid-seventeenth century as a dignified, ceremonial warriors' triumphal march. The polonaise appears in classical ballet, for example, in "Swan Lake.") Theatregoers may have seen a transformation of the polka in Jerome Robbins's staged rendition called "Circus Polka."

The soft-shoe, also called a "song and dance," was light-hearted entertainment. At the turn of the century the jig, a happy dance, lost its popularity, as did the clog. Soft leather replaced wood soles. A blend of dance that was part of minstrelsy and later common in Broadway jazz, the soft-shoe stressed elegance, well-dressed strutters, delicacy, and ease. Minstrelsy's most famous dance, "The Essence of Old Virginia," came from the shuffle, a dragging, sliding step, and led to the early soft-shoe. The latter had slow tempo, old-fashioned "darkey" steps, bastard clog, and southern tunes.

The headline "Tom Puccio and Bill Webster/The Soft-Shoe Dancers" covers a story about "Abscam" investigations and attempted evasiveness. Nat Hentoff says at one point, "Puccio executed a not particularly skillful soft-shoe dance around the defense attorneys' questions, concerning a book about his Justice Department career." [32] In another case, we read "Cable TV Song and Dance"—"A traveling road show featuring some of Prince George's County's most prominent political figures has been roaming from town to town, like a local version of 'The Music Man,' spinning a tale of riches and glamor available to town officials through the wonders of cable television." [33]

Entertainers often rode the nightclub circuit, and musical shows were written about these people who often beguiled their audiences. In this case one representative of two national cable television companies was a former vaudeville-style song-and-dance man. Americans are known to say, "Don't give me that song and dance," or "I got it for a song and dance" to refer to something that is frivolous and not worth much. [34]

The tango originated about 1880 in Argentina at houses of prostitution. [35] Experiences of a transient, isolated, and frustrated existence in addition to fears of social, economic, and sexual failures constitute the lore of the tango. The dance reflects the pimp's repertory of carefully studied postures and gestures. His straight, unmoving upper body and smooth steps reflect patterns in the underworld's duels. The slightly forward tilt of the spine perhaps results from the pimp's elegant high-heeled shoes. Male-female relations are the central theme of what was a daringly suggestive dance: an active, powerful, dominant man and a passive, docile, submissive female. The man advances slightly inclined over the woman, who never escapes his embrace and overpowering control. This close embrace caused the pope to issue a judgment on the morality of the tango when respectable men learned the scandalous dance in brothels and took it to Paris, and it then spread throughout the world.

The tango has had its metamorphoses. In 1912 New York City cafes inaugurated afternoon dances called "thé dansants" or "tango teas." For the price of a drink or a relatively small admission fee, single and married women could dance; management hired partners for them. [36] These thé dansants were inaugurated about the same time in England and lasted into the 1930s. New Yorkers could participate in a thé dansant at the Pierre as late as the end of the 1960s.

In the theatre we see the tango in Eliot Feld's "A Soldier's Tale." It is about the horrors of war, including the pimp and prostitute who prey upon its men, living and dead. The dance evokes mixed feelings: arousal and contempt. For the New York City Ballet's 1982 Stravinsky Festival, George Balanchine choreographed "Tango," emphasizing the emotion of love. Hans van Manen created "Five Tangos"; Luc de Layresse, "Three Easy Tangos."

An article titled "The 'Coup Tango' and Other Political Hits and Misses: By One Measure, Madrid Cools Down" is about Spain's terrorists and an attempted coup.[37] Colonel Tejero, locked up and awaiting trial, has his praises sung in "the hottest street cassette around—'The Coup Tango,' by Juan Palacios, which is laced with amusing vulgarities. But the effect of commercial lionization has been to turn the seditious Civil Guard officer into a popular buffoon, not a serious hero." The tango, at one point in history the epitome of degradation, in metaphorical transformation mocks political failure in this case with its shame and humiliation. An article titled "The Budget Tango: How Yes Turns into No" describes the United States Congress giving Reagan's economic program a roller-coaster ride and explains the complexities of the politics of the budget process.[38] The tango is danced in 4/4 time with deliberate slow, slow, quick-quick, slow steps in one direction followed by retracing the steps in the opposite one.

In an article called "Latest Tango in Ho Chi Minh City Plays with a Russian Leading," William Branigin describes a Saturday night at the Rex nightclub: "The large but light-footed Russian glides gracefully across the floor to the strains of a tango, followed expertly by a lithe Vietnamese girl looking like a wisp against his enormous girth."[39] The portrayal of taxi dancers for rent serves as a point of departure to talk about what has happened in the city formerly called Saigon. The Russian leading the Vietnamese in the dance is also a metaphor for the current Soviet political dominance that has replaced the United States' presence.

The tango appears in the title of Bernardo Bertolucci's film "Last Tango in Paris," first presented in October 1972. Some critics considered the film to be a landmark in movie history because of its powerful, emotionally charged sexuality. The title of the film links it to the origin of the tango and the "tango teas." The key character's tango performance is a metaphor for his low-class status and personal weakness. The dance climaxes at the end of two people's three-day search for pleasure with each other and their "unreal" orgiastic madness. Paul tries aggressively to escape the distress of his wife's suicide, and Jeanne tries to counter her bourgeois life. As in the original tango of the brothel, sex is separated from feelings of love and everything else during a brief affair. Afterward the couple stops for a drink in a ballroom that is holding a tango contest. Jeanne, an attractive twenty-year-old, and Paul, a washed-up, middle-aged man, dance outrageously in a squalid parody of what the tango had become after transcending its bordello origins. When the judges remove the couple, Paul bares his ass. The tango is old-fashioned, like the film's focus on the dominating male and adoring subservient woman. Breaking the rules of the tango clinches the end of the couple's relationship and precludes the beginning of one in which Paul wants to love Jeanne as a person.

A publication called the *South African Digest* refers to the "Last Tango in Namibia" in its assessment of the prospects of South Africa at last being able to establish what it considered a sensible relationship with an American administration concerning the question of Namibian independence, certainly an emotional issue among Africans.[40]

The waltz of the 1800s contrasts with the courtly minuet that preceded the French Revolution.[41] Danced by nobility, the minuet, as noted earlier, was a concise expression of rationality, detachment, and discipline, rarely performed elsewhere than at the courts. A mere twenty or thirty years, but a whole historical epoch, separates the age of the courtly minuet from that of the waltz. This is appositely seen at the 1814/15 Congress of Vienna, where the crowned heads of Europe assembled, in company with their chief ministers and the high society of the Austrian capital. Their purpose was to reestablish an ultraconservative Europe freed from the democratic spectre. While the diplomats worked at map-covered tables, the kings danced, but this time to the musical strains of the waltz. This dance combined the Landler traditional whirling steps of Austria's German-speaking mountain peasantry and the gliding motion of the more sedate Schleifer dance. With its 3/4 rhythm and emphasis on the first beat, the waltz conquered more than the Congress of Vienna. It soon dominated the middle-class festivities of a whole continent. The minuet disappeared fast; the polonaise survived longer. There is some irony in the triumph of the ecstatic waltz at so conservative a time; with the basic face-to-face position of the later ballrooms, it became an assertion of individual expression such as the minuet had never been. More important, the waltz was a popular art form in the service of a freer, more open, and eventually more democratic society than the Congress ever envisaged. During the French Revolution there was talk about putting the arts at the disposal of society in general: the waltz, independent of social hierarchy, and the petty tyrannies of the dancing master, and allowing personal choices of partner and movement, became one assertion of increased freedom in a crumbling conservative social order. By 1830 the waltz was danced in Boston assembly-rooms, in the Manchester Free Trade Hall in England, and in the cafes of the Champs Elysées. Couples held each other at arm's length or closer as they revolved around their own axes, vibrantly spinning among others. Mothers, of course, were still concerned about the backgrounds of young men willing to dance with their daughters. The waltz is now viewed as graceful, dignified, and orderly, as in George Balanchine's choreography "Waltz Scherzo" or "Vienna Waltzes." However, it scandalized many people living in the first generation of the dance. The clergy feared the lust aroused by partners grasping each other and throwing and twirling each other about. When the whirling dance entered the salon, the dancing teachers tried through formal rules to tame the waltz's spontaneity and self-expression.

Describing the Austrian economy as "a Strauss waltz," Paul Lewis begins his analysis this way:

> Every February at the famous Vienna Opera Ball, the season's debutantes, dressed in white with little silver crowns on their heads, perform a waltz with elaborate ritualistic pirouettes around a specially constructed dance floor in the Vienna opera house. Their formal entry into society—for which each father has paid $700—is then made with sweeping curtsies to the gilt-encrusted red velvet imperial box where Emperor Franz Josef once sat. In it today sit the applauding members of Chancellor Bruno Kriesky's Socialist Government, in white ties and tails, sipping champagne.
>
> The presence of Austria's Socialist leadership at Vienna's grandest society ball reveals the secret of why this country now has the most successful economy in Western Europe. Austrians themselves readily attribute their achievements to a remarkable social consensus—an almost-complete meeting of minds on economic matters between Socialists and conservatives, bosses and workers, rich and poor.[42]

Lewis's economic analysis concludes with a dance metaphor: "This is still a better performance than most other European countries can expect. . . ." The re-created dance imagery thus evokes sentiments of excitement and communal sharing.

After the 1980 United States presidential elections, it would have been difficult for readers to miss the front-page headline "Reagan Asks for a First Waltz and Wins Hearts in the Capital."[43] Continued on another page was the head "President-Elect Waltzing Washington." Making his entry into Washington society, Reagan was courting the establishment with dinners. The waltz herein refers to the winning diplomacy of the Congress of Vienna that gave impetus to the waltz as well as to the gracious elegance of the dance and the dizzying speed of its turning movements. Nearly a year later, however, the Democratic leader and Speaker of the House of Representatives, Tip O'Neill, indicated that the Democrats will "refuse Ronald Reagan's new invitation to the waltz." They would not enter a bipartisan approach to social security.[44]

About the New York City government we read "New Steps in Budget Waltz Help Ease the Go Around."[45] Feelings of dizziness are associated with the waltz. The journalist says, "For years, the final city budget negotiations among the City Council, the Board of Estimate and the Mayor have been conducted in the spirit of a 1930s dance marathon—the last people left on their feet would win. While this process had a sort of morbid charm, it has occurred to the various dancers over the years that it may not be the best way to produce a sensible budget."

"Coal Contract Talks: Dancing on Deadline" heads an article that begins, "The negotiating dance between the United Mine Workers of America and the Bituminous Coal Operators Association continued yesterday as the two sides waltzed around the bargaining table, trying to find a peaceful stopping point before the music stops at 12:01 A.M. Tuesday."[46]

DANCE IN LITERATURE

The dance experience has more than an emotional impact that reverberates in the transformations of metaphorical vernacular and new flesh-and-blood dancing. Dance also appears as metaphor and device in plays, novels, and poetry to document still further the punch of performance. Colleagues in the literary field have called the following illustrations to my attention.[47]

During Shakespeare's time, dance was part of folk tradition and court entertainment. Dancing was a common way of wooing in Renaissance Europe. Because dance was deeply rooted in social life and appealed to various strata, the use of dance as symbol, emotional stimulus, and comment about character and plot could be readily grasped by all. Bella Maryanne Mirabella speaks of dance as a storehouse of imagery and dramatic technique that becomes a mute rhetoric complementing the dialogue in Shakespeare's plays.[48]

*Much Ado about Nothing*, probably written in 1598, is suggestive. The play begins with the return of Don Pedro, prince of Aragon, and his officers from a war. Leonato, governor of Messina; Hero, his daughter; and Beatrice, his niece, welcome the men. Later, Leonato remarks that his niece's tongue will keep her from getting a husband. He tells her, "If the prince do solicit you in that kind, you know your answer." Beatrice replies (II. i. 60–69):

> The fault will be in the music, cousin, if you be not wooed in good time: if the prince be too important, tell him there is measure in every thing, and

so dance out the answer. For, hear me, Hero:—wooing, wedding, and re-
penting, is as a Scotch jig, a measure, and a cinque-pace: the first suit is hot
and hasty, like a Scotch jig, and full as fantastical; the wedding, mannerly-
modest, as a measure, full of state and ancientry; and then comes repentance, and, with his bad legs, falls into the cinque-pace faster and faster,
till he sink into his grave.

By introducing the notion of dancing out an answer, Mirabella explains
that Shakespeare employs dance as a dramatic technique for allowing
lovers to speak indirectly to one another. Shakespeare's audience was
familiar with specific dances and could understand the metaphorical allusions to sexuality and courtship and empathize with the emotions.
Beatrice speaks about the "hot and hasty" qualities of the jig and the
early stages of courtship. Since the word *measure* refers to dance and degree, the possibilities for pun and wordplay are great. Vigorous dances
such as the jig and galliard (a lively, seductive dance in which the couples
dance variations around each other), were favored courtship dances.
The galliard is performed with four leg thrusts alternating from right to
left and culminates in a leap, the most difficult step, which is called a
cinquepace.

Langdon Elsbree tells us that several novelists used dance scenes as an
index of the degree of emotional tension between the claims of the individual and the social being.[49] The occasion of the dance, preparations for
it, and events which follow dramatized the individual's and group's sense
of identity. Novelists used dance as a metaphor for milieu, tradition, and
community as well as stages in courtship and love that a community or
tradition permitted. Country-dances, quadrilles, and waltzes epitomize
the late eighteenth century gentry and lesser aristocracy. The dance gives
form to emotions which transcend those of fidelity and complaisance.

Novelists also used dance as different forms of play, which usually signify feelings of happiness. "In Jane Austen the dance is the purest kind of
play . . . in George Eliot the dance is symptomatic of the corruption of
the play element . . . in [Thomas] Hardy the dance signifies the disap-
pearance of the play element and the community underlying it . . . In
[D. H.] Lawrence the dance becomes a means for apprehending and di-
agnosing a deeper self than the purely social ego."[50] To Austen, dance
announces a character's feelings of sexual maturity and describes a
group's values. Eliot relies upon the dance to suggest a genuine escape in
childhood and a delusive one in adulthood (*The Mill on the Floss*).

Hardy's tendency to rely upon briefer, sometimes barely allusive dance
scenes to begin to conclude the downfall of a Henchard or Tess is an expression of his pessimism about the viability of this order of existence. The
country-dance is forgotten by the educated Grace Melburys, and becomes

an orgy for rootless farm laborers. The purely social couple dance, the polka or society ball, promises the eternal play of romantic love and happiness in the new order of knowledge and power. For those of the old order, the end is the world of Jude, one where there is no play and no dance.[51]

In Hardy's *Tess of the D'Urbervilles*, the dance motif has these functions:

Thematically, it dramatizes Tess's youthful innocence and ardor; her initial craving for Angel Clare, his failure to choose her as a partner, and the foreshadowed doom of their marriage; the farmers' loss of their Teutonic past; and, in the orgiastic dances at Chaseborough, the farm hands' rootlessness and moral confusion. Structurally, the dance introduces Tess to the reader and Angel Clare to Tess and becomes a leitmotif. Historically, the dance isolates a transitional period in which the farm community, subjected to the complex social forces of the late Victorian era, has already forgotten the meaning and is neglecting the customs of its past.[52]

Lawrence conceives of dance as "pure play, in which there is freedom and wholeness of self, but also as a means of asserting class superiority or identity, by such fashionable steps as the minuet and valeta, and on such occasions as the fancy-dress ball or the dancing school."[53] A constant in his work is the association of dance with natural playfulness, accompanied by the emotions of vitality, happiness, and the sheer celebration of being.[54]

Lawrence rejects much in Western culture and searches for renewing historic forms. He has contempt for the charleston and other dances of the twenties and admires Mexican ritual dances or the tarantella. The tango and charleston, he thinks, have lost the play element and are in direct opposition to sexuality. These couple-dances were narrowed to "either bounding toward copulation, or sliding and shaking and waggling, to elude it."[55]

Judith Simpson White describes how Yeats's work with dance theatre influenced his verse drama.[56] The changes in his theories of poetic drama resulted from his work with dancers Michio Ito and Ninette de Valois. His study of Japanese dance-drama, she suggests, was "a logical part of his search for a poetic drama which communicated through symbol and rhythm." The French championed dance as a wordless poetry. The evolution of the use of dance from image to symbol in Yeats's poems and plays particularizes his development as a writer. He consciously uses the dance as a metaphor for the feeling of life and the experience of phenomena in a cosmic order. The pattern of the dance becomes an expression of the "threshold experience" where the natural and supernatural conjoin. Clinton Vickers suggests that Yeats uses the dance erotically to denote physical generation with the element earth, ideally to portray visionary experience with the element air, metaphorically to depict the creation of art with the element fire, and rhythmically to portray the flow of life with the element water.[57] As each element gave birth to another and each potentially incorporated the whole in a cyclic procession of birth and decay, so Yeats uses various manifestations of the dance.

For Yeats, dance represents the moment when discovery takes place, the emotion of surprise. He draws upon the dancing Salome before the severed head of John the Baptist, the precursor of the Christian god-man and a new cycle of history. This is important in Yeats, because his theory of history involved cycles and transitional points. Vickers finds the archetypal dancing figure of Salome hidden behind all Yeats's dancing females. Chapter 2 included the image of Salome as an influence on some people's current feeling about dance. In *A Vision* Yeats explained: "When I think of the moment before revelation I think of Salome—she, too, delicately tinted or maybe mahogany dark—dancing before Herod and receiving the Prophet's head in her indifferent hands, and wonder if what seems to us decadence was not in reality the exaltation of the muscular flesh and of civilization perfectly achieved."[58] Yeats's beautiful woman whose body moves like that of a dancer in rhythms that the poet's song creates is perfection. Yet Yeats drew upon more than the biblical source; Celtic literature and painting also provided inspiration. Furthermore, like other literary and artistic individuals, Yeats fixed on the dancers of the "decadent" music halls of the 1890s.

The perfect moment of the dance is not labor but being, the feeling of joy. Yeats is well known for the last section of his poem "Among School Children."

Labour is blossoming or dancing where
The body is not bruised to pleasure soul,
Nor beauty born out of its own despair,
Nor blear-eyed wisdom out of midnight oil.
O chestnut-tree, great-rooted blossomer,
Are you the leaf, the blossom or the bole?
O body swayed to music, O brightening glance,
How can we know the dancer from the dance?[59]

As we have seen in exploring the Smithsonian dance concert series, this question is critical in the reconstruction of earlier dances (see, for example, chapter 5).

I have presented some illustrations of how the sentient dance influences the way creative writers express their thoughts. These creations reverberate and, in turn, influence nonfiction authors. For example, Catherine J. Allen refers to Yeats in suggesting that the self, the dancer, cannot be abstracted from the dance. She explores the formulation of a Quechua self through the "dance" of hallpay or coca chewing that creates an altered state of feeling. The symbolism of this dance defines a cultural structure. "Participation in this cultural dance puts the . . . [Quechua person] into a sacred contract to participate in Quechua tradition with his fellows and with spiritual beings. When an individual stops chewing coca, he or she seeks new cultural dances and a new definition of self." [60]

Charles Williams's novel *The Greater Trumps* gave T. S. Eliot the image of the dance around the "still point" ("Burnt Norton"):

> At the still point of the turning world.
>     Neither flesh nor fleshless:
> Neither from nor towards; at the still point,
>     There the dance is.
> But neither arrest nor movement.
>     And do not call it fixity, where past and future are gathered.
> Neither movement from nor towards,
> Neither ascent nor decline. Except for the point,
>     the still point,
> There would be no dance, and there is only the dance. [61]

In the novel the figures of the Tarot pack dance around the Fool at the still center of a magical model of the universe. "Except for the . . . only the dance" refers to the life of perfect harmony and feeling of tranquillity which is the only sort of life worth having. It depends on that life being centered on the "still point." Life is a "dance" of reconciled opposites. The point of departure is a vision of eternity "at the still point of the turning world," where past and future gather and a motionless source of movement and unchanging agent of change merge. Commonplace in the Middle Ages and Elizabethan world was the notion that the created universe with its time and divisions was one perpetual dance. And motion is part of nearly all emotions. [62]

I have considered some examples of the interdependence of stage and page in order to suggest the conjoining of modes of knowing and feeling—kinetic visual images with verbal language. Stage presentation may dramatize and enliven text. In turn the text inspires replays and new plays of choreography and live performance.

POSTWORD

Our odyssey into some puzzling areas of human communication has drawn to a close. We have explored the communication of emotion in dance: the history of attitudes that create expectations for what performers do and spectators understand, what dancers intend to convey onstage and what audience members perceive in specially selected live concerts, and what emotional traces of some past performances linger in society through the metaphors that help guide us to the exterior and interior movements of our own lives and create and re-create the performer-audience connection.

Dance in its first incarnation of live performance, and dance in its metaphoric and new dance transformations, reflects human innovative potential through historical time and across geographical space. Different dances arise from specific situations and individuals. These dances often evoke cultural images of their times. Separated from their physical presence such dance transformations serve as benchmarks in social history.

Not only is dance salient for dance devotees and professionals who earn their livelihood from dance production; the rousing dance form of human expression reaches beyond footlights and other theatrical settings to become a gloss or device for reflecting on and emotionally influencing social interaction elsewhere. This language creates the background for making dances, audience behavior, and shared culture. In taking a rarely trodden path to examine connections between performer intention and audience reception, ways to convey emotions, clues to identify them, and reciprocal influences between dance and society, my intent has been to illuminate the realm of dance as significant human behavior and to shed further light on human thought, feeling, and action.

Because this is a unique study, it has an essentially preliminary quality and many limitations. Certainly I have raised more questions than I have answered. But the work is a beginning and does point to possible pathways for future exploration to discover some of the secrets of human communication. Hopefully, this effort will stimulate further forays into the performer-audience connection; the "house will not remain dark," and the curtain will continue to rise.

# Appendix. Some Conceptual and Methodological Issues

This study explores the performer-audience connection: the performer's intention and effectiveness in conveying emotion through different channels in a live presentation. Did audience members perceive the intended or inadvertent messages? What clues did they use to identify emotions? There are no right or wrong answers. That is, the measure of accurate communication is the overlapping of performer intention and audience perception. The goal of the study is to assess—in a Webster's dictionary, commonsense way—sender-receiver correspondence and to identify some background characteristics that show relationships to the patterns of identified emotions and clues to them. The spectators' reported emotions in response to a particular dance suggest the dancer's evocative power of empathy.

## FOCUS OF THE PERFORMER-AUDIENCE CONNECTION

A live encounter in theatrical and everyday performance has the excitement of the possibility of the unexpected that filmed performance lacks, and film's two dimensions create some distortion in presenting the three-dimensionality of dance. Therefore, a decision was made to conduct research on live concerts rather than audience responses to filmed performance (see the chapter on the Cowles/Davies performance for further discussion of filmed and live images). Since limited resources precluded paying selected informants and performers for their time in a statistically representative sample, a combination of humanities and social science approaches was used. The absence of a representative sample limits the kinds of conclusions that can be drawn.

In addition to the excitement of the unknown in live performances that other kinds of communication studies lack, and the distortion of film, there are difficulties with alternative approaches. (see Ashworth, 1979: 75–77, Rosenthal 1979, Plutchik 1980, and Kendon 1983 for discussions of some of these.) Some research uses posed pictures of individuals

APPENDIX TABLE 1. Audience Perceptions of Emotions at Concerts

| Emotion | Tap | Kuchi-pudi | RDT | Dunn | Kabuki | Philip-pine | Katha-kali |
|---|---|---|---|---|---|---|---|
| Anger[d] | 2 | 87[b] | 3 | 11 | 7 | 0 | 96 |
| Boredom | 2 | 4 | 0 | 27 | 5 | 1 | 0 |
| Caring[e] | 21 | 23 | 30 | 31 | 61 | 48 | 65 |
| Competition[f] | 5 | 69 | 10 | 29 | 1 | 16 | 40 |
| Disgust | 2 | 28 | 0 | 10 | 6 | 2 | 65 |
| Ecstasy[g] | 11 | 28 | 73 | 10 | 19 | 12 | 15 |
| Eroticism[h] | 2 | 15 | 37 | 40 | 26 | 22 | 21 |
| Fatigue | 0 | 9 | 20 | 25 | 29 | 2 | 8 |
| Happiness[i] | 67 | 43 | 83 | 12 | 63 | 85 | 42 |
| Nostalgia[j] | 8 | 4 | 13 | 7 | 35 | 13 | 13 |
| Playfulness[k] | 36 | 34 | 67 | 55 | 89 | 90 | 58 |
| Pride[l] | 15 | 69 | 23 | 13 | 17 | 48 | 69 |
| Sadness[m] | 18 | 11 | 3 | 18 | 64 | 2 | 56 |
| Shame | 0 | 4 | 0 | 11 | 13 | 0 | 0 |
| Surprise[n] | 11 | 17 | 9 | 11 | 16 | 11 | 0 |
| Vitality[o] | 23 | 26 | 83 | 30 | 35 | 62 | 52 |
| Other[p] | 17 | 17 | 12 | 19 | 21 | 0 | 21 |
| No Emotion | 4 | 1 | 0 | 46 | 4 | 7 | 0 |
| N[c] | 61 | 137 | 30 | 113 | 121 | 87 | 48 |

*Percent of Audience Who Perceived Emotions[a]*

[a] Percentages are based on the proportion of returned questionnaires with responses that could be compared. See appendix table 2.
[b] Underlined figures represent response rates high enough to warrant discussion in the text.
[c] N indicates the number of returned questionnaires in the sample.
[d] synonyms: cruelty.
[e] concentration, appreciation, eagerness, determination, friendship, camaraderie, respect, affection, reluctance to leave stage.
[f] striving, combative, machism, threatening, aggressive, conflict.
[g] exultation, exhilaration, contagious high.
[h] desire, flirtation.
[i] glee, upbeat, pleasure, enjoyment, carefree, joyous, relaxed, entertaining, satisfaction.
[j] pride in past.
[k] spontaneity, fun, teasing, satire, humorous, funny.

[l] self-satisfaction, self-confident, self-exhibition.
[m] grief, slight despair.
[n] wonderment, thrill, excitement, amazement.
[o] enthusiasm, warm, exuberant, release, energy, dynamic, vigorous, madcap animation.
[p] At each concert none of the following was perceived by more than three people: humility, fear, optimism, hope, self-fulfillment, gamut, pensive, controlled, mature, peacefulness, transcendence, resolution, benediction, repose, transmutation, resolve, prayer, menace, strength, benevolence, power, control, tension, bloodthirsty, praise, anticipation, indifferent, annoyance, alienation, fascination, restlessness, stress, tension, mechanistic, self-centered, limited emotion, passivity, wistful, uncertainty, puzzled range, discipline, loneliness, irritation, irony, desire to please, decorous, graceful, submissive, scorn, superiority, pleading, revenge, sarcasm, contempt, comfort, forgiveness, shyness, coyness, coquetishness, drunkenness.

---

displaying an emotion to elicit information about the communication of emotion. However, posed pictures are not the way people perceive emotions in social interaction. Subjects are often allowed to look at a picture for a long time in order to decide which emotion(s) is depicted. Some research asks people to adopt the movement corresponding to an emotion. This can lead to exaggerated or conventionalized expressions that may differ from spontaneous acts that people are not aware of. Emotions enacted on film may be contrived (Ekman and Oster 1979: 544). Such studies appear distanced from what occurs in daily and theatrical life: social participants receive input continuously and rapidly, and they often respond in a similar way.

THE PERFORMER
Prior to performances (before, during, and after rehearsal) as time, logistics, and performer preference permitted, I interviewed choreographers and dancers (sometimes they were the same). An attempt was made to follow a similar procedure for each concert. After concerts performers were busy with receptions or packing (costumes and other belongings) to leave. With interviewees' permission, open-ended questions and answers were tape-recorded for later transcription, analysis, coding, and comparison with audience responses. Performer views on the motivation of movement (whether feeling elicits the movement, vice versa, or another factor is involved) were compared. Dancer intentions—emotions and how they thought they conveyed them—were compared with audience survey-reported perceptions of what emotions the dancers actually got across to

APPENDIX TABLE 2. Performance Sample

| Day | Date | Title | Auditorium | Seating—Maximum | # of Forms Distributed | Returned | Percent | Actual Sample[a] | Specific Problems |
|---|---|---|---|---|---|---|---|---|---|
| M | 9-8-80 | American Tap Masters (A) | Baird | 550 | 490 | 110 | 22 | 61 | hot auditorium, concert long, people left |
| Su | 10-26-80 | Kuchipudi (W) | Baird | 550 | 350 | 139 | 40 | 137 | |
| M | 10-27-80 | Modern Dance in America (A) | Marvin | 384 | 324 | 34 | 10 | 30 | anti-intellectual philos. of mod. aud., nonsubscription, high exodus |
| M | 1-12-81 | Post-Modern Dance (A) | Marvin | 384 | 265 | 125 | 47 | 113 | |
| Su | 2-22-81 | Kabuki Dance (W) | Baird | 550 | 468 | 141 | 30 | 121 | non-English speakers in aud. |
| M | 2-23-81 | Dance and the Camera (A) | Hirshhorn | 280 | 250 | 14 | 5 | 0 | mail in, people left |
| Su | 3-15-81 | Philippine Dance Co. (W) | Baird | 550 | 235 | 91 | 39 | 87 | |
| W | 5-27-81 | Kathakali (W)[b] | Baird | 550 | 300 | 24 | 8 | } 48 | ⅔ people left; subscriber saturation |
| Th | 5-28-81 | Kathakali (W) | Baird | 183 | 160 | 29 | 18 | | non-English speakers |

Note: Series (A) American Dance Experience (W) World Explorer

[a] The N in the various tables differs because people did not always provide comparable data.

[b] Concert samples were combined.

**APPENDIX TABLE 3.** Dimensions of Conveying Emotion

1. *Action:* gesture (movement in space that does not carry weight)
   locomotion (movement through space that does carry weight)
   posture (lying, tilting, standing, stance, carriage)
2. *Body Parts:* face/parts of face
   eyes
   chest/back
   abdomen/waist } upper torso

   pelvis/hips/buttocks
   shoulder
   arms
   hands/fingers
   leg/knee
   feet
   whole body/all parts/muscles
3. *Quality of Movement:*
   A. Dancers' Interpersonal Dynamics (touching, holding, copying, relating to each other, lack of interaction, hugging)
   B. Soul/Charisma (attitude, awareness, presence, self-centered, aura, independence of action, nonchalance toward audience)
   C. Use of Energy (strength of movement, whole body stillness, flow, bound quality, thrust, breath, dynamics, change of effort, no energy, light/heavy)
   D. Use of Time (speed, rhythm, pace, tempo)
   E. Use of Space (directions, open/closed)
   F. Other (technical, abstract, pure, singleness, repetition, total manner, mechanical, purposeful, central, deliberate, persuasive, no meaning, outside force, robot-like, confused, cool, awkward, flexible, distant, drunk, inventive, intellectual, precise, detached, hauteur, one character becoming another, narrative expressed by dance)
4. *Nondance Factors* (costume, scenery, music, words)

them and how (see appendix tables 1, 2, 3). Although there were some audience interviews, their opinions were obtained primarily through surveys.

The rationale for not also administering a questionnaire form to the dancers is that an interview can ask the same questions. In addition, the potential for in-depth and broader understanding of intentions and reasons can be realized. This is essential in a subject area that has not been explored, as noted in chapter 1. Besides, performers are accustomed to being interviewed and are more amenable to conversations than forms.

Some interviews with performers led to more exploration than others. Extended discussion occurred when performers showed interest in dialogue and had time or when their dance genre had an ancient, classical tradition. Extended discussion led to a more detailed description of the dance form and its history in this study.

## THE AUDIENCE

Audience members are also more likely to talk than to fill out forms. But it is not feasible to talk to more than a few people, given the time available at intermission. The limited memory most people have for the information being solicited precluded fruitful discussions at a later time.

At eight performances, two to six assistants and I distributed questionnaires to audience members after ushers took their tickets at the door. We loaned small golf pencils as needed, and if there were only a few people entering at a time, we warmly invited their cooperation in the study to encourage a positive response. When the concert was over, assistants stood at the exits to collect forms as audience members left.

Who are the respondents in the survey? They are audience members who volunteered to fill out the survey. On the basis of written and oral comments, we know that these respondents are interested in dance, the visual kinesthetic experience, exploring a new phenomenon, or merely joining friends who invite them along. Respondents include Smithsonian dance series subscribers as well as nonsubscribers. The museum generally attracts people who are interested in continuing education. As at most theatre events, the audience tends to be white, middle-class (above median income and college-educated), and female. Tickets were $7.50 per concert; the sites of most of the performances were not adjacent to residential areas and consequently required traveling to the performances. According to a survey of audience social files based upon 270 audience studies (DiMaggio et al. 1978), the Smithsonian sample is biased in a way that is representative of performing arts audiences in general. The dance culture—consuming public is better educated with higher status jobs and incomes than the general public, and audiences for dance are heavily female.

Moreover, the respondents do not constitute a random sample of the dance concert audience. People who fill forms may be those individuals who are receptive to questionnaires at an educational/entertainment event, find the form understandable and interesting, and have time (people often must use the restrooms or telephone, or leave before a concert is over). The survey form included this Smithsonian Institution statement: "Note: information furnished by you on this survey is purely voluntary."

Although the sample lacks representativeness of the entire audience, there is a range of respondents (i.e., individuals with different backgrounds) which allows us to examine a woefully unexplored slice of social life. This voluntary sample provides information on what some members of a dance audience perceive, how these perceptions correspond with performer intentions, and what relationships exist between perceptions and backgrounds. The percentage of audience surveys returned ranges from one-third to one-half at most of the performances (see appendix table 2). At several concerts, as audience members entered the theatre, an assistant standing at each entrance made an "eyeball" account of the total audience population, characterizing individuals by gender, ethnicity, and age category on a check sheet. There was a rough correspondence to the survey returns.

Voluntarily excluded as respondents were newspaper and magazine dance critics (one to six attended each performance), who concentrate on their own ways of viewing performances. Also excluded were children under 15, those handicapped in ability to write (including the very elderly and those who leave their glasses at home), people who entered the theatre after the lights dimmed or left before the end of a performance, and non–English speaking individuals.

People subscribed to one or both Smithsonian dance series or bought a ticket for a specific performance without any expectation of filling out a survey form. People had various reasons for participating in the study. They expressed these in writing or orally. Let us consider the reasons for "uncooperative" responses.

(1) Some people are opposed to surveys of any type because they are associated with government intervention in their lives.

(2) A respondent pointed out that people "hate to commit themselves." Some individuals were concerned with the accuracy of their responses when a dance rapidly conveyed many emotions and they were viewing it for the first time. However, note that in everyday social interaction and in special relationships such as teacher/student, people make quick, immediate judgments that are conscious or out of explicit awareness as they attempt to grasp the mercurial immediacy and meaning of an exchange. Not all actions get attention. Sometimes time elapses and the meaning of an act is reinterpreted, or if an act was not explicitly considered when it occurred, it is later recollected and considered. In most social relations people do not look for the emotional messages to which they respond. Thus a survey of this type was a new experience for most audience members, and some found it difficult.

(3) A few spectators said that filling out a form interfered with their enjoyment of the performance. There is a philosophical position that the arts should be enjoyed not analyzed. For example, the first full-time critic for the *New York Times*, John Martin, called his students at UCLA who had an analytic bent "dried up intellectuals." Poor response to the RDT concert of American modern dance may be attributed to what

critic/historian Marcia Siegel (1976) refers to as the American modern dance movement inheritance of a cultural indifference to analysis and interpretation. Because there were two Smithsonian dance series concerts at the same time and two RDT performances, the RDT audience that was surveyed was not primarily a broad series subscription audience but one comprised of devotees of American modern dance. In chapter 2, I noted early modern dance pioneer Mary Wigman's concern that the audience not view dance from an intellectual point of view. This attitude has continued to influence modern dance audiences.

(4) Perceived difficulty (including forgetting one's glasses or sitting far from the stage and lack of time) precluded some audience members from filling out the form.

(5) Emotion is not a focus of attention for a number of viewers, who, for example, look at the basic elements of dance and their combination or the general overall feeling of the dance as opposed to specific feelings expressed at particular times. Thus some audience members found the form irrelevant to their way of responding to the arts.

(6) Several seriesgoers had filled out the form once or more and said that those experiences sufficed.

(7) Some audience members left a performance while it was in progress and did not find an usher in the dark to take the form if they had filled it out earlier; nor did they opt to mail it in, although the form had my name, address, and phone number. People who left early because they disliked a performance may have had no interest in responding to a survey about that performance. At two of the four American Dance Experience Series concerts, at least one-third of the audience left before the end. Because there was a single exit at the Sage Cowles/Molly Davies concert, an accurate exodus count was possible: 38 percent. Physical discomfort may have discouraged a high questionnaire response. One spectator angrily asked, "What happened to the air conditioner? Are we still conserving energy?" Thus the audience size and theatre condition had a bearing on the return rate.

(8) At an Indian dance concert, three people wrote on the form that they performed Indian dance themselves and did not feel that they should comment. They offered no further explanation. These dancers did not place themselves in the "audience" category even though their responses were desired.

Since this pilot study was interested in ways to increase audience response, for several of the concerts, before the performance began, the series organizer went onstage to make some introductory remarks about the program. At that time, in order to promote survey returns, the following comments were made to clarify and legitimate the study: "Dr. Judith Lynne Hanna, author of *To Dance Is Human*, is studying performances. You are invited to share your views on the (name) dance before the first intermission. Your cooperation would be appreciated. At intermission she will be in the lobby to speak in person with those who are interested." The announcement may have increased audience return by about 10 percent, judging from figures on the concert prior to using this procedure. However, the Smithsonian felt the announcement was too intrusive for some of the concerts.

In order to investigate variables which affected audience return response rates, two other approaches to administering the questionnaire were tried, one out of necessity, the other out of opportunity (explained in the chapters on each concert). At the "Dance and the Camera" concert, audience members were asked to mail in their forms out of necessity, because there was to be no intermission, and the auditorium had to be emptied immediately after the concert for custodial needs. Consequently an assistant offered addressed/stamped envelopes to audience members as they left the auditorium. The return was poor in comparison with the usual procedure of collecting the forms at the end of the concert. Perhaps the major reason was because nearly half of the audience had left before the end of the performance. At the first of two Kathakali performances we followed the usual procedure of distribution and collection of forms at the door. At the second performance we used another procedure to see its effect on the response rate. This time a letter of explanation along with the survey and a pencil were fixed to every third seat in the auditorium. The return rate was more than double that for the previous night. However, the fact that the response rate was still lower than other concert return rates may have been due primarily to the high number of Indian families at the second concert and possible lack of English skills.

What are some of the reasons why audience members shared their views?

(1) These individuals might have seen value in learning what goes on in an exchange. They filled out the form and gave their names and addresses so that they might receive information on the study.

(2) Some spectators found that the form asked for new ways of interpreting a dance performance. Thus they found the exercise a challenge.

(3) There are audience members who like to cooperate with friendly people who ask for their assistance.

(4) Some spectators had strong positive or negative feelings that they wanted to express and the form was a vehicle for their sentiment.

The reponses given at the concerts offer a repertoire of perceptions of emotions and clues to them and should provide guidance for further, more systematic research. Heretofore most reactions to performance have been from armchair philosophers and critics. However, very few write about the same performance, and critics are not typical of most concertgoers. Furthermore, they rarely discuss the questions posed in this study.

QUALITY OF RESPONSES
There is difficulty in achieving rigorous inter-subject reliability about the meaning of an emotion. Yet, it should be noted that through history, performance theory has evolved without any systematic empirical exploration. At the first concert an open-ended survey was used in which respondents were asked to list the emotions they perceived in the dance before the first intermission. In response to audience member comments, at subsequent concerts the emotions mentioned were grouped into categories by synonyms, following Webster's *New Collegiate Dictionary* and Izard (1980: 204–205), the number (16) determined by the spatial constraints of a one-page, two-sided survey form. The form also provided spaces for emotions which audience members saw or felt but which were not listed and for "no emotion." There are about 400 names of emotions in English (Wallace and Carson 1973; de Rivera 1977; Boucher 1979). Named emotions may mean different things to different people, and labeling has a potential cultural bias, situational relevance, and personally specific assumptions. A word like *love*, for example, may refer to feelings toward all humans, a mother's affection for her child, or an individual's sexual activity. However, it is assumed that the audience-named emotions also have some commonality and contrasts. When foreigners use the English language to identify emotions, it is likely that they share these meanings.

Although the survey form focuses responses on the communication of emotion, it does not tap all the complexities of emotional communication, such as intensity of emotion or primary and secondary emotions (see Plutchik 1980: 131). A great deal happens in a performance, and observers can only process a certain amount of material at a time. If a dance is complex, with a succession of multiple emotions, not all may be recalled. However, people are usually bombarded with multiple stimuli, and their selective impressions are the bases for action. A person's mood or distance from the stage may affect perception. If more than one dancer is onstage, it may not be clear which one is being discussed. More than one person onstage may diffuse a spectator's attention, as may the question of whether a dance has a set choreography or is improvised. The form relies upon audience introspection and recall. Plutchik (1980: 102) calls attention to some of the problems with this approach. He focuses on verbal self-reports of an inner emotional state and not on the perception of intended and unintended emotions conveyed onstage. Some of his remarks are inapplicable to audiences (for example, those about infants, children, and the mentally ill). Of relevance to the performer-audience connection study is the fact that verbal reports may be deliberately or unconsciously distorted and are dependent on an individual's particular conditioning history, facility with words, and memory and on the inherent ambiguity of language. Plutchik reminds us that "requests for a report of one's immediate emotional state create the problem that the process of observing generally changes the thing observed" (1980: 102).

The audience responses and their agreement (mention of the same emotions and ways of expressing them) with the performer's intentions may be the result of expectations developed through prior knowledge. For example, the "message" of the piece may be suggested in the program notes, title, performer's explanation, advance publicity, familiarity with the genre of dance through training, reading, or observing, choreographer's aesthetic philosophy, and the survey form itself. Looking at the questions prior to a performance, or having filled out the form at a previous concert, may have sensitized respondents to look for something in a performance that they might not have observed otherwise. Since setting expectations in this way may create a bias toward uniform responses, findings of diversity are especially credible. It is important to point out that all social interaction is influenced by expectations as well as by the reaction to momentary stimuli as they occur. The element of surprise is never ruled out. The vagaries of the staged and offstage life encounters are such that the unexpected can be counted on when it is least expected.

Some individuals may not consciously perceive emotion. Thus there is a question about whether respondents really perceive what they report they have seen. In this study I accept self-reports and verbal recall as valid data even though they may be tied to thought more than feeling and may be a rationalization of what is out of awareness. When the nonverbal is verbalized, we do not know what "reality" of observation is lost in the communication process. It is noteworthy that two people preferred to express themselves through pictures rather than words.

Trained dancers and individuals of analytical professions may be able to break down their observations into verbal abstractions more easily than other people. Differences among people are inherent.

Variations in perceptual learning and intellectual interests may lead people to have varying experiences when viewing the same visual patterns from the same spatial position. Emotion and action words are learned, and maturity affects perception. Some individuals have acquired sophisticated acumen and subtlety in being able to recognize, respond to, and articulate fine nuances of feeling.

Another factor that affected the quality of audience response to the survey was the seat from which the performance was viewed. Distance and angle from the stage affect an individual's perception of what occurs there.

A few people misinterpreted the instructions concerning which dance was the focus of audience views or were confused by last minute program changes. This may have led some people to respond to all the dances in a suite or all the dances before the first intermission.

## CODING

The audience response rate is higher than the number of surveys coded (see performance sample table A2). As noted earlier, some people wrote essays on emotions and aesthetics that did not lend themselves to comparison with other audience member responses on emotions perceived, clues to them, and emotions felt.

An assistant, working with me to resolve any response that was not clear-cut, coded the Dunn concert, and I coded the rest. The code for face included head, although there should have been a separate code for each. For example, a smile or frown differs from a head tilt or sway, a much grosser movement, which may include an immobile face.

## SURVEY DATA PROCESSING

For each concert respondents were examined for about 200 variables. After one-way frequency tables were computed for all variables, we decided on subsequent analysis to examine only the six most frequently perceived emotions and the six most frequently perceived clues to identify each emotion for each concert except when a frequency was below ten. Frequencies on the remaining variables were too low for consideration. Due to the categorical nature of all variables, two-way contingency tables were used to analyze relationships. Chi-square tests were then performed to assess the strengths of those relationships. Chi-square test relationships, significant at the .05 level, guide analyses. The power of this statistic is restricted by the nature of the sample. Although some findings could be statistically significant, we relied on contrastive patterns of frequency distributions as indicators of meaningful relationships.

Because of low frequency distributions for the ethnic categories on the questionnaire, we grouped them into United States white, United States black, Filipino, Indian, and other. In the description of survey respondent characteristics the "no answer" response category accounts for figures within the background categories not totaling 100 percent.

The coding dimensions for conveying emotion were drawn from audience responses and clustered into categories based on analyses in human kinesiology, nonverbal communication, the work of Rudolf Laban and his followers, and modern dance movement and choreography manuals. Because people could mention more than one clue to identify an emotion, we calculated the total number of clues noticed to identify an emotion and presented the distributions according to dimensions and the percentage of clues within a category out of the total number to identify an emotion.

This study dealt with the presence and absence of clues to identifying emotion. There is, of course, an important aspect that remains to be explored. Clues may appear as indices for other than emotions. That is, a clenched fist may signify not anger, but the possibility of anger. Another example is that dance about anger may express not the performer's anger but a person who is paid to participate in a dance on behalf of someone who is angry.

For the Cross-Concert analysis, I focused on the six most commonly perceived emotions and the six most frequently identified clues. In this aggregation of respondents, it is possible that a person who filled out surveys at several concerts was counted more than once. About half of the audience members may have been subscribers to one or the other dance series. Fewer were likely to subscribe to both. Several subscribers who filled out a questionnaire once or twice said they did not choose to participate in the survey again. Close to half of the audience members at a particular concert were respondents. If the distributions of subscribers and respondents are independent, the overlap might be at most a fourth.

## CONCLUSION

Like all studies, this one has conceptual and methodological problems that are important to point out. The difficulties I have discussed do not make the study invalid. However, they do represent limits on any conclusions that one can draw. Furthermore, they suggest areas for attention in future conceptualization and empirical research. It may be, of course, that some of the problems are insoluble.

---

## AUDIENCE VIEWS ON THE DANCE
## BEFORE FIRST INTERMISSION

How do people communicate feelings to each other? We are trying to learn *how performers send messages of emotion to their audiences and how audiences receive the messages.*

With the assistance of the Smithsonian Performing Arts Dance Series, Dr. Judith Lynne Hanna, University of Maryland, College Park, Md. 20742 (author of *To Dance Is Human*), is conducting a study of communication. She is asking performers in person about their views on conveying emotion and asking you please to take a few minutes at intermission to share your views by filling out this form. A report will be published and be useful to all kinds of performers. Your cooperation would be appreciated.

Please return this form and pencil, if borrowed, to usher. Thank you.

| (A)  Check (√) *emotion(s)* *conveyed* on stage in the dance before first intermission | (B)  State *place* in dance where emotion is displayed, e.g., beginning (b) middle (m) end (e) throughout (t) | (C)  State *how dancer expressed emotion* (e.g., through which body parts, kinds of movement, or other means) | (D)  How did *you feel* in response to the emotion(s) conveyed? |
|---|---|---|---|
| anger | | | |
| boredom | | | |
| caring | | | |
| competitiveness | | | |
| disgust | | | |
| ecstasy | | | |
| eroticism | | | |
| fatigue | | | |
| happiness | | | |
| nostalgia | | | |
| playfulness | | | |
| pride | | | |
| sadness | | | |
| shame | | | |
| surprise | | | |
| vitality | | | |
| other | | | |
| no emotion | | | |

So that your views can be placed in context, please provide us with some information about yourself. Check the appropriate places and fill in additional information in the places provided.

Birthplace:

___ rural

___ urban

if U.S., state _____

If outside U.S.,

   country _____

Sex:

___ female

___ male

Age:

___ under 20 years

___ 20–30

___ 31–40 years

___ 41–65 years

___ over 65

Religious upbringing; note sect

___ Christian _____

___ Jewish _____

___ Muslim _____

___ Hindu _____

___ Other _____

___ None

How do you identify yourself in
terms of ethnic group (for example,
Anglo-American, Afro-American,
Navajo, Japanese-American)?

_____

Occupation _____

Education:

___ high school

___ some college

___ college graduate

___ postgraduate

How knowledgeable about dance do
you consider yourself?

___ very

___ somewhat

___ not at all

Family income:

___ under $20,000

___ $21,000–$30,000

___ $31,000–$40,000

___ over $40,000

Are you a Smithsonian Series
Subscriber?

___ yes

___ no

How did you learn about this
performance? _____

Comments:

If you wish information on this study, please give your

Name _____

Street _____

City _____

State _____ Zip _____

Phone _____

NOTE: *Information furnished by you on this survey is purely voluntary and
will be used only for the purpose stated. Personally identifying information will
be used only for supplying you with information on this study.*

# *Notes*

CHAPTER 1

1. Cf. Schechner 1977:144. Complete references appear in the bibliography.
2. *New York Times* 1980:4.
3. *U.S. News and World Report* 1977:50; Jedlicka 1979.
4. Schjeldahl 1981:67.
5. See Blacking 1977, Spindler 1978, A. Cohen 1980, Hsu 1980. De Rivera (1977:38, *passim*) discusses "The Movements of the Emotions." He presents diagrams of movements of a person in relation to the self or another person, the bodily movement, and the typical emotion. For example, a tender movement toward another person involves the bodily movement of extension which expresses the typical emotion of love.

   Three kinds of movement are distinguished: autonomic movement of the physiological system in response to an external stimulus (e.g., blushing, dilation and contraction of the eye, withdrawing one's hand from a hot object), movement in everyday living (e.g., walking, sitting), and movement in dance (from the dancer's perspective, purposeful, culturally patterned, intentionally rhythmical, nonverbal body movements other than ordinary motor activity, the motion having inherent aesthetic value). See Hanna 1979a for an elaboration. Dance participant conceptualizations are presented throughout this book.
6. Building upon the work of Erving Goffman, Hochschild (1979) asks why the emotive experience of normal adults in daily life is as orderly as it is.
7. Quoted in Bain 1980:11.
8. Izard 1979:7.
9. Kemper (1981) and Ashworth (1979) provide useful reviews of the cognitive social/cultural constructionist/interactionist theory of emotion.
10. Batcher 1981:171.
11. Geertz 1973:82.
12. See Burke (1941), Goffman (1959), and Turner (1974), who are among those who examine social life from a dramaturgical perspective. This is discussed further in chapter 12.
13. Hanna 1979a, 1979b.
14. Quoted in S. Cohen 1974:2.

15. Wundt 1921 (rpt. 1973). Later Wiener et al. (1972) challenged the view that all nonverbal behavior communicates an emotional state.

16. Goodenough 1957; Kroeber and Parsons 1958.

17. Hanna 1982.

18. Plutchik 1980 and Ashworth 1979 summarize various approaches experimental psychologists have used and point out a number of their shortcomings. Focusing specifically on the face, Eibl-Eibesfeldt (1972, 1979) concludes that facial expressions are universal. Ekman and Friesen (1969, and in their later work) documented universal biologically based yet culturally influenced communication patterns and the assessment of meaning. Culture determines emotional responses in various contexts, dictates the proper degree of emotion that can be shown, and teaches people what to do after they have shown a particular emotion (Ekman 1980). More recently there has been concern with other channels of nonverbal communication. See Davis 1979 and Kendon 1983 for overviews. Scheflen (1964) has examined postural arrangements and Rosenthal (1979) sensitivity over eleven separate dimensions (face, torso, entire figure, two vocal, and six first-order combinations of the five pure).

19. See, for example, Efron 1941, La Barre 1947, E. Hall 1966, Birdwhistell 1970, Seaford 1975, K. Johnson 1976, Nine Curt 1976, Erickson 1979, and Hanna 1979a. Kemper (1978:4) points out that "the theories of emotion that have an evolutionary cast must appreciate that social stimulus conditions constitute the largest part of the human environment." According to Boucher (1979:161), the universal versus culturally determined expression debate is a classic case of the intrusion of discipline and orthodoxy to such an extent that two quite distinct camps have formed.

Rosenthal (1979) and his colleagues, in their program of research on the measurement of sensitivity of individuals to nonverbal communication presented in motion picture film, found measurable differences among various groups, especially women, in their ability to understand meaning in nonverbal communication transmitted through different nonverbal channels in a non-naturalistic setting. When researchers have assessed accuracy, they have used unicultural standards of skills in intensifying emotions among children, adolescents, and adults (e.g., Izard 1971, J. Johnson 1975, Fry 1976, Greenspan et al. 1976, Rosenthal 1979). These standards might obscure cultural diversity.

20. Ekman and Friesen 1975. See D. Morris et al. 1979 on gesture in Europe and Efron 1941 on Italian use of gesture to illustrate objects and actions and European and Jewish use of abstract gestures to indicate the structure or logical progression of a discussion.

21. Henley 1977, J. Hall 1979, Rosenthal 1979, Mayo and Henley 1981.

22. Durkheim 1964:336.

23. See Kemper 1981.

24. Batcher 1981.

25. Hanna 1979a, 1979b, Shapiro 1981, Steiner 1981, Sebeok 1983. Philosophers have, of course, reflected upon the expression of emotion. Cf. Sirridge and Armelagos 1977, who critique the classical expression theory; they do

not accept the premise that the dancer-audience interaction is rooted in everyday behavioral interaction. They argue that style is more important than expression, yet the way emotion is communicated may be an aspect of style. See also Goodman 1968, who criticizes earlier expression theories and discusses the functions of emotion in art. Chapter 2 discusses some of the views of philosophers and other performance theorists.

26. An illustrative exception is Brown's 1979 survey of audience perception of feelings and ideas evoked by music performance. Berlyne (1971, 1974) conducted experimental studies of observer reaction to visual arts.

27. Guthrie 1976, Vlahos 1979.

28. Stanislavski 1936, Shawn 1954, Sachs 1937, Laban 1974, Langer 1953.

29. DiMaggio et al. 1978.

30. C. Morris 1955; rpt. 1971.

31. Hanna 1979*b*, 1982.

32. Barnes 1976 and Canadian conference on critics and society 1978; English 1979.

33. Mimeograph distributed at concert.

34. Kriegsman 1981*a*.

35. Quoted in Krucoff 1980.

36. Quoted in C. Hall 1980.

37. Kriegsman 1980*a*: F3.

38. Savitsky and Eby 1979.

39. Schieffelin 1979: 128.

40. Kapferer 1979.

41. Ellis 1923.

42. Kaiser 1980: A1.

43. *Washington Post*, August 21, 1980, A16.

44. Anderson 1980: E65.

## CHAPTER 2

1. J. Martin 1936: 92–93.

2. Jowitt 1981*b*: 75.

3. For example, Marett 1914, Radcliffe-Brown 1922 (rpt. 1933), Simmel (Wolf) 1950, Durkheim and Mauss 1963, and Durkheim 1964. Malinowski (1922) was concerned with phatic function. Evans-Pritchard (1965: 142) and Fernandez (1974) were aware that many feelings and concepts are inchoate. Linking these to visible objects enables the human mind to grasp them. The human experience of corporeal life makes the body an important communicative vehicle. Such scholars as Turner (1969), Geertz (1973), Blacking (1977), Heller (1979), and Hochschild (1979) are concerned with different aspects of the impact of human emotion in both sacred and secular life.

4. Taylor 1967: 68–69. See also Oesterley 1923, G. Mead 1926, Clive 1961.

5. Ries 1977.

6. Quoted in S. Cohen 1974: 2.

7. Quoted in Taylor 1967: 71.

8. Quoted in G. Mead 1926: 38.

9. The dances of Matthew 14: 6 and Mark 6: 21–29, Dance of Amalekites (1

Samuel 30:16), Incident of the Golden Calf (Exodus 32:1–6), and other kinds of unrestrained sensual forms of dance caused a negative reaction. See Backman 1952, Clive 1961, Taylor 1967:67.
10. National Council of Churches 1946, quoted in Taylor 1967.
11. Backman 1952:159 ff.
12. Taylor 1967:121–122.
13. Cole 1942.
14. Andrews 1940.
15. Kern 1975:93.
16. Benthall 1976:68.
17. Quoted in Yenckel 1980:C5.
18. Shawn 1954.
19. Ibid.:11.
20. Kandinsky 1977:71.
21. Quoted in Kaprelian 1979:55–56.
22. Stanislavski 1936:233; see Wiles 1980.
23. Foster 1977:39.
24. Ibid.:75.
25. Ibid.:123.
26. Sachs 1937:24.
27. Langer 1953:182.
28. Ibid.:187.
29. Spiegel and Machotka 1974:24–25.
30. Langer, 1953:177–178; see also p. 184.
31. Langer 1957:26.
32. Davitz 1964:193; Hanna 1979a:39–45, 86–89; see also M. Cohen 1981 for other problems with Langer's theory.
33. Quoted in S. Cohen 1974:59; see Beaumont 1935.
34. Quoted in S. Cohen 1974:62.
35. Quoted in Sorell 1981:305.
36. Duncan 1927, 1928.
37. Quoted in Beaumont 1935.
38. Hargrave 1980.
39. Quoted in Romola Nijinsky 1937:17, 92–93.
40. Kendall 1979:51.
41. Quoted in ibid.:202.
42. Ibid.:203.
43. Quoted in Kaprelian 1979:56.
44. Quoted in S. Cohen 1974:152.
45. Quoted in ibid.:136.
46. Graham 1973.
47. Quoted in Kisselgoff 1981b.
48. Quoted in Sorell 1981:395.
49. Quoted in S. Cohen 1974:191.
50. Quoted in Kriegsman 1980b.
51. Banes 1980.
52. Kisselgoff 1981a.

53. Paul 1980:58.
54. Quoted in ibid.:58.
55. Ibid.:61.
56. Quoted in C. Martin 1980:40.
57. Jowitt 1981*a*:65.
58. Ibid.
59. Ibid.

CHAPTER 3

1. Hanna 1976, 1979*a*, 1980, 1983*a*.
2. See Stearns and Stearns 1968.
3. P'Bitek 1966.
4. Quoted in Kriegsman 1980*a*.
5. See Emery 1972.
6. For an example of what is taught, see Ames and Siegelman 1977.
7. Croce 1980.
8. See appendix for discussion of methodology.
9. See appendix table 3 for a range of dimensions of conveying emotion.
10. Although happy eyes roll or follow another dancer's movement and sad eyes droop, one way black women offstage show anger is by rolling their eyes at an adversary (Hanna 1984).

CHAPTER 4

1. Bowers 1953:9.
2. Ibid.:31. See chapter 10 for further discussion of these concepts.
3. Chaki-Sircar and Sircar 1982.
4. Bowers 1953:30.
5. Devi 1972; see also Rao 1959.
6. Bowers 1956:31.
7. Vatsyayan 1962:51.
8. Ibid.
9. Ibid.
10. Khokar, mimeograph distributed at concert.
11. Quoted in program.
12. Jackson 1980.
13. See appendix for a discussion of methodology.
14. See appendix table 3 for a range of dimensions that convey emotion.
15. Vatsyayan 1962:53.

CHAPTER 5

1. Terry 1980; see also Carroll 1981, who reports on a four-day festival devoted to early American modern dance.
2. Warren 1980:16.
3. J. Martin 1936:9.
4. Barnes 1981.
5. Forsberg 1980:E9.
6. Stowe 1980.

7. Kriegsman 1980*c*:E11.
8. Goldner 1980.
9. Welsh 1980:C1, 22.
10. Quoted in Lloyd 1949:143.
11. Quoted in ibid.:139.
12. Schlundt 1972:28.
13. Ibid.:7.
14. See appendix for a discussion of methodology.
15. See appendix table 3 for a range of dimensions that convey emotion.

CHAPTER 6

Note: Parts of this chapter and the introduction were presented at the "Signs in the Field: Semiotic Perspectives on Ethnographic Research" panel of the Annual Meeting of the American Anthropologial Association, December 1981, and the "Symposium on Perception and Criticism" of the Annual Meeting of the Society for Ethnomusicology, November 1982. I thank the panelists, especially Michael Herzfeld, for their helpful comments.
1. The people who exited during the performance became a stage through their distraction of other performance participants.
2. Brown and Dunn 1976.
3. Riesman 1950.
4. Schjeldahl 1981:67.
5. Kriegsman 1981*a*:B9.
6. Welsh 1981*a*:D5.
7. See appendix for a discussion of methodology.
8. See appendix table 3 for a range of dimensions that convey emotion.
9. This is the only concert for which religion was examined as a background characteristic. Too few respondents reported on this category at other concerts.
10. Banes (1980) provides the key background source on post-modern.
11. Kriegsman 1981*b*:32.
12. J. Morris 1981:1.

CHAPTER 7

1. Gunji 1970:71. Leonard Pronko is gratefully acknowledged for his most helpful comments on an earlier draft of this chapter.
2. Shively 1978:4.
3. Kincaid 1925.
4. Bowers 1952:42.
5. Quoted in Ernst 1956:165.
6. Kincaid 1925:60.
7. Pronko 1977:27.
8. Ibid.:68.
9. Ibid.:65.
10. Havens 1982:chapter 8.
11. Ibid.:54.
12. Ernst 1956:170–171.

13. Gunji 1970:120.
14. Bowers 1952:179.
15. Ernst 1956:73.
16. Ibid.:76.
17. Ibid.:86.
18. Gunji 1970:67.
19. Ito 1979:273.
20. Gunji 1970:68.
21. Ibid.:71.
22. Ernst 1956:87.
23. Jackson 1981.
24. See appendix for a discussion of methodology.
25. Sullivan 1927:52.
26. See appendix table 3 for a range of dimensions that convey emotion.

CHAPTER 8

1. Robertson 1980. (References 1–6 are from S. A. Kriegsman's file.)
2. Dyer 1981; Hutera 1980.
3. Hutera 1980.
4. Robertson 1980.
5. Ibid.
6. Hutera 1980.
7. Van Camp 1981.

CHAPTER 9

1. Tolentino 1935, 1946.
2. Alejandro 1978.
3. According to Dane Harwood (personal communication), the candle-dance is ubiquitous in Southeast Asia. In this case the Spanish fandango has been adapted to the purpose.
4. Jowitt 1980.
5. See appendix for a discussion of methodology.
6. See appendix table 3 for a range of dimensions that convey emotion.

CHAPTER 10

1. Jones and Jones 1970:12.
2. Chaki-Sircar and Sircar 1982.
3. Bowers 1953:98.
4. The concepts of *bhava* and *rasa* are interrelated.
5. Vatsyayan 1968.
6. Jowitt 1981c.
7. Kisselgoff 1981c.
8. Kriegsman 1981c.
9. Welsh 1981b.
10. See appendix for a discussion of methodology.
11. See appendix table 3 for a range of dimensions that convey emotion.

CHAPTER 11
1. Darwin 1965 ed.:365.
2. See Hanna 1979*a* for a review of findings on psychobiological bases of dance.
3. Louis 1980:92.
4. Martin 1936:117.
5. Lumsden and Wilson 1981.
6. Wigman (Europa 1/1, [May–July 1933]) in S. Cohen 1974:149.
7. Kirstein 1973:82.
8. Selden 1935:177.
9. Humphrey 1959.
10. See appendix table 3 for a range of dimensions that convey emotion.
11. Cf. Kagan 1958.
12. Martin 1936:114–115.
13. See Hanna 1965.
14. Levy 1980:42.
15. Quoted in Mokwa 1980.
16. Martin 1936:85.
17. Hanna 1983*b*.

CHAPTER 12
1. Cf. Perkins and Leondar 1977.
2. Lakoff and Johnson 1980, Ortony 1979. They build upon forebears: Freud explored the meanings of individuals' metaphors, and Durkheim concentrated on collective representations. I wish to acknowledge my appreciation to Barbara Kirshenblatt-Gimblatt, Langdon Elsbree, Jack Anderson, Anne Marie Welsh, and Lena Orlin, who called to my attention proverbs and literary materials, and to Janet Goodridge and Jean Cunningham, for quotations in London publications. I am most grateful to Orlin, Cunningham, Allan Cunningham, Joan and Barry Stahl, Barry Laine, and William John Hanna for their helpful and insightful comments on portions or earlier drafts of this chapter. Some of the material has appeared in "Dancing Off-Stage," *Stagebill* 11/3 (1982):25–26, 29–30, 37, and in the session on Semantic Processes in the Culture of Language, Annual Meeting of the American Anthropological Association, 1982.
3. Kenneth Burke articulated the dramaturgical model for social life that has been implicit in common parlance since Shakespeare's image of the world as a stage. There is yet classical precedent. Burke viewed human life as the interplay of scenes, acts, actors, agencies, and purposes. The view of the world as a stage, further elaborated by Erving Goffman and Victor Turner, has become a common principle in contemporary social science.
4. The dramaturgical model as a metaphorical explanatory strategy appears in the press. For example: "Lights, Camera, Fire" headlines an article on the United States shooting of Libyan aircraft in retaliation for being fired upon in what the United States considered international space. The mass media "would explain the theatrical nature. . . . When it is judged on its merits as dramatic presentation rather than as military exploit, President Reagan and

Col. Muammar Qaddafi appear as co-producers." Both countries have been engaged for several years in conflict. Therefore, they appeared to have been "playing to secondary audiences. Reagan wished to 'make American power impressive' [to the world] . . . Qaddafi wished to rally Arab opinion to the standard of anti-imperialism" (Lapham 1981:20).

5. Louis 1980:26.
6. Jackson 1977.
7. Proverbs come from Apperson 1929, Davidoff 1946, Smith 1948, Stevenson 1948, Tilley 1950, Wilson 1970, and Henke 1979.
8. Gilliam 1981.
9. *Newsweek* 1980.
10. Henke 1979:63–64.
11. Gorney 1981*a*.
12. Anderson 1980.
13. Prochnau 1981.
14. *Economist* 1981.
15. Gorney 1981*b*.
16. *New York Times* 1981*a*.
17. Evans and Novak 1981.
18. Williams 1981.
19. O'Neill 1981.
20. *Washington Post* 1981*c*.
21. *Washington Post* 1981*a*.
22. Washington Post *1981b*.
23. New York Times 1981*b*.
24. *Guardian* 1981.
25. Young 1981.
26. *Los Angeles Times* 1981.
27. Wynne 1970, S. Cohen 1974:42–51.
28. C. Hall 1980.
29. Anderson 1981.
30. Crossette 1979, Stampfel 1981.
31. Keil 1979.
32. Hentoff 1981. "Abscam" stands for the United States Federal Bureau of Investigation's Arab scam operation, the entrapment of congressmen through an undercover agent posing as an Arab and offering a gift in exchange for a favor. Seven congressmen were convicted on bribery and conspiracy charges.
33. Shapiro and Bauer 1980.
34. Safire 1981.
35. J. Taylor 1976.
36. Erenberg 1981.
37. Markham 1981.
38. Dewar 1981.
39. Branigan 1981.
40. *South African Digest* 1981.
41. Katz 1973.
42. Lewis 1981.

43. Rosellini 1980.
44. McGory 1981.
45. Ivins 1981.
46. W. Brown 1981.
47. In this discussion I do not provide illustrations of the term *dance* or the name of a particular dance used metaphorically in book or play titles (e.g., anthropologist Robert Briffaualt's *Fandango* [New York: Scribners, 1940], or Eric Redman's *The Dance of Legislation* [New York: Simon and Schuster, 1973]). This exclusion is due to my limited knowledge of the literature and the lack of a study on the meanings of such titles.
48. Mirabella 1979.
49. Elsbree 1961.
50. Elsbree 1972:364.
51. Ibid.:366.
52. Elsbree 1961:607–608.
53. Elsbree 1972:367.
54. Dance recurs as a leitmotif to signify weapons of class distinction and the complete failure of the play element. Lawrence rejects the rivalry, competition, and release-through-winning kind of play in favor of Johan Huizinga's "sacred play"—the human effort to realize cosmic dynamics of birth, growth, and death and to participate in these. In his *Homo Ludens: A Study of the Play Element in Culture*, Huizinga contends "that culture arises in the form of play." Hence "When Lawrence's dancers transcend play and achieve sacred play, they achieve order and unity . . . almost all of Lawrence's dancers, however they fail, at least crave what Lawrence himself found in the dance—a vital playfulness and integrity" (Elsbree 1968:28).
55. Elsbree 1968:4.
56. White 1979.
57. Vickers 1974.
58. Quoted in Vickers 1974:26.
59. Quoted in Anderson 1972:52.
60. Allen 1981:167.
61. Quoted in Gardner 1978:85.
62. According to Derek Traversi (1976:112), the image of "dance" is "a figure of our experience in its temporal guise or 'movement', distinguished by the intuitive presence of form, 'pattern', from mere anarchic flow. The 'dance', . . . might be comprehensible as a reflection of the central point of reference in relation to which its successive motions fall into place."

# References

Alejandro, Reynaldo G.
   1978   *Philippine Dance: Mainstream and Crosscurrents.* Philippines: Vera-Reyes.
Allen, Catherine J.
   1981.   "To Be Quechua: The Symbolism of Coca Chewing in Highland Peru." *American Anthropologist* 8/1 : 157–167.
Ames, Jerry, and Jim Siegelman
   1977   *The Book of Tap.* New York: David McKay.
Anderson, Jack (ed.)
   1972   *The Dance, the Dancer, and the Poem.* Dance Perspectives 52.
Anderson, Jack
   1980   "The Greediness of the OPEC Moguls." *Washington Post*, September 6, p. E65.
   1981   "The Mitterand Minuet." *Washington Post*, July 19, p. C7.
Andrews, Edwards
   1940   *The Gift to Be Simple: Song, Dances and Rituals of the American Shakers.* New York: Dover.
Apperson, George Latimer
   1929   *English Proverbs and Proverbial Phrases.* New York: Dutton.
Ashworth, P. D.
   1979   *Social Interaction and Consciousness.* New York: Wiley and Sons.
Backman, E. Louis
   1952   *Religious Dances in the Christian Church and in Popular Medicine.* Trans. E. Classen. London: George Allen and Unwin.
Bain, Sandy Kyle
   1980   "Teaching Candidates to Beat the Press." *Washington Post*, June 22, p. L1.
Banes, Sally
   1980   *Terpsichore in Sneakers: Post-Modern Dance.* Boston: Houghton Mifflin.
Barnes, Clive
   1976   "The 'Terrible Power' of Critics over Institutions." *New York Times*, July 25, pp. 10, 16.

1978   "Dance Criticism." *Stagebill* 8/3 : 33 – 34, 43 – 44.
1981   "Yesterday Modern Dance at Riverside." *New York Post*, April 5.
Batcher, Elaine
1981   *Emotion in the Classroom: A Study of Children's Experience*. New York: Praeger.
Beaumont, Cyril W.
1935   *Michel Fokine and His Ballets*. London: Beaumont.
Benthall, Jonathan
1976   *Body Electric: Patterns of Western Industrial Culture*. London: Thames and Hudson.
Berlyne, D. E.
1971   *Aesthetics and Psychobiology*. New York: Appleton-Century-Crofts.
1974   *Studies in the New Experimental Aesthetics: Steps toward an Objective Psychology of Aesthetic Appreciation*. New York: John Wiley.
Birdwhistell, Ray L.
1970   *Kinesics and Context: Essays on Body Motion Communication*. Philadelphia: University of Pennsylvania Press.
p'Bitek, Okot
1966   *Song of Lawino*. Nairobi: East African Publishing House.
Blacking, John (ed.)
1977   *The Anthropology of the Body*. A.S.A. Monograph 15. London: Academic Press.
Boucher, Jerry D.
1979.  "Culture and Emotion." In *Perspectives on Cross-Cultural Psychology*, ed. Anthony J. Marsella, Roland G. Tharp, and Thomas J. Ciborowski, pp. 159 – 178. New York: Academic Press.
Bowers, Faubion
1952   *Japanese Theater*. Westport, Conn.: Greenwood Press.
1953   *The Dance in India*. New York: Columbia University Press.
1956   *Theatre in the East*. New York: Thomas Nelson.
Branigin, William
1981   "Latest Tango in Ho Chi Minh City Plays with a Russian Leading." *Washington Post*, August 23, p. A19.
Brown, Roger
1979   "Music and Language." Paper presented at the Ann Arbor Symposium.
Brown, Trish, and Douglas Dunn
1976   "Dialogue on Dance." *Performing Arts Journal* 1/2 : 76 – 83.
Brown, Warren
1981   "Coal Contract Talks: Dancing on Deadline." *Washington Post*, March 16, p. A2.
Burke, Kenneth
1941   *The Philosophy of Literary Form*. New York: Random House.
Carroll, Noel
1981   "The Early Years, American Modern Dance from 1900 through the 1930s." *Dancemagazine* (August): 24 – 25, 72 – 74, 84 – 85.
Chaki-Sircar, Manjusri, and Parbati K. Sircar
1982   "Indian Dance: Classical Unity and Regional Variation." In *India: Cul-*

*tural Patterns and Processes*, ed. Allen G. Noble and Ashok K. Dutt, pp. 147–164. Boulder: Westview Press.

Clive, H. P.
1961 "The Calvinists and the Question of Dancing in the Sixteenth Century." *Bibliothèque d'Humanisme et Renaissance* 23:296–323.

Cohen, Abner
1980 "Drama and Politics in the Development of a London Carnival." *Man* 15/1:65–87.

Cohen, Marshall
1981 "Primitivism, Modernism and Dance Theory." In *Philosophical Essays on Dance*, ed. Gordon Fancher and Gerald Myers, pp. 138–166. New York: Dance Horizons.

Cohen, Selma Jeanne (ed. and commentator)
1974 Dance as a Theatre Art. New York: Dodd, Mead and Co.

Cole, Arthur
1942 "The Puritan and Fair Terpshichore." *Mississippi Valley Historical Review* 29/1, *Dance Horizons* reprint.

Croce, Arlene
1980 "Dancing: Doing the Old Low Down." *New Yorker*, April 28, pp. 133–136.

Crossette, Barbara
1979 "Ten Days and Nights of Polka Upstate." *New York Times*, August 10, p. C25.

Darwin, Charles
1965 *The Expression of the Emotions in Man and Animals*. Chicago: University of Chicago Press. Reprint of 1872 edition.

Davidoff, Henry
1946 *A World Treasury of Proverbs*. New York: Random House.

Davis, Martha
1979 "The State of the Art." In *Nonverbal Behavior*, ed. Aaron Wolfgang, pp. 51–66. New York: Academic Press.

Davitz, Joel, with Michael Beldoch et al.
1964 *The Communication of Emotional Meaning*. Westport, Conn.: Greenwood Press.

Devi, Ragini
1972 *Dance Dialects of India*. Delhi: Vikas Publications.

Dewar, Helen
1981. "The Budget Tango: How Yes Turns into No." *Washington Post*, April 11, p. A5.

DiMaggio, Paul, Michael Useem, and Paula Brown
1978 *Audience Studies of the Performing Arts and Museums: A Critical Review*. Washington, D.C.: National Endowment for the Arts, Research Division Report No. 9.

Duncan, Isadora
1927 *My Life*. New York: Liveright.
1928 *The Art of the Dance*. New York: Theatre Arts Books.

Durkheim, Emile
   1964   "The Dualism of Human Nature and Its Social Conditions." Trans. C.
          Blend. In *Essays on Sociology and Philosophy*, ed. K. H. Wolff. New
          York: Harper Torchbooks.
Durkheim, Emile, and Marcel Mauss
   1963   *Primitive Classification*. London: Cohen and West. Reprint of 1903
          edition.
*Economist* (UK)
   1981   "Hu's in Hua's Out." July 4–10, pp. 34, 36.
Efron, David
   1941   *Gesture and Environment*. New York: King's Crown Press.
Eibl-Eibesfeldt, Irenäus
   1972   "Similarities and Differences between Cultures in Expressive Move-
          ments." In *Nonverbal Communication*, ed. R. A. Hinde, pp. 297–314.
          Cambridge: Cambridge University Press.
   1979   "Universals in Human Expressive Behavior." In *Nonverbal Behavior*,
          ed. Aaron Wolfgang, pp. 17–30. New York: Academic Press.
Ekman, Paul
   1980   *The Face of Man*. New York: Garlant STPM Press.
Ekman, Paul, and Wallace V. Friesen
   1969   "The Repertoire of Nonverbal Behavior: Categories, Origins, Usage,
          and Coding." *Semiotica* 1 : 49–98.
   1975   *Unmasking the Face*. Englewood Cliffs: Prentice-Hall.
Ekman, Paul, and Harriet Oster
   1979   "Facial Expressions of Emotion." *Annual Review of Psychology*
          30 : 527–554.
Ellis, Havelock
   1923   *The Dance of Life*. Boston: Houghton Mifflin.
Elsbree, Langdon
   1961   "Tess and the Local Cerealia." *Philological Quarterly* 40/4 : 606–613.
   1968   "D. H. Lawrence, Homo Ludens, and the Dance." *D. H. Lawrence Re-
          view* 1 : 1–30.
   1972   "The Purest and Most Perfect Form of Play: Some Novelists and the
          Dance." *Criticism* 14/4 : 361–372.
Emery, Lynne Fauley
   1972   *Black Dance in the United States from 1619 to 1970*. Palo Alto: Na-
          tional Book Press.
English, John W.
   1979   *Criticizing the Critics*. New York: Hastings House.
Erenberg, Lewis A.
   1981   *Steppin' Out: New York Nightlife and the Transformation of American
          Culture 1890–1930*. Westport, Conn.: Greenwood Press.
Erickson, Frederick
   1979   "Talking Down: Some Cultural Sources of Miscommunication in Inter-
          racial Interviews." In *Nonverbal Behavior*, ed. Aaron Wolfgang, pp.
          100–126. New York: Academic Press.

Ernst, Earle
1956   *The Kabuki Theatre.* New York: Oxford University Press.
Evans, Rowland, and Robert Novak
1981   "Big Business Is Furious, Too." *Washington Post,* June 8, p. A15.
Evans-Pritchard, E. E.
1965   *Theories of Primitive Religion.* Oxford: Clarendon Press.
Fernandez, James
1974   "The Mission of Metaphor in Expressive Culture." *Current Anthropology* 15/2: 119–145.
Forsberg, Helen
1980   "RDT Brings Modern Dance History to Stage." *Salt Lake Tribune,* March 16, p. E9.
Foster, John
1977   *The Influences of Rudolf Laban.* London: Lepus.
Fry, P. S.
1976   "Children's Social Sensitivity, Altruism, and Self-Gratification." *Journal of Social Psychology* 98: 77–88.
Gardner, Helen
1978   *The Composition of "Four Quartets".* New York: Oxford University Press.
Geertz, Clifford
1973   *The Interpretation of Culture.* New York: Basic Books.
Gilliam, Dorothy
1981   "Sidestepping: The Dance of Two Mayors under Fire." *Washington Post,* April 13, p. B2.
Goffman, Erving
1959   *The Presentation of Self in Everyday Life.* New York: Doubleday.
Goldner, Nancy
1980   "Raising Your Consciousness." *Soho Weekly Review,* April 9.
Goodenough, Ward H.
1957   "Cultural Anthropology and Linguistics." In *Report of the Seventh Annual Round Table Meeting on Linguistics and Language Study,* ed. P. L. Garvin. Washington: Georgetown University Monograph Series on Linguistics No. 9.
Goodman, Nelson
1968   *Languages of Art.* New York: Bobbs-Merrill.
Gorney, Cynthia
1981a   "Coping: 'Equivocado' Telephones, Appliances That Dance." *Washington Post,* February 22, p. A23.
1981b   "Argentina Dances 'The Process,' a Slow Martial Step." *Washington Post,* October 3, p. 1.
Graham, Martha
1973   *The Notebooks of Martha Graham.* New York: Harcourt Brace Jovanovich.
Greenspan, Stephen, Carl Barenboim, and Michael J. Chandler
1976   "Empathy and Pseudoempathy: The Affective Judgements of First- and Third-Graders." *Journal of Genetic Psychology* 129: 77–88.

*Guardian* (UK)
  1981   "Fleet Street Takes a Gamble on Bingo." October 16, p. 4.
Gunji, Masakatsu
  1970   *Buyo: The Classical Dance.* New York: Walker/Weatherhill.
Guthrie, R. Dale
  1976   *Body Hot Spots: The Anatomy of Social Organs and Behavior.* New York: Van Nostrand Reinhold.
Hall, Carla
  1980   "The Great Post-Election Memoir Minuet." *Washington Post*, November 26, p. B1.
Hall, Edward T.
  1966   *The Hidden Dimension.* Garden City, N.Y.: Doubleday.
Hall, Judith A.
  1979   "Gender, Gender Roles, and Nonverbal Communication Skills." In *Skill in Nonverbal Communication: Individual Differences*, ed. Robert Rosenthal, pp. 32–67. Cambridge, Mass.: Oelgeschlager, Gunn and Hain.
Hanna, Judith Lynne
  1965   "Africa's New Traditional Dance." *Ethnomusicology* 9:13–21.
  1976   "The Anthropology of Dance Ritual: Nigeria's Ubakala Nkwa di Iche Iche." Ph.D. dissertation, Columbia University. Ann Arbor: University Microfilms (#76-28, 657).
  1979a  *To Dance Is Human: A Theory of Nonverbal Communication.* Austin: University of Texas Press.
  1979b  "Toward Semantic Analysis of Movement Behavior: Concepts and Problems." *Semiotica* 25/1–2:77–110.
  1980   "African Dance Research: Past, Present, and Future." *Africana Journal* 11/1:33–51.
  1982   "Public Social Policy and the Children's World: Implications of Ethnographic Research for Desegregated Schooling." In *Doing the Ethnography of Schooling: Educational Anthropology in Action*, ed. George D. Spindler, pp. 316–355. New York: Holt, Rinehart and Winston.
  1983a  "Movement in African Performance." In *Bibliographic Anthology of Theatre Movement*, ed. Bob Fleshman. Metuchen: Scarecrow Press.
  1983b  "The Mentality and Matter of Dance." *Art Education* (special issue on Arts and the Mind, ed. Martin Engel) 3/2:42–46.
  1984   "Black/White Nonverbal Differences, Dance, and Dissonance." In *Second International Conference on Nonverbal Behavior: An Intercultural Perspective*, ed. Aaron Wolfgang. Toronto.
Hargrave, Susan Lee
  1980   "The Choreographic Innovations of Vaslov Nijinsky." Ph.D. dissertation. Cornell University.
Havens, Thomas R. H.
  1982   *Artist and Patron in Postwar Japan: Dance, Music, Theatre and the Visual Arts 1955–1980.* Princeton: Princeton University Press.

Heller, Agnes
1979 "Towards an Anthropology of Feeling." *Dialectical Anthropology* 4/1 : 1 – 20.
Henke, James T.
1979 *Courtesans and Cuckolds: A Glossary of Renaissance Dramatic Bawdy (Exclusive of Shakespeare).* New York: Garland.
Henley, Nancy
1977 *Body Politics, Power, Sex and Nonverbal Communication.* Englewood Cliffs: Prentice-Hall.
Hentoff, Nat
1981 "Tom Puccio and Bill Webster/The Soft-Shoe Dancers." *Village Voice,* March 18 – 24, p. 8.
Hochschild, Arlie Russell
1979 "Emotion Work, Feeling Rules and Social Structure." *American Journal of Sociology* 85/3 : 551 – 575.
Horst, Louis, and Carroll Russell
1961 *Modern Dance Forms in Relation to the Other Modern Arts.* San Francisco: Impulse Publications.
Hsu, Francis L. K.
1980 "Margaret Mead and Psychological Anthropology." *American Anthropologist* 82/2 : 349 – 353.
Huizinga, Johan
1950 Homo Ludens: A Study of the Play Element in Culture. Boston: Beacon.
Humphrey, Doris
1959 *The Art of Making Dances.* New York: Rinehart.
Hutera, Donald
1980 "Sage Cowles and Molly Davies." *Twin Cities Reader,* May 21.
Ito, Sachiyo
1979 "Some Characteristics of Japanese Expression as They Appear in Dance." In *Dance Research Collage,* pp. 267 – 281. New York: Congress on Research in Dance.
Ivins, Molly
1981 "New Steps in Budget Waltz Help Ease the Go Around." *New York Times,* June 19, p. B3.
Izard, Carroll E.
1971 *The Face of Emotion.* New York: Appleton-Century-Crofts.
1979 (ed.) *Emotions in Personality and Psychopathology.* New York: Plenum.
1980 "Cross-Cultural Perspectives on Emotion and Emotion Communication." In *Handbook of Cross-cultural Psychology,* ed. Harry C. Triandis and William Wilson Lambert, vol. 3. pp. 185 – 221. Boston: Allyn and Bacon.
Jackson, George
1977 "Viennese Waltzes." *New York City Ballet Program Notes.*
1980 "Indrani." *Washington Post,* October 29, p. B2.
1981 "Sachiyo Ito." *Washington Post,* February 23, p. D7.

Jedlicka, Judith Ann
  1979  "Business Is Investing in Dance: It Makes Good Business Sense." *Grants Magazine* 2/1 : 41 – 47.
Johnson, J. W.
  1975  "Affective Perspective Taking and Cooperative Pre-Disposition." *Developmental Psychology* 11 : 869 – 870.
Johnson, Kenneth R.
  1976  "Black Kinesics: Some Non-verbal Communication Patterns in the Black Culture." In *Intercultural Communication*, 2nd ed., ed. Larry A. Samovar and Richard E. Porter, pp. 259 – 268. Belmont, Ca.: Wadsworth.
Jones, Clifford R., and Betty True Jones
  1970  *Kathakali.* San Francisco: American Society for Eastern Arts.
Jowitt, Deborah
  1980  "Better a Link than the End of the Line." *Village Voice*, September 24 – 30, p. 77.
  1981a "Abandoning the Ivory Tower." *Village Voice*, January 7 – 13, p. 65.
  1981b "A Slack String Won't Resonate: A Tight One May Snap." *Village Voice*, February 4 – 10, p. 75.
  1981c "I'll Give You the Answer—If You've Got a Week." *Village Voice*, May 6 – 12, p. 81.
Kagan, Jerome
  1958  "The Concept of Identification." *Psychological Review* 65 : 296 – 305.
Kaiser, Robert G.
  1980  "The Morning After." *Washington Post*, September 23, p. A1.
Kandinsky, Wassily
  1977  *Concerning the Spiritual in Art.* Unabridged republication of *The Art of Spiritual Harmony.* New York: Dover.
Kapferer, Bruce
  1979  "Emotion and Feeling in Sinhalese Healing Rites." *Social Analysis* 1 : 153 – 176.
Kaprelian, Mary H.
  1979  "Parallel Trends in the Development of German Expressionist Painting and Modern Dance." In *New Directions in Dance (Collected Writings from the Seventh Dance in Canada Conference Held at the University of Waterloo)*, ed. Diana Theodores Taplin, pp. 51 – 59. Toronto: Pergamon.
Katz, Ruth
  1973  "The Egalitarian Waltz." *Comparative Studies in Society and History* 15 : 368 – 377.
Keil, Charles
  1979  "Class and Ethnicity in Polish-America." *Journal of Ethnic Studies* 7/2 : 37 – 45.
Kemper, Theodore D.
  1978  *A Social Interactional Theory of Emotions.* New York: John Wiley.
  1981  "Social Constructionist and Positivist Approaches to the Sociology of Emotions." *American Journal of Sociology* 87/2 : 336 – 362.

Kendall, Elizabeth
1979  *Where She Danced.* New York: Alfred A. Knopf.
Kendon, Adam
1983  "Nonverbal Communication." In *Encyclopedic Dictionary of Semiotics,* ed. Thomas A. Sebeok. Bloomington and London: Indiana University Press and Macmillan.
Kern, Stephen
1975  *Anatomy and Destiny: A Cultural History of the Human Body.* New York: Bobbs-Merrill.
Khokar, Mohan
1979  *Traditions of Indian Classical Dance.* Delhi: Clarion Books.
Kincaid, Zoe
1925  *Kabuki: The Popular Stage of Japan.* New York: Macmillan.
Kirstein, Lincoln
1973  *The New York City Ballet.* New York: Knopf.
Kisselgoff, Anna
1981*a*  "Recent Choreographic Novelties." *New York Times,* January 4, pp. 18–19.
1981*b*  "Dance: Martha Graham in Washington." *New York Times,* February 28.
1981*c*  "Dance: Indian Kathakali." *New York Times,* April 26, p. 38.
Kriegsman, Alan M.
1980*a*  "Honi Coles, Tapping His Feet." *Washington Post,* August 16, p. D3.
1980*b*  "Tahl." *Washington Post,* September 26, p. F3.
1980*c*  "Utah Repertory Dance." *Washington Post,* October 27, p. E11.
1981*a*  "Douglas Dunn, in Step." *Washington Post,* January 12, p. C2.
1981*b*  "Douglas Dunn." *Washington Post,* January 14, p. B9.
1981*c*  "Kathakali Dancers." *Washington Post,* May 29, p. C2.
Kroeber Alfred, and Talcott Parsons
1958  "The Concept of Culture and of Social System." *American Sociological Review* 23 : 582–583.
Krucoff, Carol
1980  "You: Sending Out Messages of Muggability?" *Washington Post,* December 9, p. B5.
Laban, Rudolf
1974  *The Language of Movement: A Guidebook to Choreutics,* annotated and ed. Lisa Ullmann. Boston: Plays. Reprint of 1966 edition.
La Barre, Weston
1947  "The Cultural Basis of Emotions and Gesture." *Journal of Personality* 16 : 49–68.
Lakoff, George, and Mark Johnson
1980  *Metaphors We Live By.* Chicago: University of Chicago Press.
Langer, Susanne K.
1953  *Feeling and Form: A Theory of Art Developed from Philosophy in a New Key.* New York: Charles Scribner's Sons.
1957  *Philosophy in a New Key: A Study of the Symbolism of Reason, Rite and Art.* 3rd ed. Cambridge, Mass.: Harvard University Press.

Lapham, Lewis H.
    1981   "Lights, Camera, Fire!" *Washington Post*, August 29, p. 20.
Levy, Sidney J.
    1980   "Arts, Consumers and Aesthetic Attributes." In Marketing the Arts, ed.
            Michael P. Mokwa, William M. Dawson, and E. Arthur Prieve, pp.
            29–46. New York: Praeger.
Lewis, Paul
    1981   "The Austrian Economy Is a Strauss Waltz." *New York Times*, March
            22, p. 8.
Lloyd, Margaret
    1949   *The Borzoi Book of Modern Dance*. New York: Knopf.
*Los Angeles Times*
    1981   "Struggling at the Tuition Door." August 18.
Louis, Murray
    1980   *Inside Dance*. New York: St. Martin's Press.
Lucian
    1905   "On the Dance (De Saltatione)." *The Works of Lucian of Samosata*,
            trans. H. W. Fowler and F. G. Fowler, 4 volumes, vol. 2.
Lumsden, Charles J., and Edward O. Wilson
    1981   Genes, Mind and Culture. Cambridge, Mass.: Harvard University Press.
McGory, Mary
    1981   "Court Advice to Democrats on Really Reforming Social Security."
            *Washington Post*, September 17, p. A3.
Malinowski, Bronislaw
    1922   *Argonauts of the Western Pacific*. London: Routledge and Sons.
Marett, R. R.
    1914   *The Threshold of Religion*. London: Methuen.
Markham, James M.
    1981   "The 'Coup Tango' and Other Political Hits and Misses: By One Mea-
            sure, Madrid Cools Down." *New York Times*, July 26, p. E2.
Martin, Carol
    1980   "Joanna Boyce: An Interview." *Dance Scope* 14/4 : 35–50.
Martin, John
    1936   *America Dancing*. New York: Dodge.
Mayo, Clara, and Nancy M. Henley (eds.)
    1981   Gender and Nonverbal Behavior. New York: Springer-Verlag.
Mead, George Herbert
    1934   *Mind, Self and Society*. Chicago: University of Chicago Press.
Mead, G. R. S. (ed.)
    1926   *The Sacred Dance in Christendom*. London: John M. Watkins.
Mirabella, Bella Maryanne
    1979   "Part I, Mute Rhetoric: Dance in Shakespeare and Marston." Ph.D. dis-
            sertation. Rutgers University.
Mokwa, Michael P., and William M. Dawson (eds.)
    1980   *Marketing the Arts*. New York: Praeger.

Morris, Charles
  1971  *Writings of the General Theory of Signs (Approaches to Semiotics 16).* The Hague: Mouton. Reprint of 1955 edition.
Morris, Desmond, Peter Collett, Peter Marsh, and Marie O'Shaughnessy
  1979  *Gestures: Their Origins and Distribution.* New York: Stein and Day.
Morris, James R.
  1981  "Balancing Acts." *Notes on the Arts* (January–February): 1.
Neisser, Ulric
  1967  *Cognitive Psychology.* New York: Appleton-Century-Crofts.
*Newsweek*
  1980  "The Legal Mating Dance." December 1, p. 111.
*New York Times*
  1980  "Ivory Coast Holding Its First Open Vote since 1960." November 9, p. 4.
  1981*a*  "100 Days." April 26, p. E22.
  1981*b*  "Soviet Asserts Reagan Sets Stage for 'Dances of Death.'" November 6, p. A7.
Nijinsky, Romola (ed.)
  1937  The Diary of Vaslav Nijinsky. London: Gollancz.
Nine Curt, Carmen Judith
  1976  *Non-verbal Communication in Puerto Rico.* Cambridge, Mass.: National Assessment and Dissemination Center ESEA, Title VII.
Oesterley, W. O. E.
  1923  *The Sacred Dance.* Cambridge: Cambridge University Press.
O'Neill, Alison
  1981  "Dance of the Ambassadors." *Washington Post*, February 4, p. B2.
Ortony, Andrew
  1979  *Metaphor and Thought.* Cambridge: Cambridge University Press.
Paul, Janice
  1980  "Judy Padow: An Analysis." *Dance Scope* 14/4:51–61.
Perkins, David, and Barbara Leondar
  1977  *The Arts and Cognition.* Baltimore: Johns Hopkins University Press.
Plutchik, Robert
  1980  *Emotion: A Psychoevolutionary Synthesis.* New York: Harper and Row.
Prochnau, Bill
  1981  "Dancer in the Goodness of Government." *Washington Post*, May 2, p. A2.
Pronko, Leonard C.
  1977  "Kabuki Dance." Unpublished ms. available from author, Pomona College, Cal.
Radcliffe-Brown, A. R.
  1933  *Adaman Islanders.* Cambridge: Cambridge University Press. Reprint of 1922 edition.
Rao, Vissa Appa
  1959  "Kuchipudi School of Dancing." *Sangeet Natak Akademi Bulletin* 11–12:1–8.

Ries, Frank W. D.
    1977   "Plato on the Dance." *Dance Scope* 11/2 : 53 – 60.
Riesman, David
    1950   *The Lonely Crowd.* New Haven: Yale University Press.
de Rivera, Joseph
    1977   "A Structural Theory of Emotions." *Psychological Issues* 10/4. Monograph 40.
Robertson, Allen
    1980   "Footsteps and Film." *Minneapolis Star*, May 16, p. C8.
Rosellini, Lynn
    1980   "Reagan Asks for a First Waltz and Wins Hearts in the Capital." *New York Times*, November 19, p. A1.
Rosenthal, Robert (ed.)
    1979   *Skill in Nonverbal Communication: Individual Differences.* Cambridge, Mass.: Oelgeschlager, Gunn and Hain.
Sachs, Curt
    1937   *World History of the Dance.* New York: W. W. Norton.
Safire, William
    1981   "On Language." *New York Times Magazine*, November 8, pp. 16, 18.
Savitsky, Jeffrey C., and Thomas Eby
    1979   "Emotion Awareness and Antisocial Behavior." In *Emotions in Personality and Psychopathology*, ed. Carroll E. Izard, pp. 475 – 492. New York: Plenum.
Schechner, Richard
    1977   *Essays on Performance Theory 1970 – 1976.* New York: Drama Books.
Scheflen, Albert E.
    1964   "The Significance of Posture in Communication Systems." *Psychiatry* 27 : 316 – 331.
Schieffelin, Edward L.
    1979   "Mediators as Metaphors: Moving a Man to Tears in Papua, New Guinea." In *The Imagination of Reality: Essays in Southeast Asian Coherence Systems*, ed. A. L. Becker and Aram A. Yengoyan, pp. 127 – 144. Norwood, N.J.: Ablex.
Schlundt, Christena L.
    1972   *Tamiris: A Chronicle of Her Dance Career: 1927 – 1955.* New York: New York Public Library; Astor, Lenox, and Tilden Foundations.
Seaford, Henry W., Jr.
    1975   "Facial Expression Dialect: An Example." In *Organization of Behavior in Face-to-Face Interaction*, ed. Adam Kendon, Richard M. Harris, and Mary Ritchie Key, pp. 151 – 155. The Hague: Mouton.
Sebeok, Thomas A. (ed.)
    1983   *Encyclopedic Dictionary of Semiotics.* Bloomington and London: Indiana University Press and Macmillan.
Selden, Elizabeth
    1935   *The Dancer's Quest.* Berkeley: University of California Press.
Shapiro, Margaret, and Pat Bauer
    1980   "Cable TV Song and Dance." *Washington Post*, December 21, p. 1.

Shapiro, Marianne
1981 "Preliminaries to a Semiotics of Ballet." In *The Sign in Music and Literature*, ed. Wendy Steiner, pp. 216–237. Austin: University of Texas Press.
Shawn, Ted
1954 *Every Little Movement: A Book about François Delsarte*. New York: Dance Horizons reprint.
Shiveley, Donald H.
1978 "The Social Environment of Tokugawa Kabuki." In *Studies in Kabuki: Its Acting, Music, and Historical Context*, ed. James R. Brandon, William P. Malm, and Donald H. Shively, pp. 1–61. Honolulu, Hawaii: East-West Center.
Shott, Susan
1979 "Emotion and Social Life: A Symbolic Interactionist Analysis." *American Journal of Sociology* 84:1317–1334.
Siegel, Marcia
1976 "Waiting for the Past to Begin." *Arts in Society: Growth of Dance in America* 13/2:228–235.
1979 *Shapes of Change*. Boston: Houghton Mifflin.
Simmel, Georg
1950 *The Sociology of Georg Simmel*, trans., ed., and intro. Kurt H. Wolff. Glencoe: Free Press.
Sirridge, Mary, and Adina Armelagos
1977 "The In's and Out's of Dance: Expression as an Aspect of Style." *Journal of Aesthetics and Art Criticism* 36/1:15–24.
Smith, William George
1948 *The Oxford Dictionary of English Proverbs*. 2nd ed. Oxford: Clarendon.
Sorell, Walter
1981 *Dance in Its Time*. Garden City, N.Y.: Anchor/Doubleday.
*South African Digest*
1981 "Last Tango in Namibia?" May 15, p. 21.
Spiegel, John, and Pavel Machotka
1974 *Messages of the Body*. New York: Free Press.
Spindler, George (ed.)
1978 *The Making of Psychological Anthropology*. Berkeley: University of California Press.
Stampfel, Peter
1981 "Confessions of a Polkaholic." *Village Voice*, July 1–7, p. 67.
Stanislavski, Constantin
1936 *An Actor Prepares*. New York: Theatre Art Books.
Stearns, Marshall, and Jean Stearns
1968 *Jazz Dance: The Story of American Vernacular Dance*. New York: Macmillan.
Steiner, Wendy (ed.)
1981 *The Sign in Music and Literature*. Austin: University of Texas Press.

Stevenson, Burton (ed.)
  1948  *The Home Book of Proverbs, Maxims, and Familiar Phrases.* New
       York: Macmillan.
Stowe, Dorothy
  1980  "RDT Shows Dance as It Was Then." *Deseret News*, March 5, p. A5.
Sullivan, J. W. N.
  1927  *Beethoven: His Spiritual Development.* New York: Knopf.
Taylor, Julie
  1976  "Tango: Theme of Class and Nation." *Ethnomusicology* 20/2:
       273–292.
Taylor, Margaret Fisk
  1967  *A Time to Dance: Symbolic Movement in Worship.* Philadelphia: United
       Church Press.
Terry, Walter
  1980  "An Effort to Save the Masterpieces of Modern Dance." *Smithsonian*
       11/7:62–69.
Tilley, Morris Palmer
  1950  *A Dictionary of the Proverbs of England in the Sixteenth and Seven-
       teenth Centuries.* Ann Arbor: University of Michigan Press.
Tolentino, Francisca Reyes [Aquino]
  1935  *Philippine Folk Dances and Games.* New York: Burdett and Co.
  1946  *Philippine National Dances.* New York: Burdett and Co.
Traversi, Derek
  1976  *T. S. Eliot: The Longer Poems.* London: Bodley Head.
Turner, Victor
  1969  *The Ritual Process: Structure and Anti-Structure.* Chicago: Aldine.
  1974  *Dramas, Fields, and Metaphor: Symbolic Action in Human Society.*
       Ithaca: Cornell University Press.
U.S. News and World Report
  1977  "The Culture Boom." 83/6:50–53, 55.
Van Camp, Julie
  1981  "Sage Cowles and Molly Davies." *Washington Dance Review*, April–
       May, p. 8.
Vatsyayan, Kapila
  1962  "The Sahrdaya—The Initiated Spectator." *Impulse: Audience for
       Dance:* 51–53.
  1968  *Classical Indian Dance in Literature and the Arts.* New Delhi: Sangeet
       Natak Akademi.
Vickers, Clinton J.
  1974  "Image into Symbol: The Evolution of the Dance into the Poetry and
       Drama of W. B. Yeats." Ph.D. dissertation. University of Massachusetts.
Vlahos, Olivia
  1979  *Body: The Ultimate Symbol.* New York: Lippincott.
Wallace, Anthony F. C., and Margaret Carson
  1973  "Sharing and Diversity in Emotion Terminology." *Ethos* 1/1:1–29.

Warren, Larry
   1980  "Dance Reconstruction." *Washington Dance View*, October–November, p. 16.
*Washington Post*
   1980  "O Politics: Wave of the Future?" August 21, p. A16.
   1981*a*  "Does Ronald Reagan Represent the West and, If So, Which West?" January 20, pp. 25, 33.
   1981*b*  "The Irish Dance of Death," January 26, p. A30.
   1981*c*  "RIF Notices Arrive in Washington Area," June 13, p. A4.
Welsh, Anne Marie
   1980  "Lifeless Effort to Recall Era." *Washington Star*, October 27, pp. C1–2.
   1981*a*  "Disappointing 'Foot Rules.'" *Washington Star*, January 13, p. D5.
   1981*b*  "A Hypnotic Form of Indian Dance." *Washington Star*, May 28, p. D2.
White, Judith Simpson
   1979  "William Yeats and the Dancer: A History of Yeats's Work with Dance Theatre." Ph.D. dissertation. University of Virginia.
Wiener, Morton, Shannon Devoe, Stuart Rubinow, and Jesse Geller
   1972  "Nonverbal Behavior and Nonverbal Communication." *Psychological Review* 79:185–214.
Wiles, Timothy J.
   1980  *The Theatre Event: Modern Theories of Performance.* Chicago: University of Chicago Press.
Williams, Juan
   1981  "Real Heroes." *Washington Post*, July 21, p. A13.
Wilson, F. P. (ed.)
   1970  *The Oxford Dictionary of English Proverbs.* Oxford: Clarendon.
Wundt, Wilhelm
   1973  *The Language of Gestures (Approaches to Semiotics 6).* The Hague: Mouton. Reprint of 1921 edition.
Wynne, Shirley
   1970  "Complaisance, An Eighteenth Century Cool." *Dance Scope* 5/1: 22–35.
Yenckel, James T.
   1980  "Leisure: Happy Toes, Smiling Feet." *Washington Post*, June 20, p. C5.
Young, Hugo
   1981  "A Sober Voice to Still the Dance of Death." *Sunday Times* (UK), October 18.

# Index